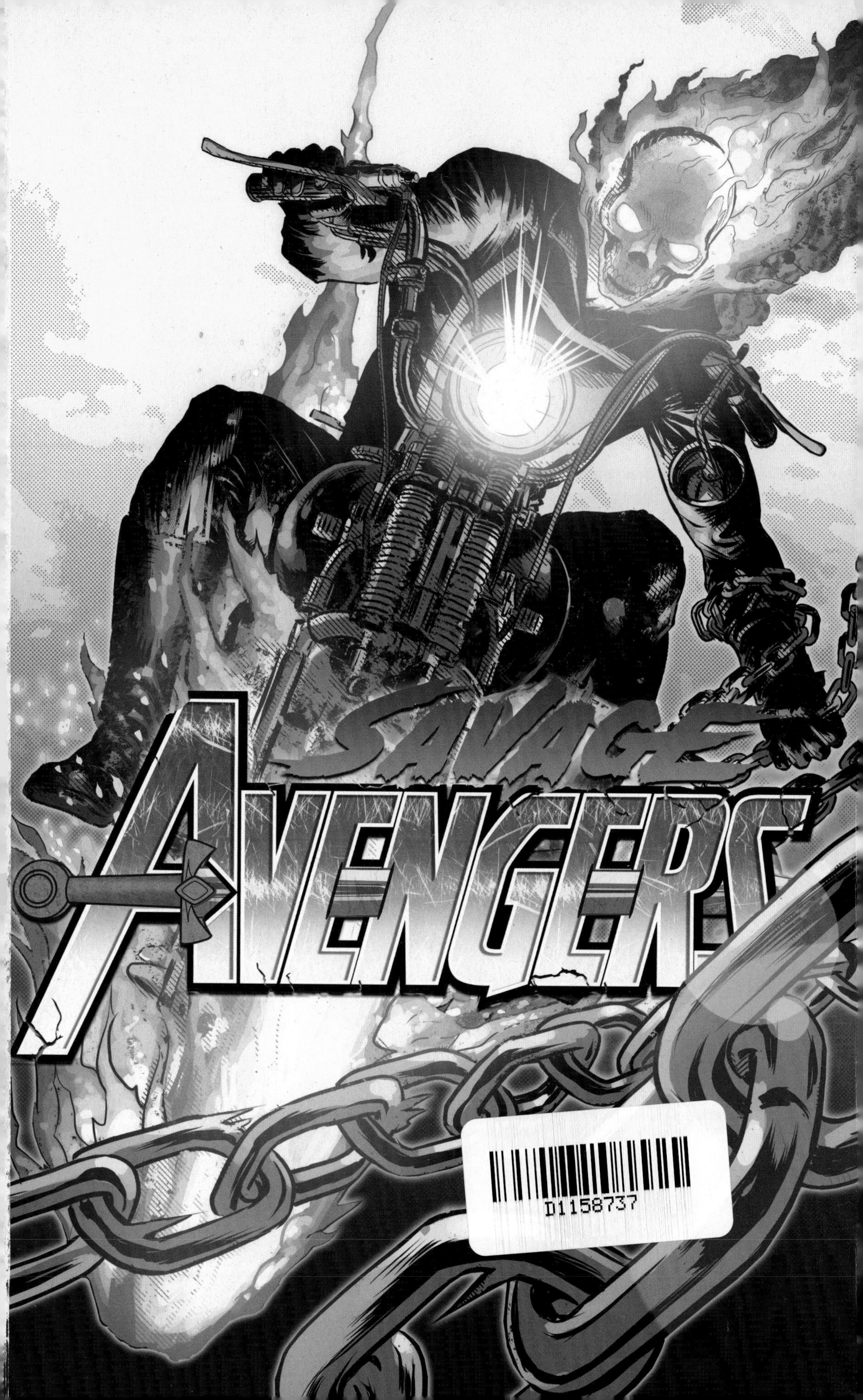
SAVAGE
AVENGERS

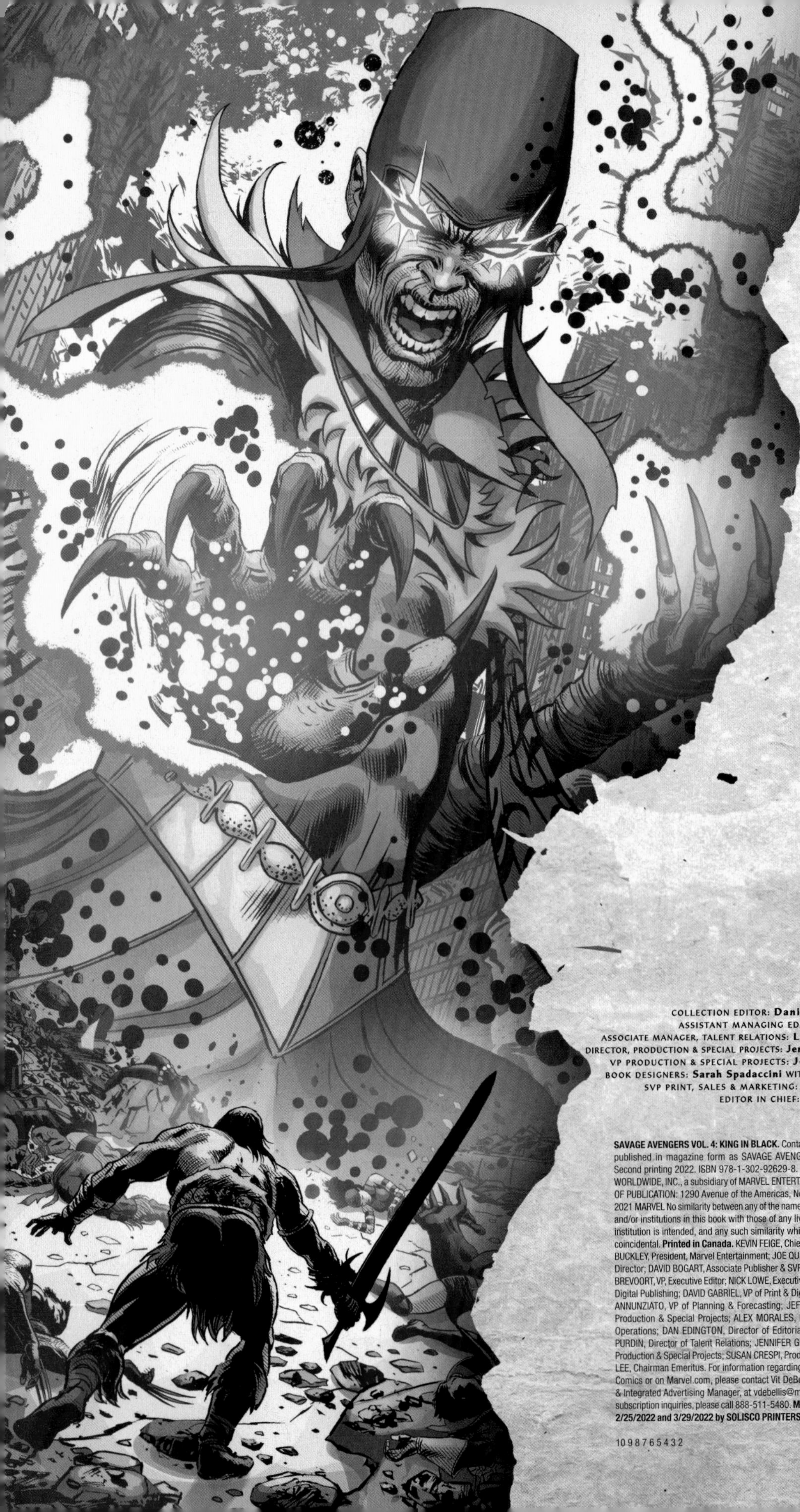

COLLECTION EDITOR: **Daniel Kirchhoffer**
ASSISTANT MANAGING EDITOR: **Maia Loy**
ASSOCIATE MANAGER, TALENT RELATIONS: **Lisa Montalbano**
DIRECTOR, PRODUCTION & SPECIAL PROJECTS: **Jennifer Grünwald**
VP PRODUCTION & SPECIAL PROJECTS: **Jeff Youngquist**
BOOK DESIGNERS: **Sarah Spadaccini** WITH **Adam Del Re**
SVP PRINT, SALES & MARKETING: **David Gabriel**
EDITOR IN CHIEF: **C.B. Cebulski**

SAVAGE AVENGERS VOL. 4: KING IN BLACK. Contains material originally published in magazine form as SAVAGE AVENGERS (2019) #17-22. Second printing 2022. ISBN 978-1-302-92629-8. Published by MARVEL WORLDWIDE, INC., a subsidiary of MARVEL ENTERTAINMENT, LLC. OFFICE OF PUBLICATION: 1290 Avenue of the Americas, New York, NY 10104. **Printed in Canada.** KEVIN FEIGE, Chief Creative Officer; DAN BUCKLEY, President, Marvel Entertainment; JOE QUESADA, EVP & Creative Director; DAVID BOGART, Associate Publisher & SVP of Talent Affairs; TOM BREVOORT, VP, Executive Editor; NICK LOWE, Executive Editor, VP of Content, Digital Publishing; DAVID GABRIEL, VP of Print & Digital Publishing; MARK ANNUNZIATO, VP of Planning & Forecasting; JEFF YOUNGQUIST, VP of Production & Special Projects; ALEX MORALES, Director of Publishing Operations; DAN EDINGTON, Director of Editorial Operations; RICKEY PURDIN, Director of Talent Relations; JENNIFER GRÜNWALD, Director of Production & Special Projects; SUSAN CRESPI, Production Manager; STAN LEE, Chairman Emeritus. For information regarding advertising in Marvel Comics or on Marvel.com, please contact Vit DeBellis, Custom Solutions & Integrated Advertising Manager, at vdebellis@marvel.com. For Marvel subscription inquiries, please call 888-511-5480. **Manufactured between 2/25/2022 and 3/29/2022 by SOLISCO PRINTERS, SCOTT, QC, CANADA.**

10 9 8 7 6 5 4 3 2

Knull, the creator and god of the alien symbiotes, has been freed from his prison at the edge of the galaxy. He led a horde of symbiote dragons across the cosmos, and now they have arrived on Earth — the galaxy's final line of defense against the King in Black.

Conan successfully aided Doctor Strange and his allies in their latest salvo against the evil sorcerer Kulan Gath, helping retrieve the second Eye of Agamotto. Once the quest was done, Conan was teleported back to New York City, and he went to celebrate his victory at the infamous super villain hangout the Bar with No Name.

SAVAGE AVENGERS

KING IN BLACK

Gerry Duggan
WRITER

Kev Walker (#17-19) & Patch Zircher (#20-22)
PENCILERS

Kev Walker (#17-18), Scott Hanna (#19) & Patch Zircher (#20-22)
INKERS

Java Tartaglia
COLOR ARTIST

VC's Travis Lanham
LETTERER

Valerio Giangiordano & Frank D'Armata
COVER ART

Martin Biro
ASSISTANT EDITOR

Alanna Smith
ASSOCIATE EDITOR

Tom Brevoort
EDITOR

FOR CONAN PROPERTIES INTERNATIONAL

Fredrik Malmberg
PRESIDENT

Jay Zetterberg
EXECUTIVE VICE PRESIDENT

Steve Booth
CHIEF OPERATING OFFICER

AVENGERS created by STAN LEE & JACK KIRBY

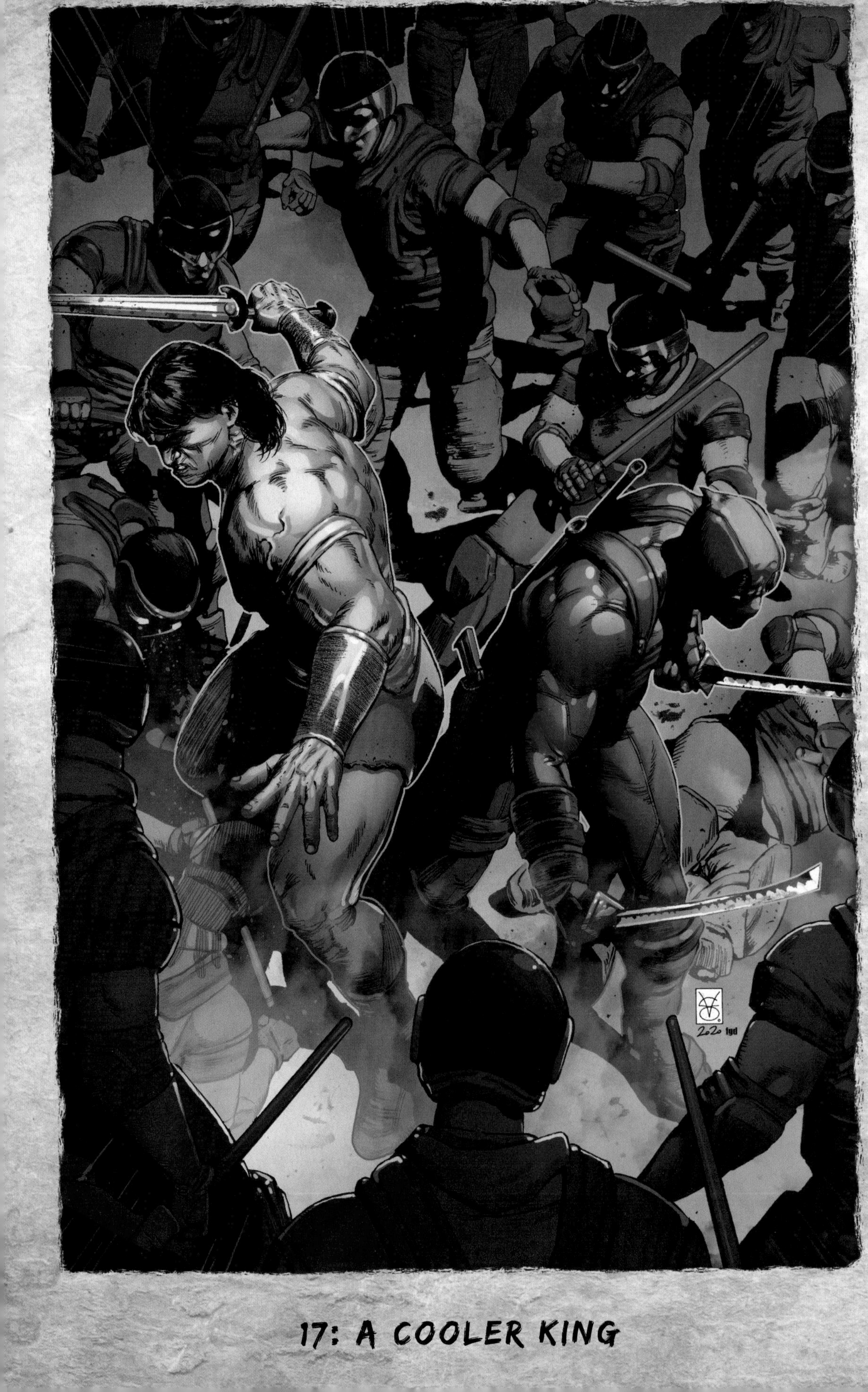

17: A COOLER KING

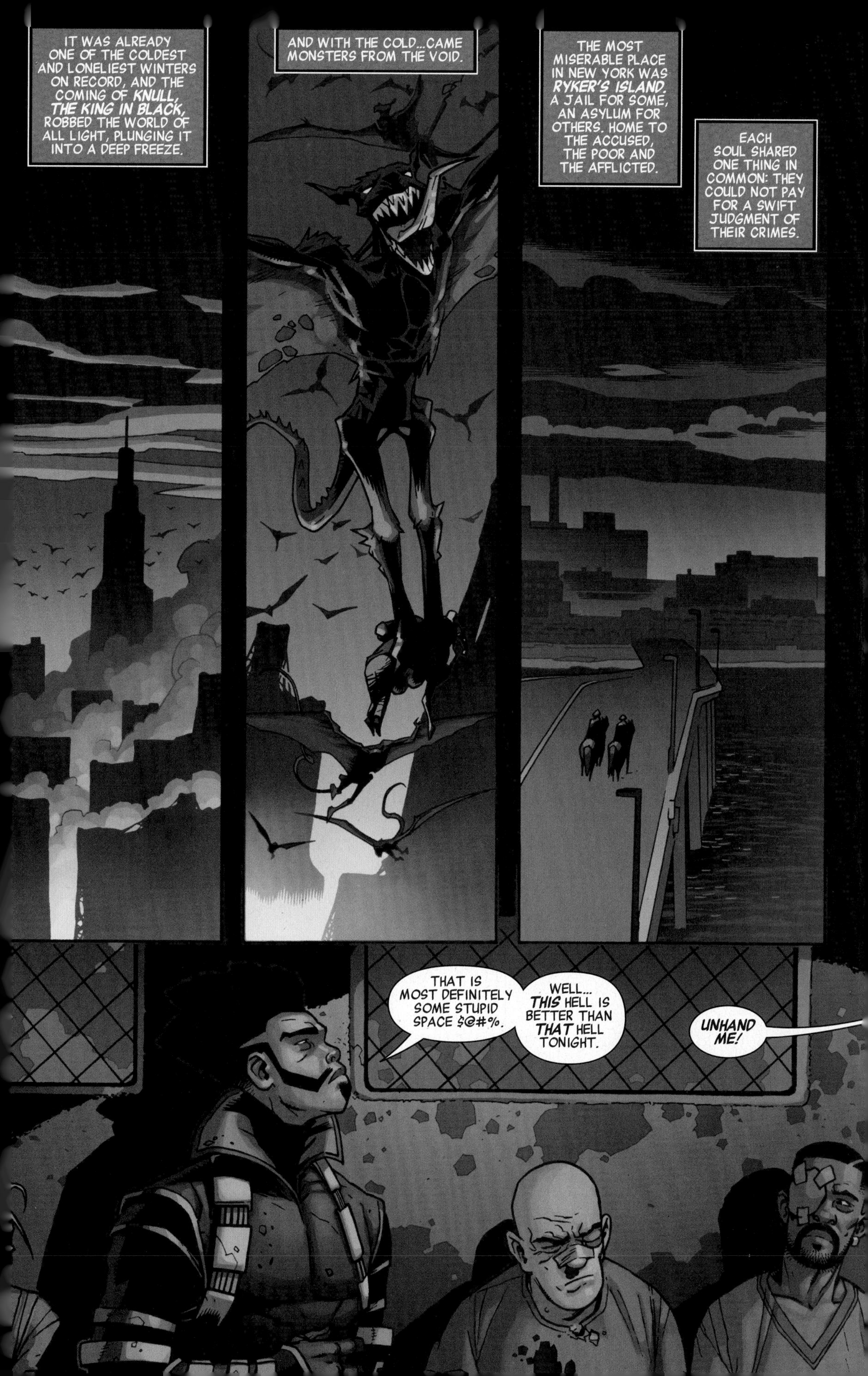
IT WAS ALREADY ONE OF THE COLDEST AND LONELIEST WINTERS ON RECORD, AND THE COMING OF KNULL, THE KING IN BLACK, ROBBED THE WORLD OF ALL LIGHT, PLUNGING IT INTO A DEEP FREEZE.
AND WITH THE COLD...CAME MONSTERS FROM THE VOID.
THE MOST MISERABLE PLACE IN NEW YORK WAS RYKER'S ISLAND. A JAIL FOR SOME, AN ASYLUM FOR OTHERS. HOME TO THE ACCUSED, THE POOR AND THE AFFLICTED.
EACH SOUL SHARED ONE THING IN COMMON: THEY COULD NOT PAY FOR A SWIFT JUDGMENT OF THEIR CRIMES.
THAT IS MOST DEFINITELY SOME STUPID SPACE $@#%.
WELL... THIS HELL IS BETTER THAN THAT HELL TONIGHT.
UNHAND ME!

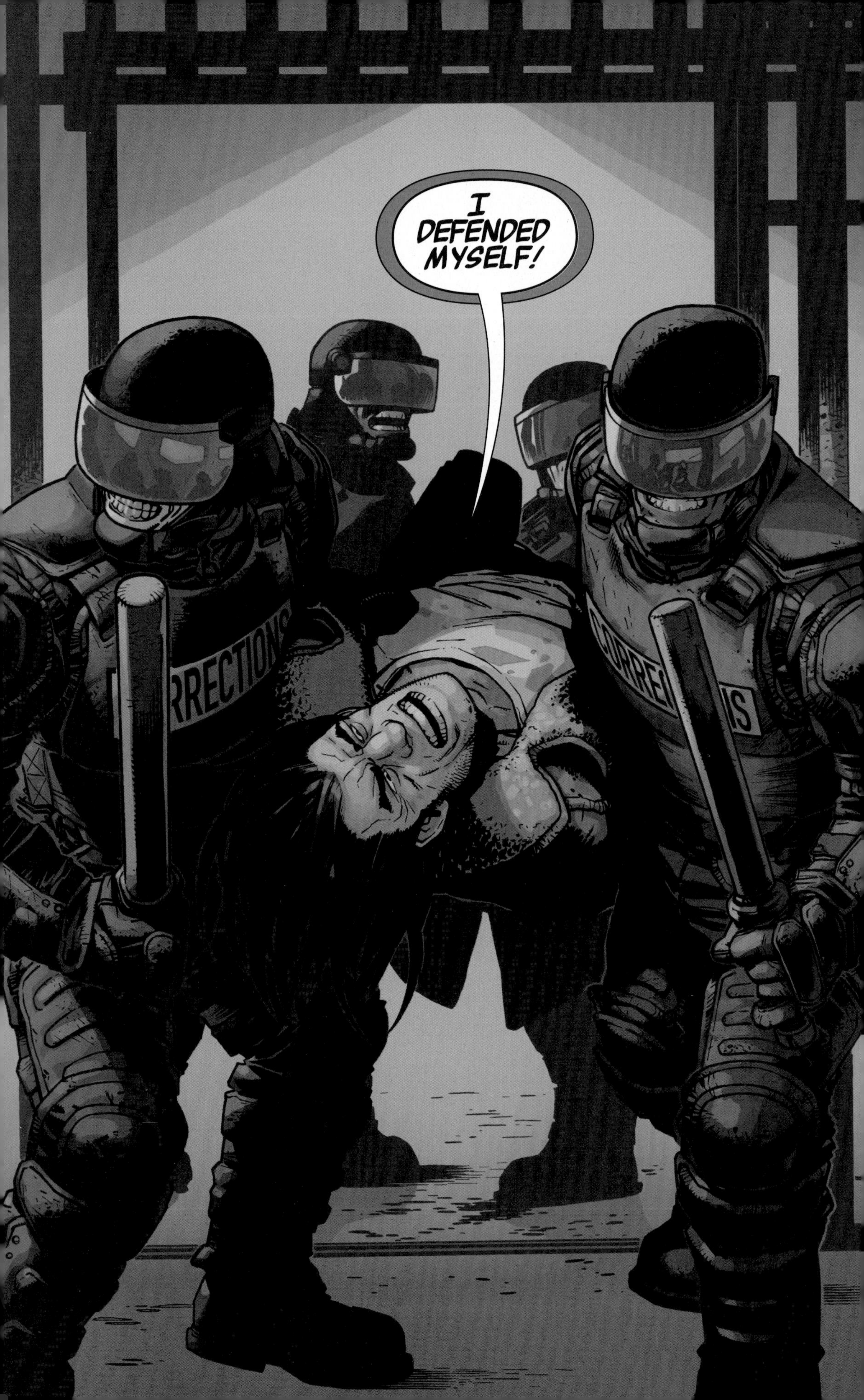
I DEFENDED MYSELF!
RRECTIONS

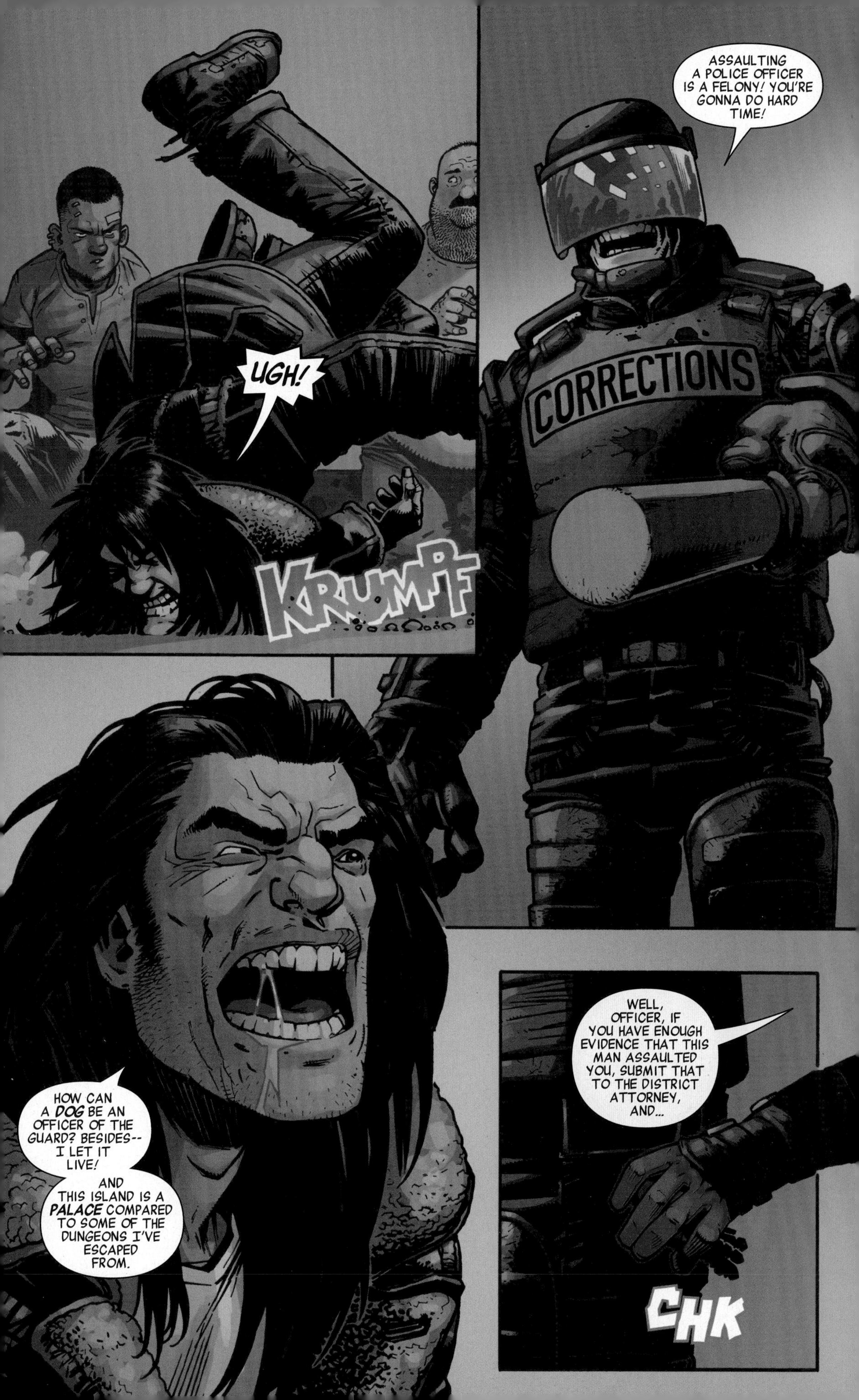
UGH!
KRUMPF
ASSAULTING A POLICE OFFICER IS A FELONY! YOU'RE GONNA DO HARD TIME!
CORRECTIONS
HOW CAN A DOG BE AN OFFICER OF THE GUARD? BESIDES-- I LET IT LIVE!
AND THIS ISLAND IS A PALACE COMPARED TO SOME OF THE DUNGEONS I'VE ESCAPED FROM.
WELL, OFFICER, IF YOU HAVE ENOUGH EVIDENCE THAT THIS MAN ASSAULTED YOU, SUBMIT THAT TO THE DISTRICT ATTORNEY, AND...
CHK

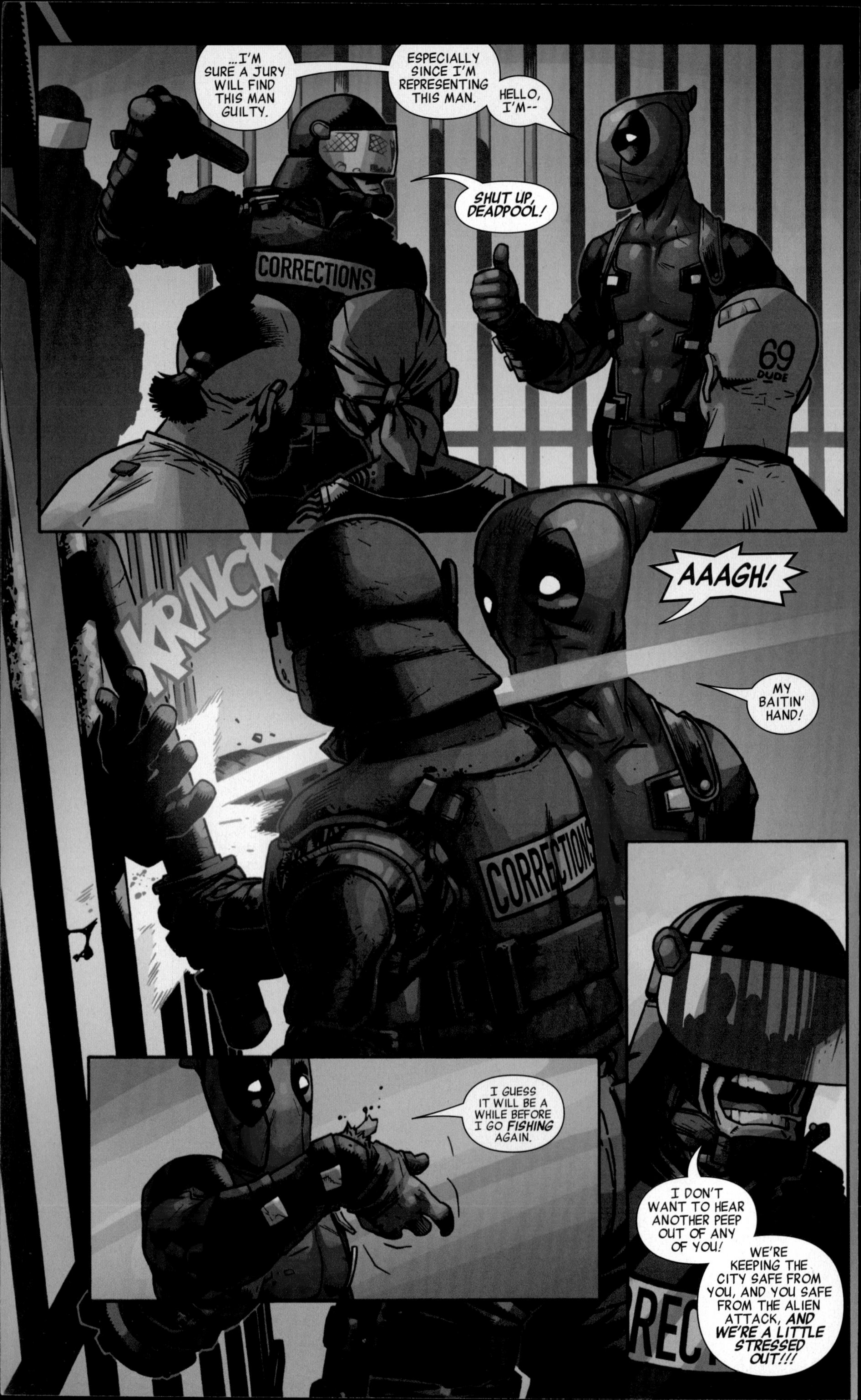
...I'M SURE A JURY WILL FIND THIS MAN GUILTY.
ESPECIALLY SINCE I'M REPRESENTING THIS MAN.
HELLO, I'M--
SHUT UP, DEADPOOL!
CORRECTIONS
69 DUDE
KRACK
AAAGH!
MY BAITIN' HAND!
CORRECTIONS
I GUESS IT WILL BE A WHILE BEFORE I GO FISHING AGAIN.
I DON'T WANT TO HEAR ANOTHER PEEP OUT OF ANY OF YOU!
WE'RE KEEPING THE CITY SAFE FROM YOU, AND YOU SAFE FROM THE ALIEN ATTACK, AND WE'RE A LITTLE STRESSED OUT!!!

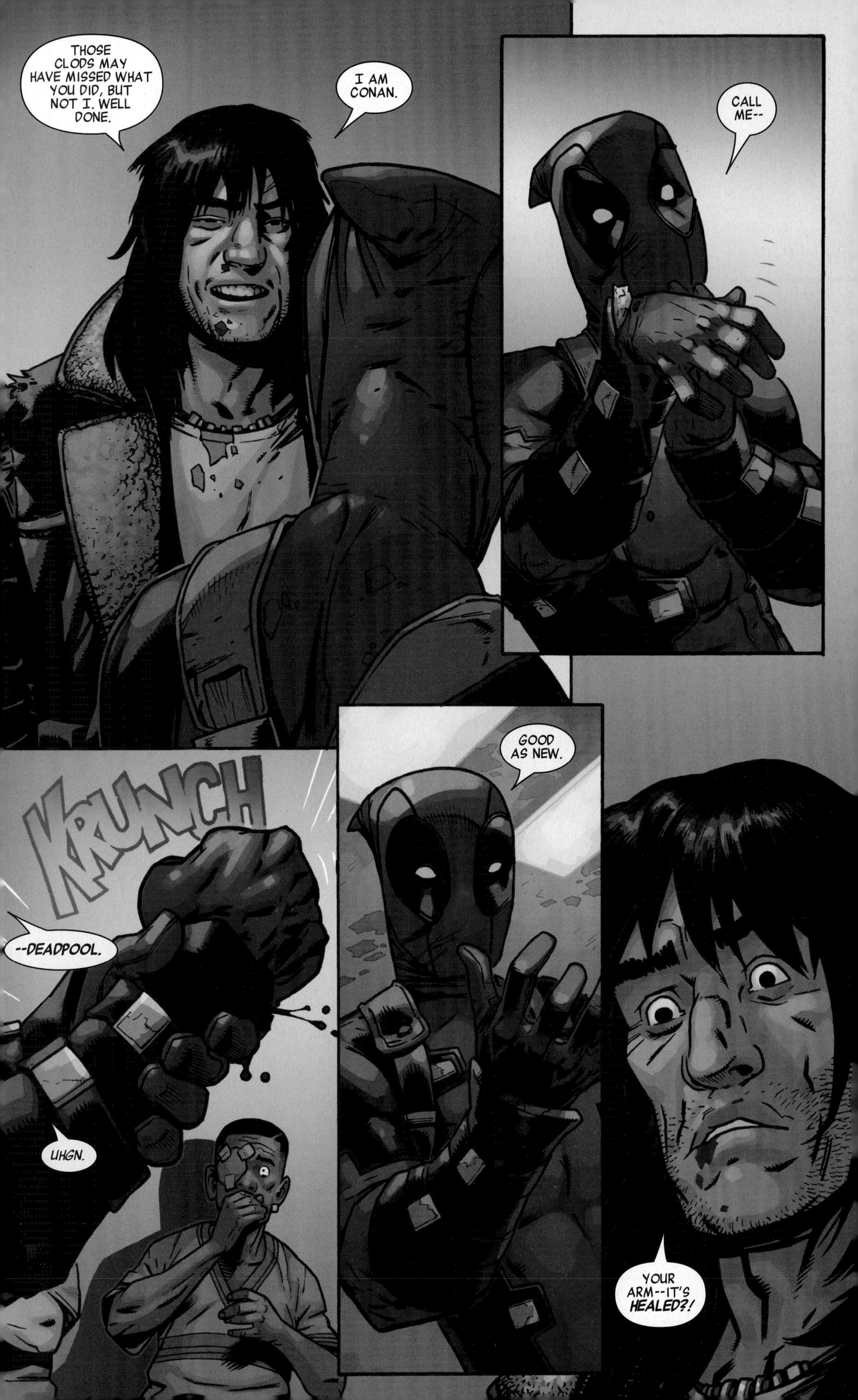
THOSE CLODS MAY HAVE MISSED WHAT YOU DID, BUT NOT I. WELL DONE.
I AM CONAN.
CALL ME--
KRUNCH
--DEADPOOL.
UHGN.
GOOD AS NEW.
YOUR ARM--IT'S HEALED?!

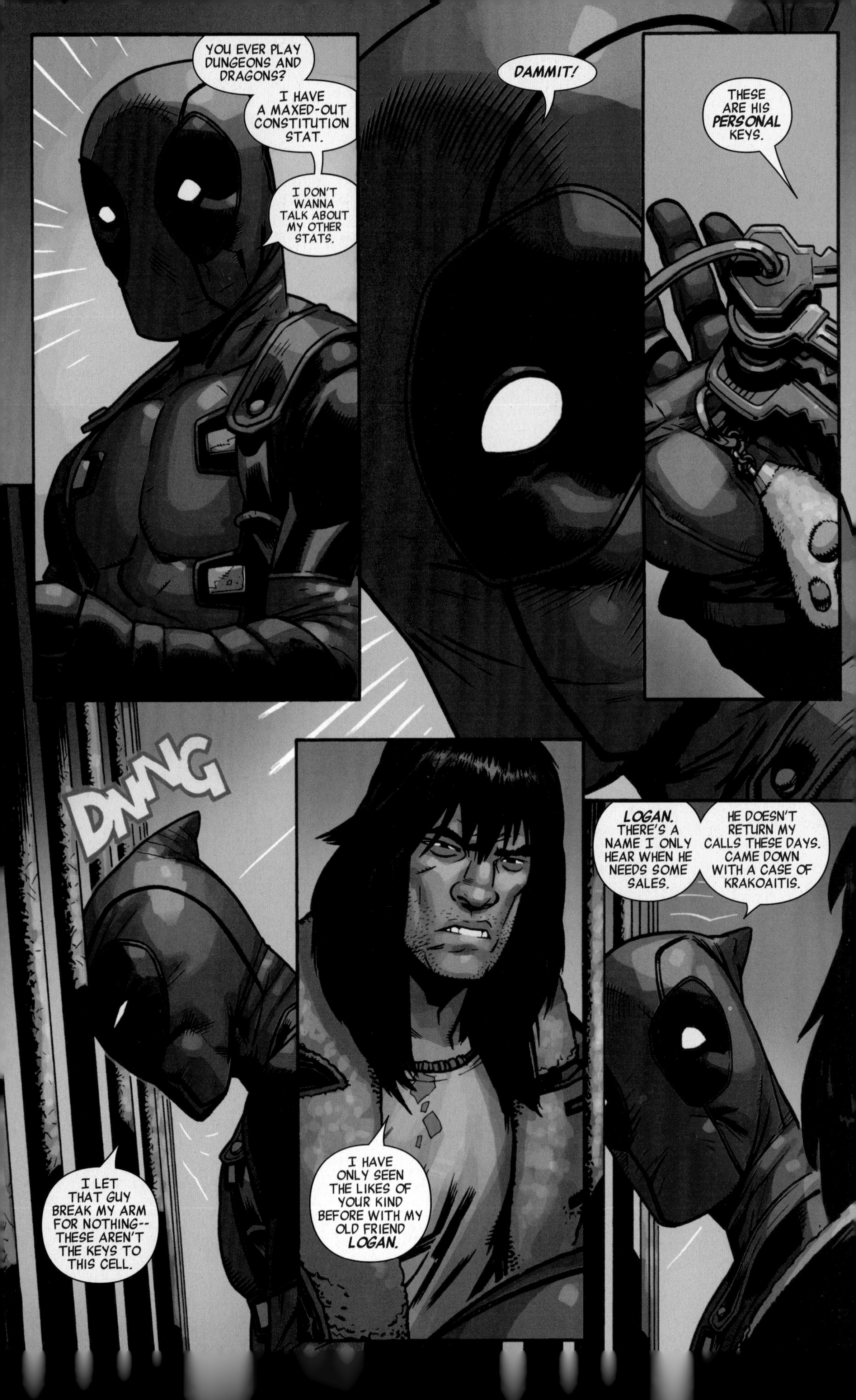
YOU EVER PLAY DUNGEONS AND DRAGONS?
I HAVE A MAXED-OUT CONSTITUTION STAT.
I DON'T WANNA TALK ABOUT MY OTHER STATS.
DAMMIT!
THESE ARE HIS PERSONAL KEYS.
DNNG
I LET THAT GUY BREAK MY ARM FOR NOTHING-- THESE AREN'T THE KEYS TO THIS CELL.
I HAVE ONLY SEEN THE LIKES OF YOUR KIND BEFORE WITH MY OLD FRIEND LOGAN.
LOGAN. THERE'S A NAME I ONLY HEAR WHEN HE NEEDS SOME SALES.
HE DOESN'T RETURN MY CALLS THESE DAYS. CAME DOWN WITH A CASE OF KRAKOAITIS.

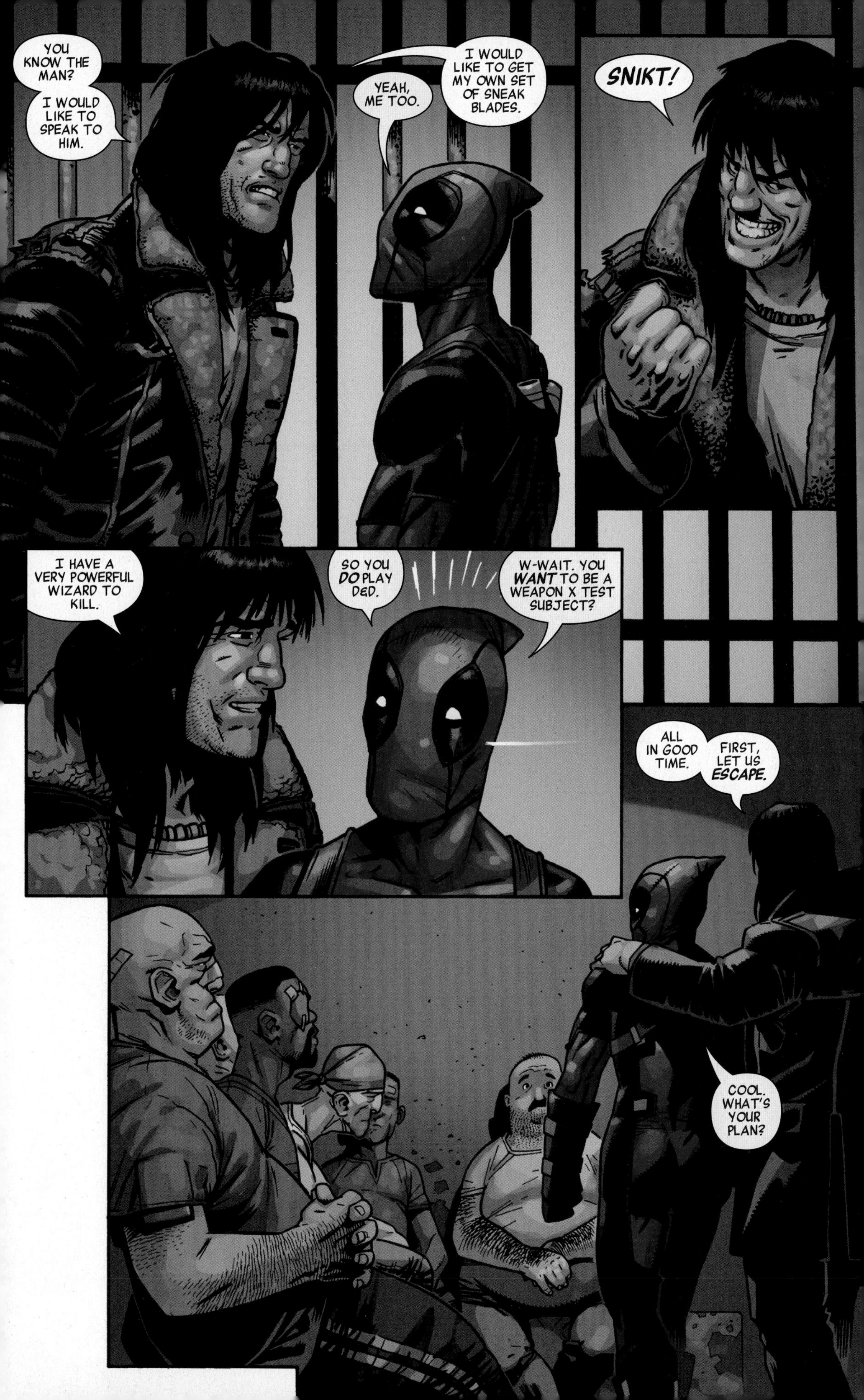
YOU KNOW THE MAN?
I WOULD LIKE TO SPEAK TO HIM.
I WOULD LIKE TO GET MY OWN SET OF SNEAK BLADES.
YEAH, ME TOO.
SNIKT!
I HAVE A VERY POWERFUL WIZARD TO KILL.
SO YOU DO PLAY DED.
W-WAIT. YOU WANT TO BE A WEAPON X TEST SUBJECT?
ALL IN GOOD TIME.
FIRST, LET US ESCAPE.
COOL. WHAT'S YOUR PLAN?

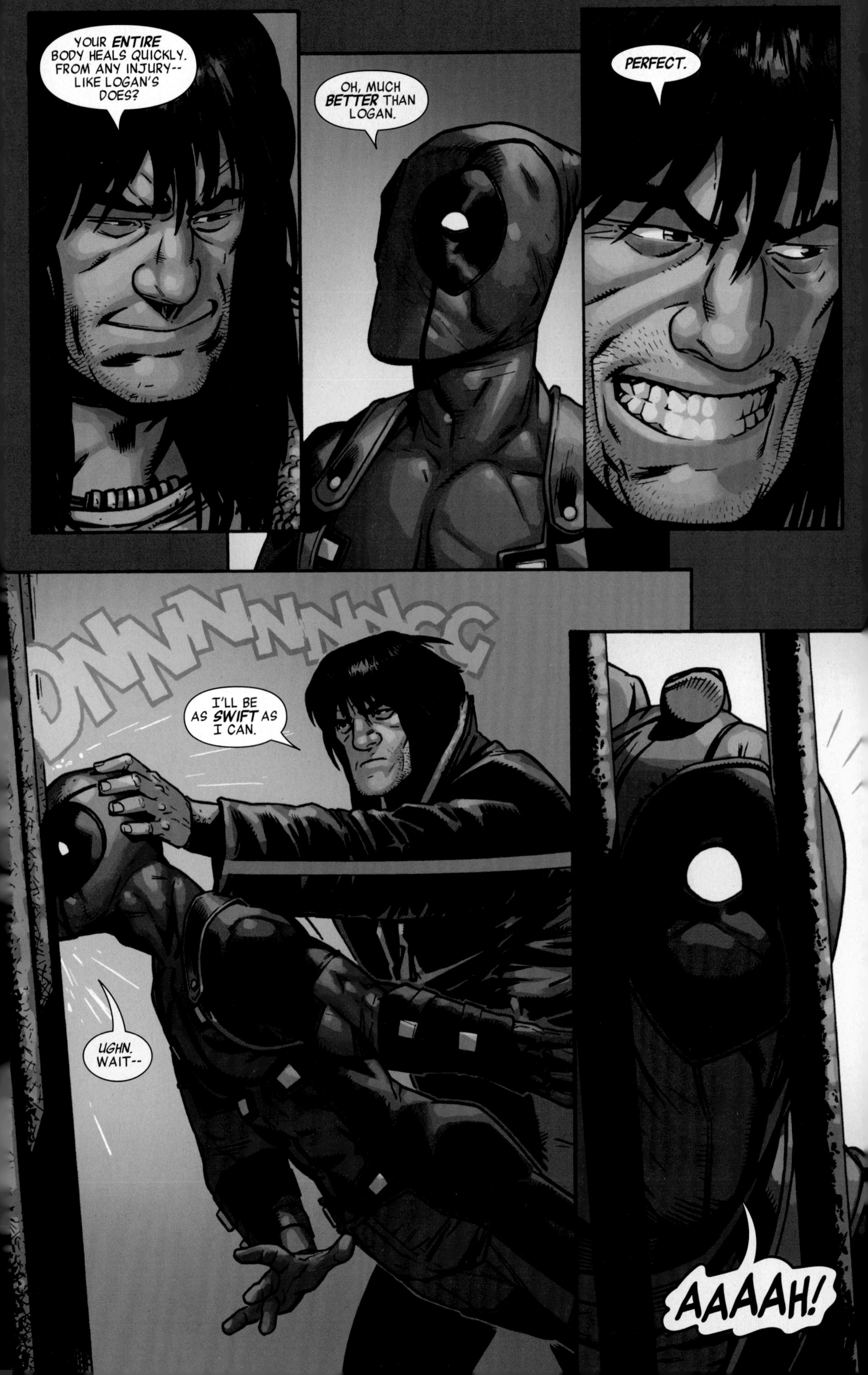
YOUR ENTIRE BODY HEALS QUICKLY. FROM ANY INJURY-- LIKE LOGAN'S DOES?
OH, MUCH BETTER THAN LOGAN.
PERFECT.
DNNNNNNGG
I'LL BE AS SWIFT AS I CAN.
UGHN. WAIT--
AAAAH!

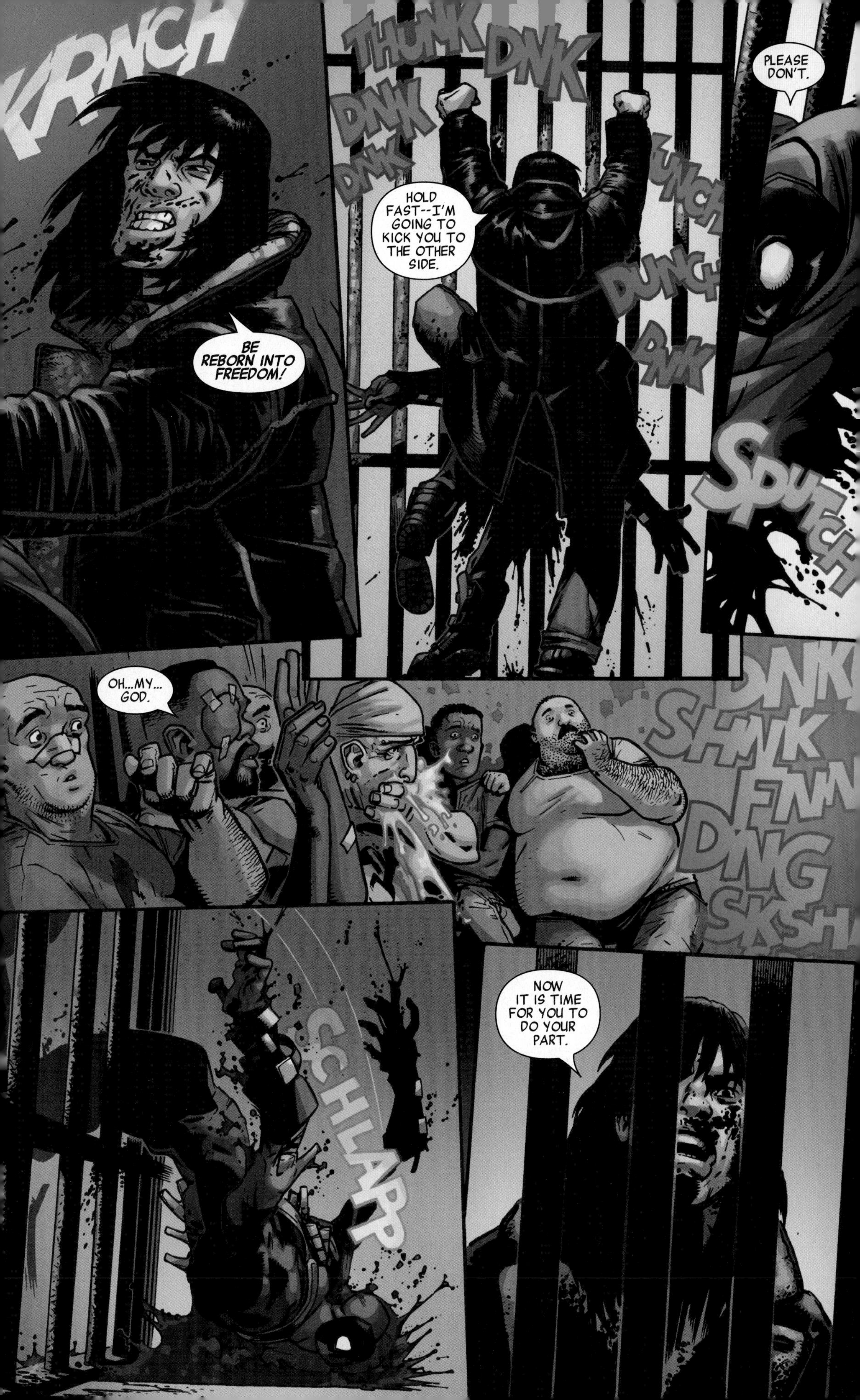
KRNCH
BE REBORN INTO FREEDOM!
THUNK
DNK
DNK
DNK
HOLD FAST--I'M GOING TO KICK YOU TO THE OTHER SIDE.
PLEASE DON'T.
SPLTCH
OH...MY... GOD.
SHNK
DNG
SCHLAPP
NOW IT IS TIME FOR YOU TO DO YOUR PART.

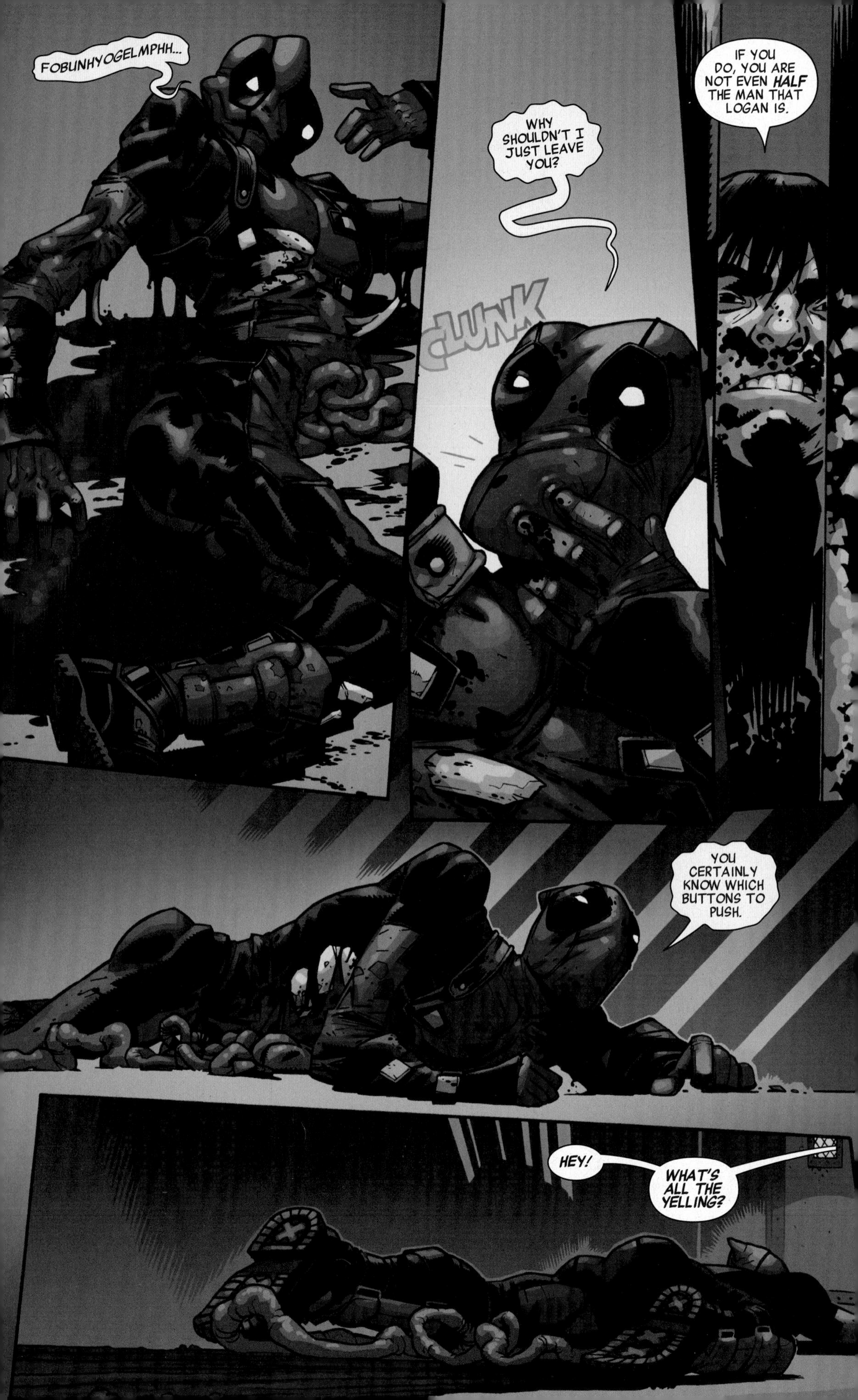
FOBUNHYOGELMPHH...
WHY SHOULDN'T I JUST LEAVE YOU?
CLUNK
IF YOU DO, YOU ARE NOT EVEN HALF THE MAN THAT LOGAN IS.
YOU CERTAINLY KNOW WHICH BUTTONS TO PUSH.
HEY!
WHAT'S ALL THE YELLING?

WHY'S IT SMELL LIKE A $@#% TOOK A PISS IN HERE?
CORRECTIONS
YEAOWP!
I DON'T KNOW HOW YOU GOT OUT--BUT I'M GONNA SHOW YOU BACK INTO THAT CELL--THROUGH THE DAMN BARS!
BECAUSE ON RYKER'S ISLAND I AM THE L--
AW, NO!
WHUDD
I AIN'T GETTING SUED.
WHUDD
EAT MY ELBOW!
WHUDD
CATCH, CONAN!

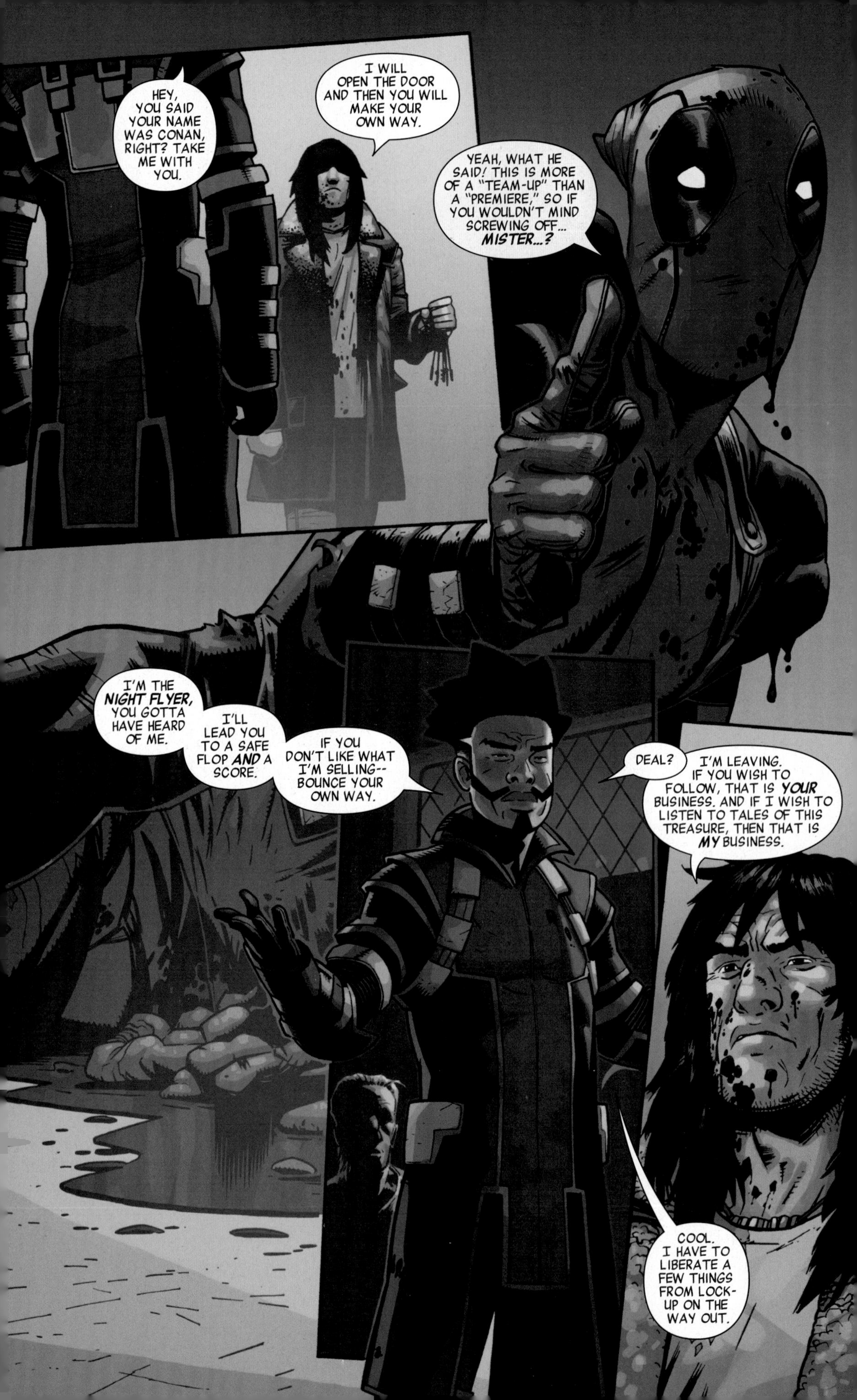
HEY, YOU SAID YOUR NAME WAS CONAN, RIGHT? TAKE ME WITH YOU.
I WILL OPEN THE DOOR AND THEN YOU WILL MAKE YOUR OWN WAY.
YEAH, WHAT HE SAID! THIS IS MORE OF A "TEAM-UP" THAN A "PREMIERE," SO IF YOU WOULDN'T MIND SCREWING OFF... **MISTER...?**
I'M THE **NIGHT FLYER,** YOU GOTTA HAVE HEARD OF ME.
I'LL LEAD YOU TO A SAFE FLOP **AND** A SCORE.
IF YOU DON'T LIKE WHAT I'M SELLING-- BOUNCE YOUR OWN WAY.
DEAL?
I'M LEAVING. IF YOU WISH TO FOLLOW, THAT IS **YOUR** BUSINESS. AND IF I WISH TO LISTEN TO TALES OF THIS TREASURE, THEN THAT IS **MY** BUSINESS.
COOL. I HAVE TO LIBERATE A FEW THINGS FROM LOCK-UP ON THE WAY OUT.

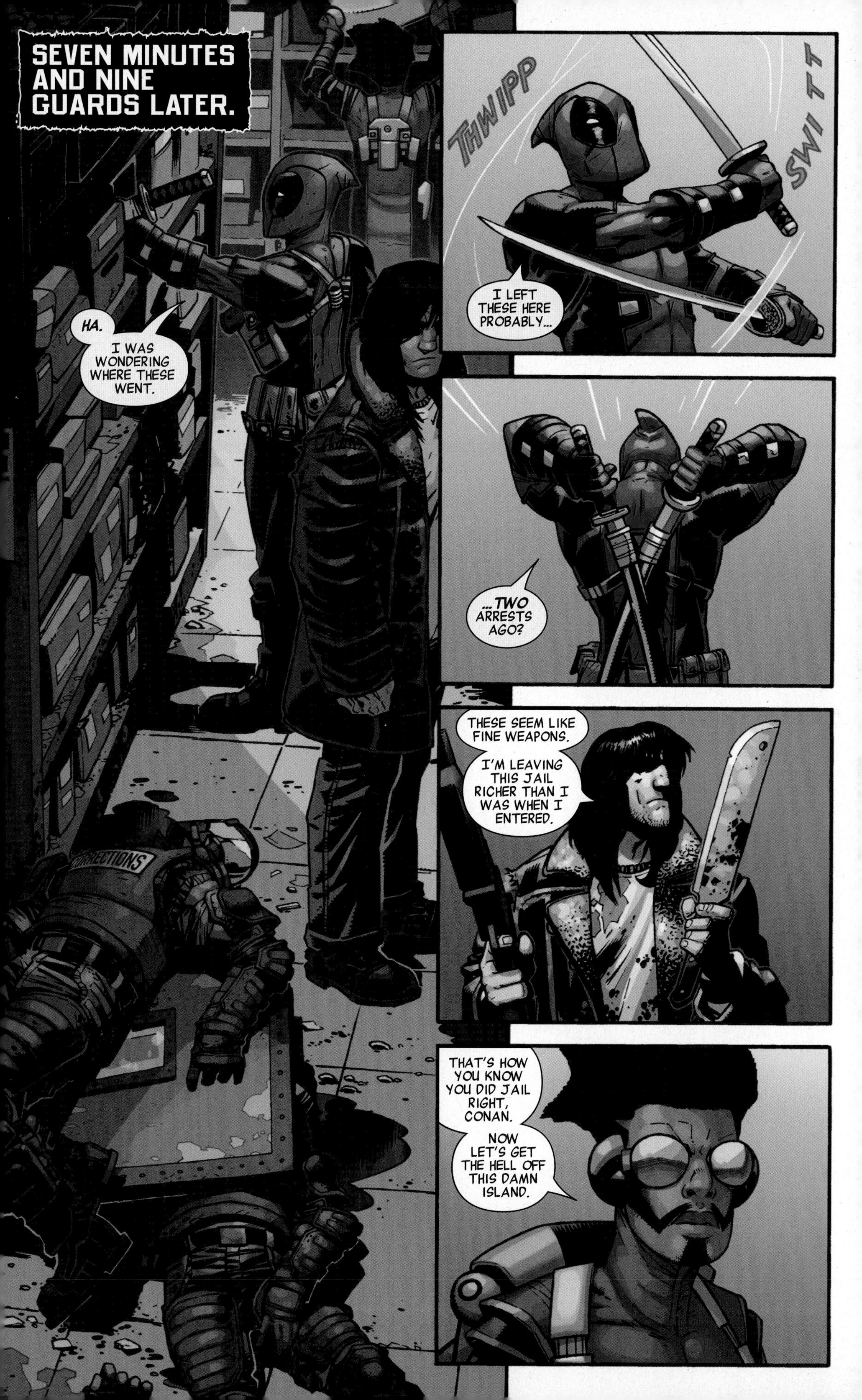
SEVEN MINUTES AND NINE GUARDS LATER.
HA.
I WAS WONDERING WHERE THESE WENT.
CORRECTIONS
THWIPP
SWI TT
I LEFT THESE HERE PROBABLY...
...TWO ARRESTS AGO?
THESE SEEM LIKE FINE WEAPONS.
I'M LEAVING THIS JAIL RICHER THAN I WAS WHEN I ENTERED.
THAT'S HOW YOU KNOW YOU DID JAIL RIGHT, CONAN.
NOW LET'S GET THE HELL OFF THIS DAMN ISLAND.

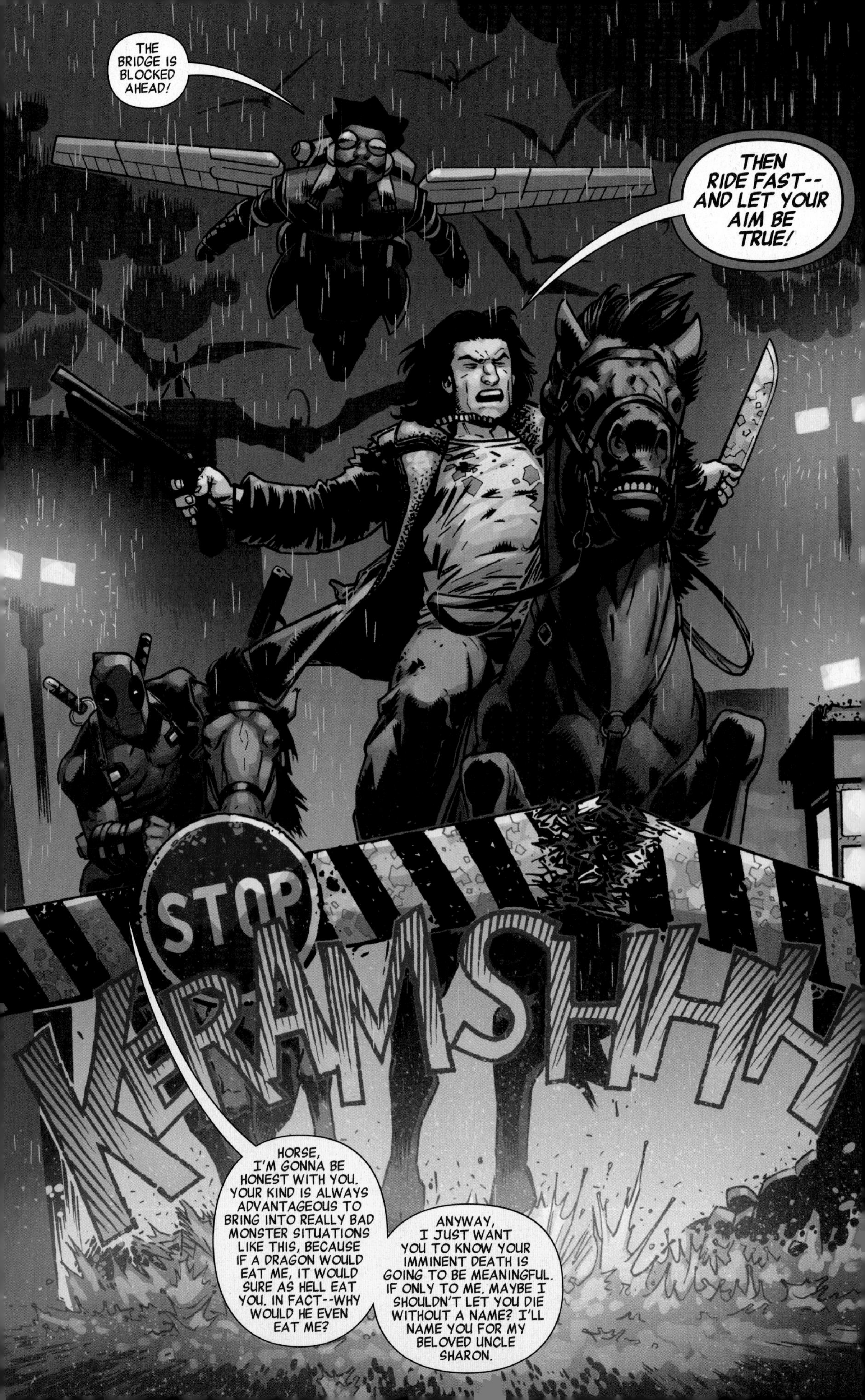
THE BRIDGE IS BLOCKED AHEAD!
THEN RIDE FAST--AND LET YOUR AIM BE TRUE!
STOP
KRAMSHHH
HORSE, I'M GONNA BE HONEST WITH YOU. YOUR KIND IS ALWAYS ADVANTAGEOUS TO BRING INTO REALLY BAD MONSTER SITUATIONS LIKE THIS, BECAUSE IF A DRAGON WOULD EAT ME, IT WOULD SURE AS HELL EAT YOU. IN FACT--WHY WOULD HE EVEN EAT ME?
ANYWAY, I JUST WANT YOU TO KNOW YOUR IMMINENT DEATH IS GOING TO BE MEANINGFUL. IF ONLY TO ME. MAYBE I SHOULDN'T LET YOU DIE WITHOUT A NAME? I'LL NAME YOU FOR MY BELOVED UNCLE SHARON.

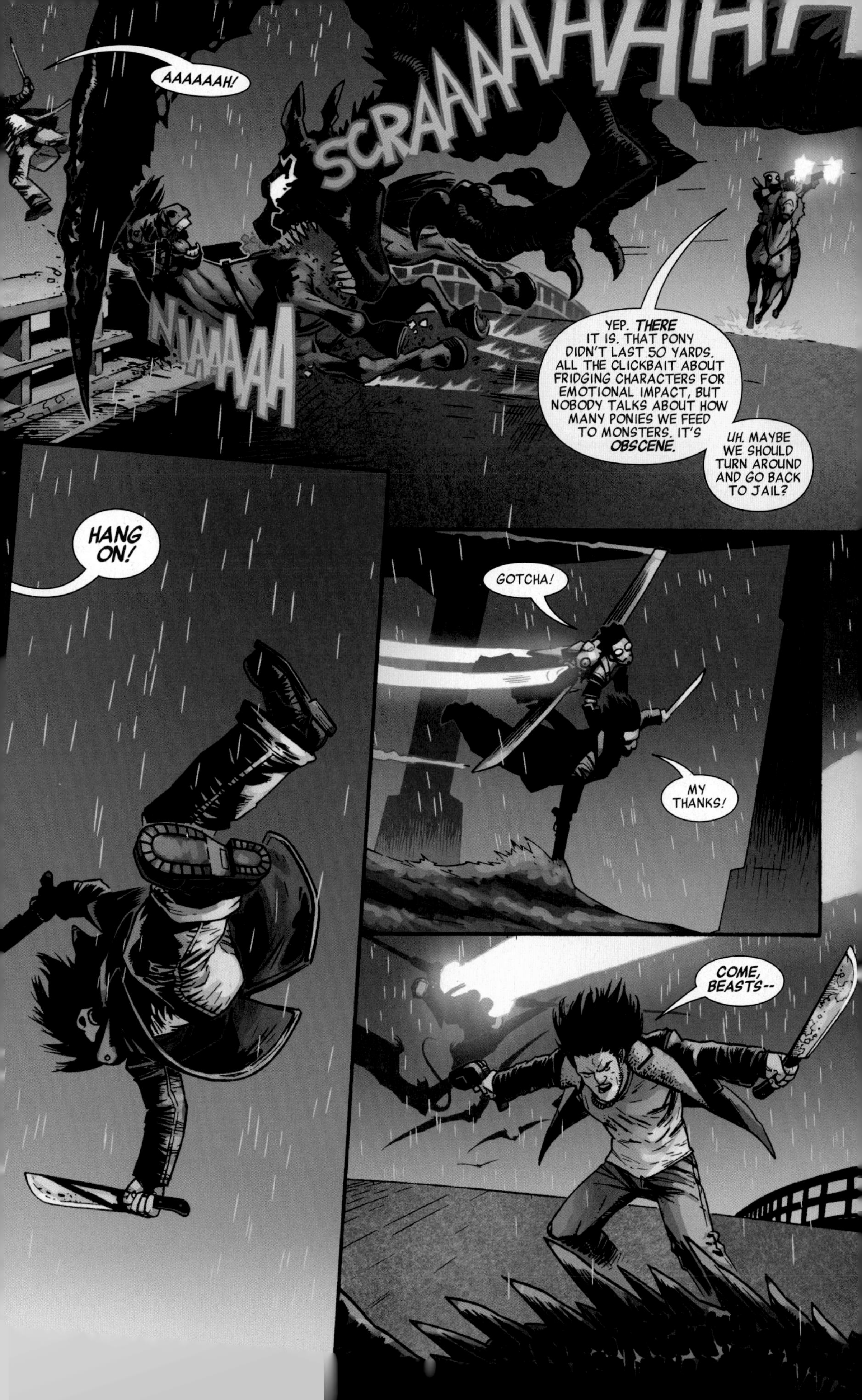
AAAAAAH!
SCRAAAAAAHHHH
NIAAAAAA
YEP. THERE IT IS. THAT PONY DIDN'T LAST 50 YARDS. ALL THE CLICKBAIT ABOUT FRIDGING CHARACTERS FOR EMOTIONAL IMPACT, BUT NOBODY TALKS ABOUT HOW MANY PONIES WE FEED TO MONSTERS. IT'S OBSCENE.
UH. MAYBE WE SHOULD TURN AROUND AND GO BACK TO JAIL?
HANG ON!
GOTCHA!
MY THANKS!
COME, BEASTS--

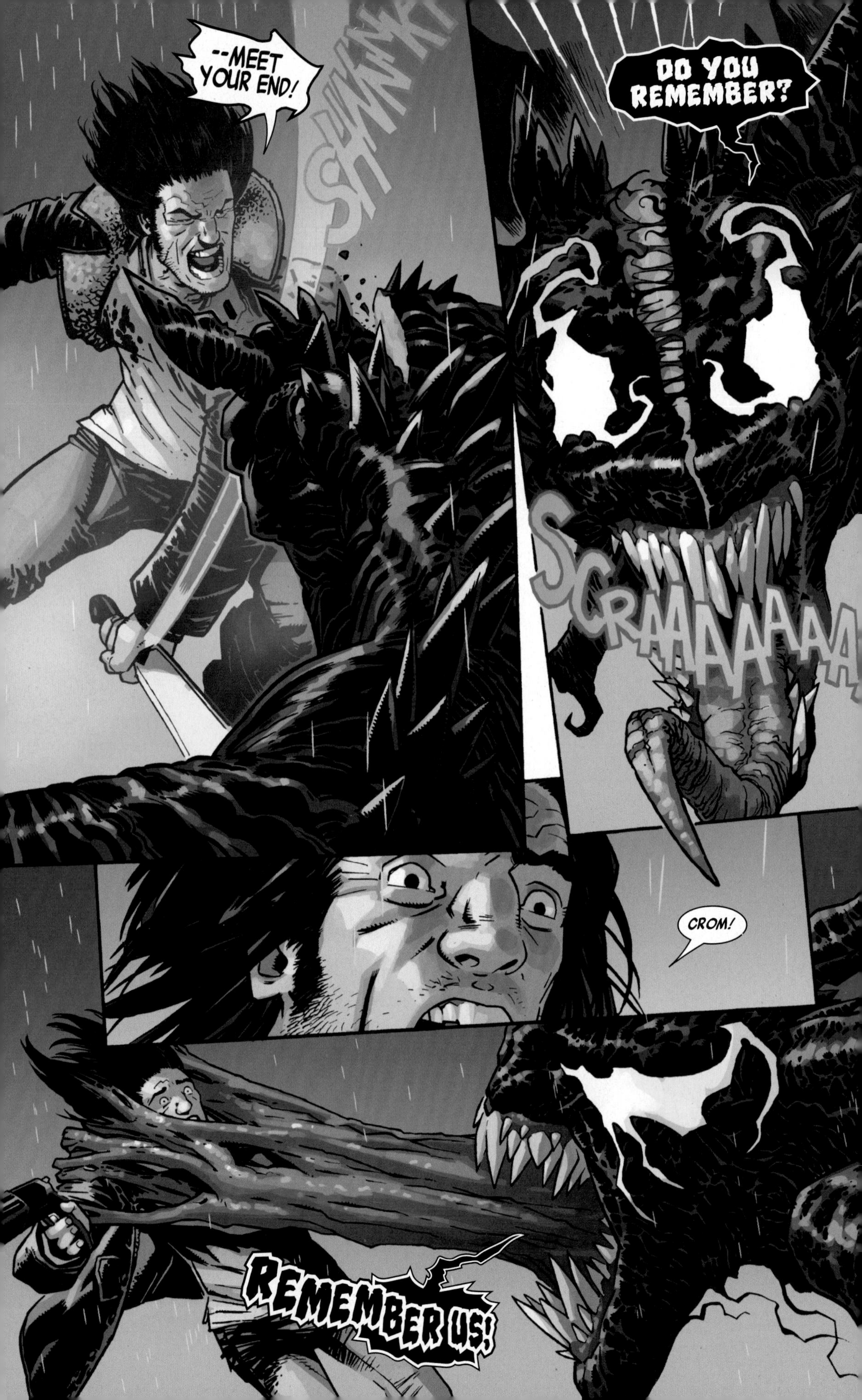
--MEET YOUR END!
SHANK!
DO YOU REMEMBER?
SCRAAAAAAA
CROM!
REMEMBER US!

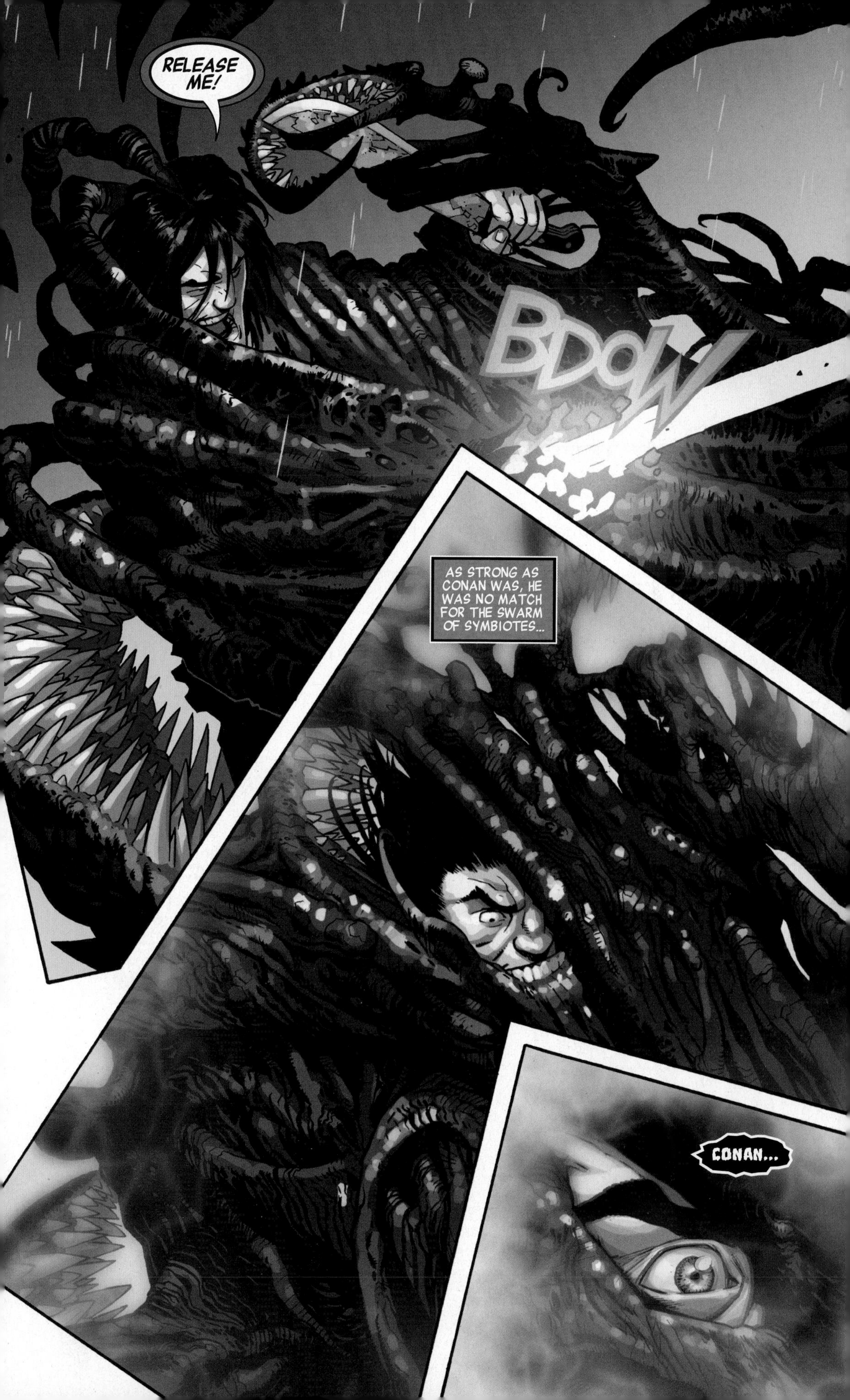
RELEASE ME!
BDOW
AS STRONG AS CONAN WAS, HE WAS NO MATCH FOR THE SWARM OF SYMBIOTES...
CONAN...

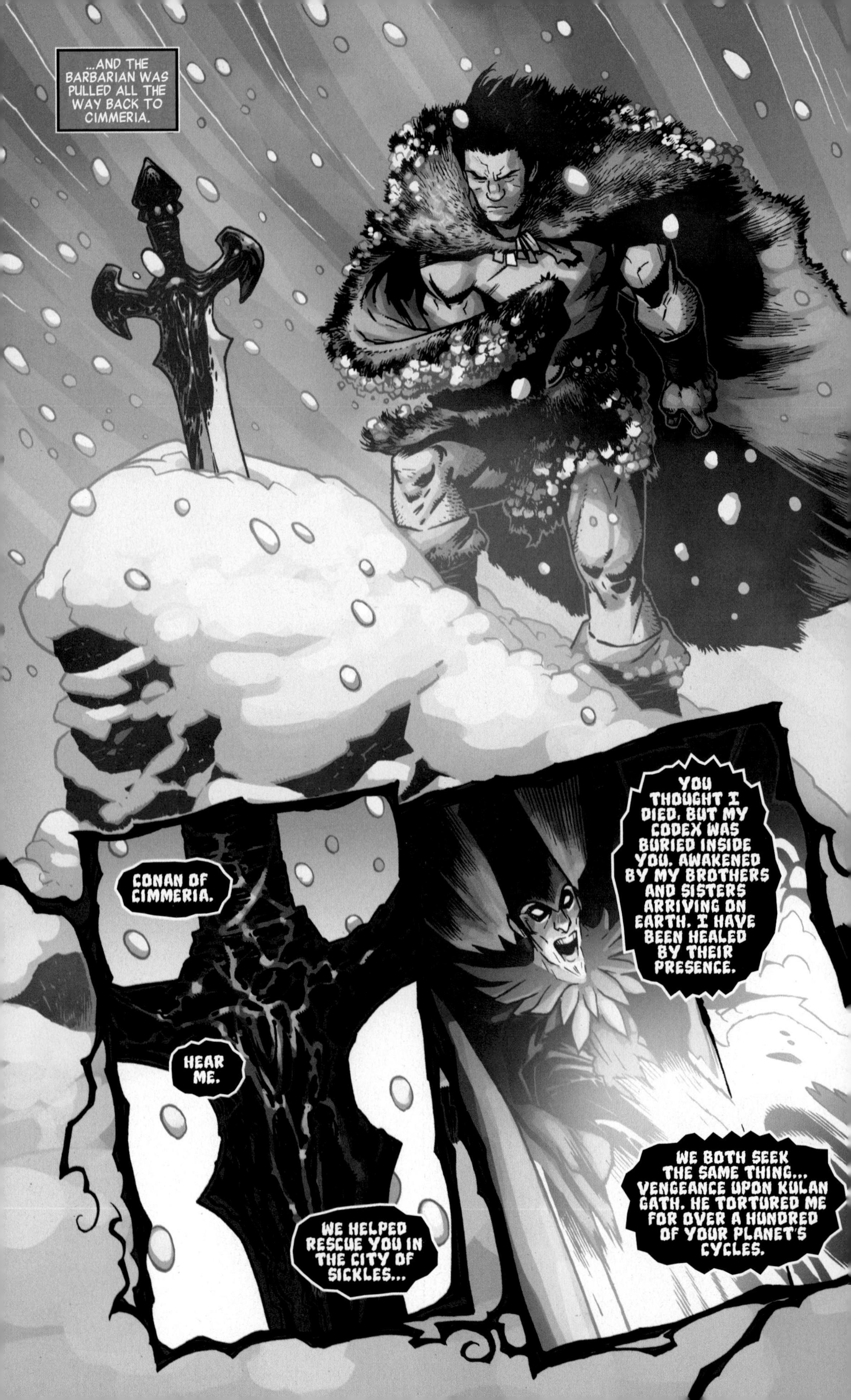
...AND THE BARBARIAN WAS PULLED ALL THE WAY BACK TO CIMMERIA.
CONAN OF CIMMERIA.
YOU THOUGHT I DIED, BUT MY CODEX WAS BURIED INSIDE YOU. AWAKENED BY MY BROTHERS AND SISTERS ARRIVING ON EARTH. I HAVE BEEN HEALED BY THEIR PRESENCE.
HEAR ME.
WE HELPED RESCUE YOU IN THE CITY OF SICKLES...
WE BOTH SEEK THE SAME THING... VENGEANCE UPON KULAN GATH. HE TORTURED ME FOR OVER A HUNDRED OF YOUR PLANET'S CYCLES.

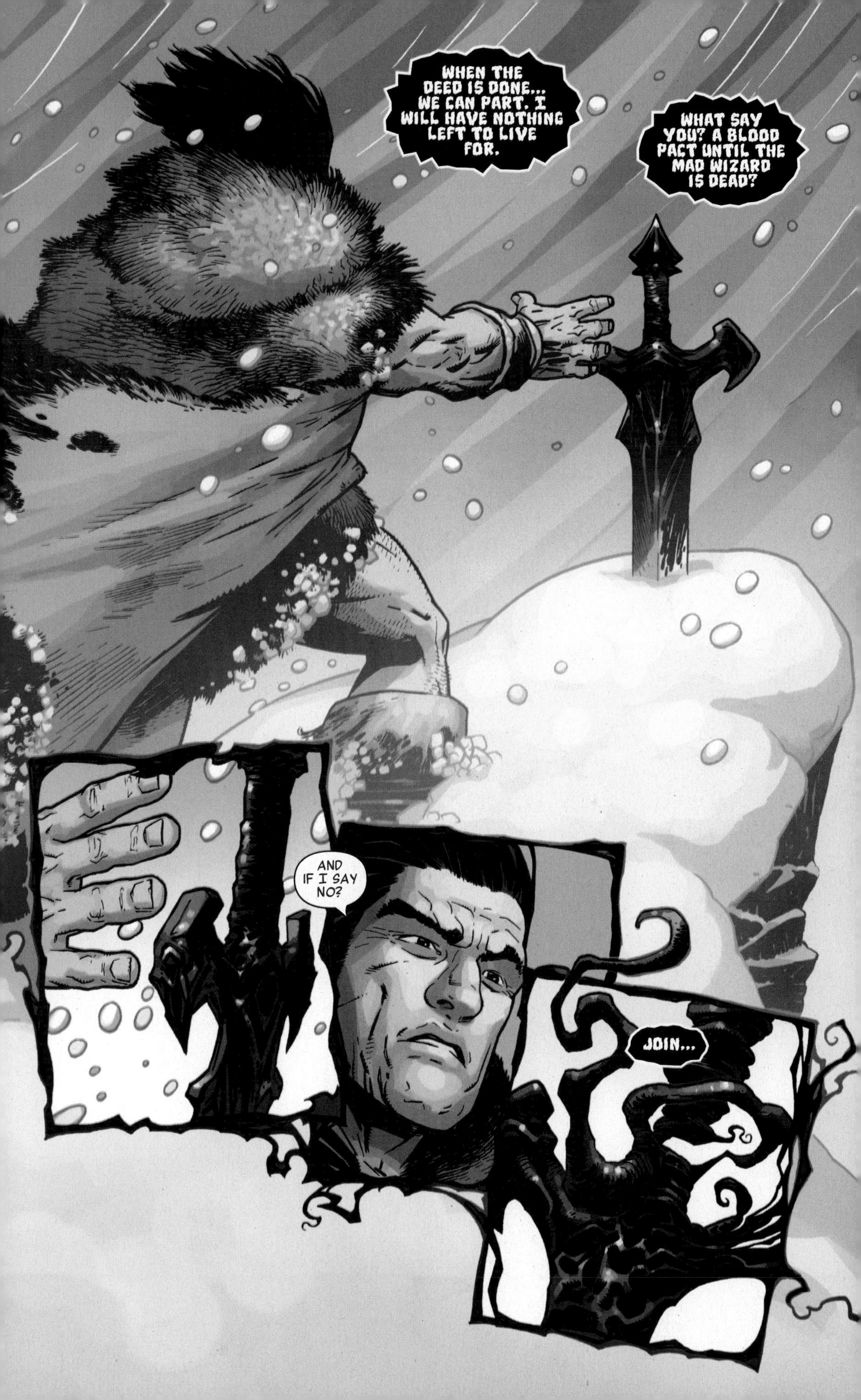
WHEN THE DEED IS DONE... WE CAN PART. I WILL HAVE NOTHING LEFT TO LIVE FOR.
WHAT SAY YOU? A BLOOD PACT UNTIL THE MAD WIZARD IS DEAD?
AND IF I SAY NO?
JOIN...

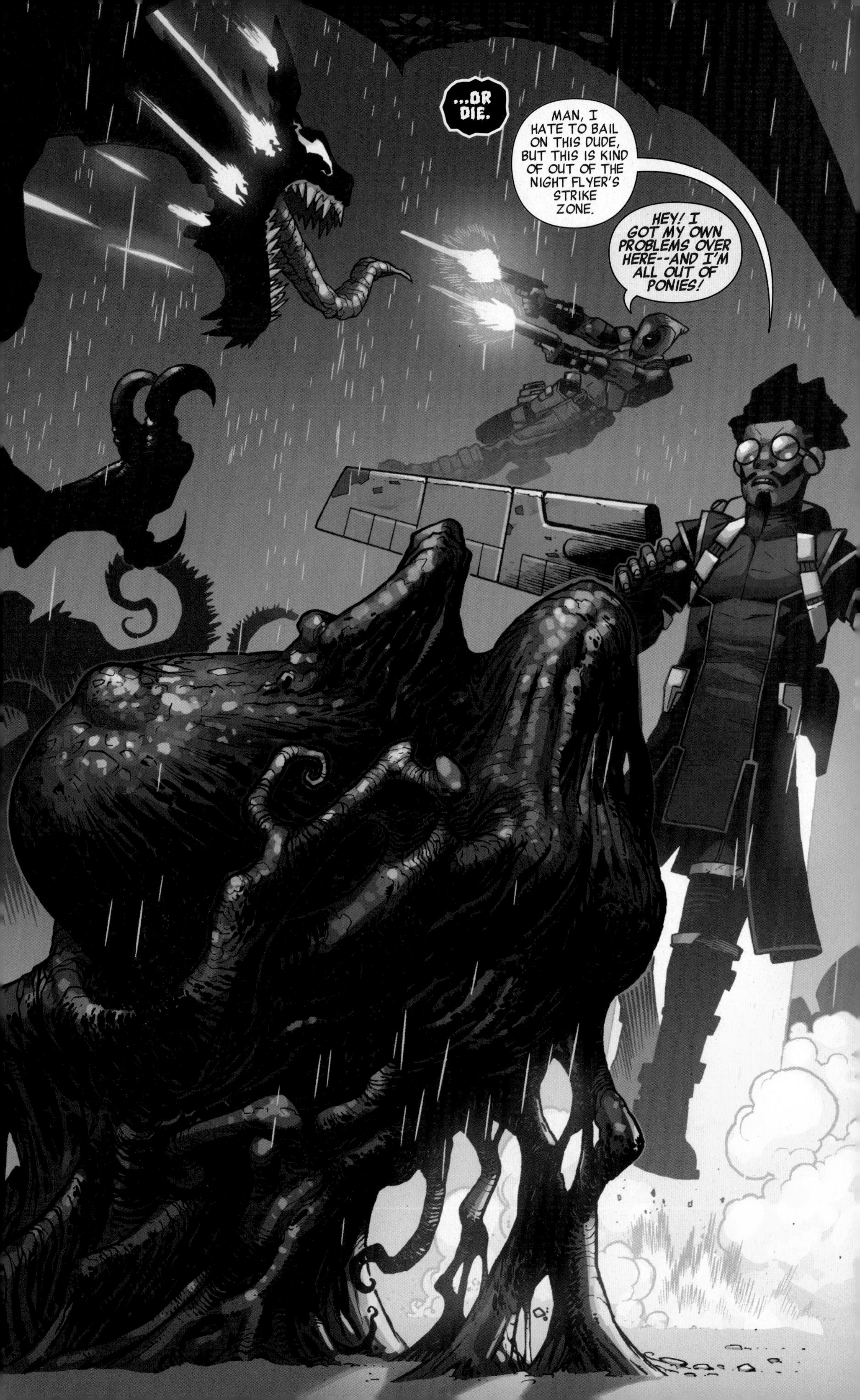
...OR DIE.
MAN, I HATE TO BAIL ON THIS DUDE, BUT THIS IS KIND OF OUT OF THE NIGHT FLYER'S STRIKE ZONE.
HEY! I GOT MY OWN PROBLEMS OVER HERE--AND I'M ALL OUT OF PONIES!

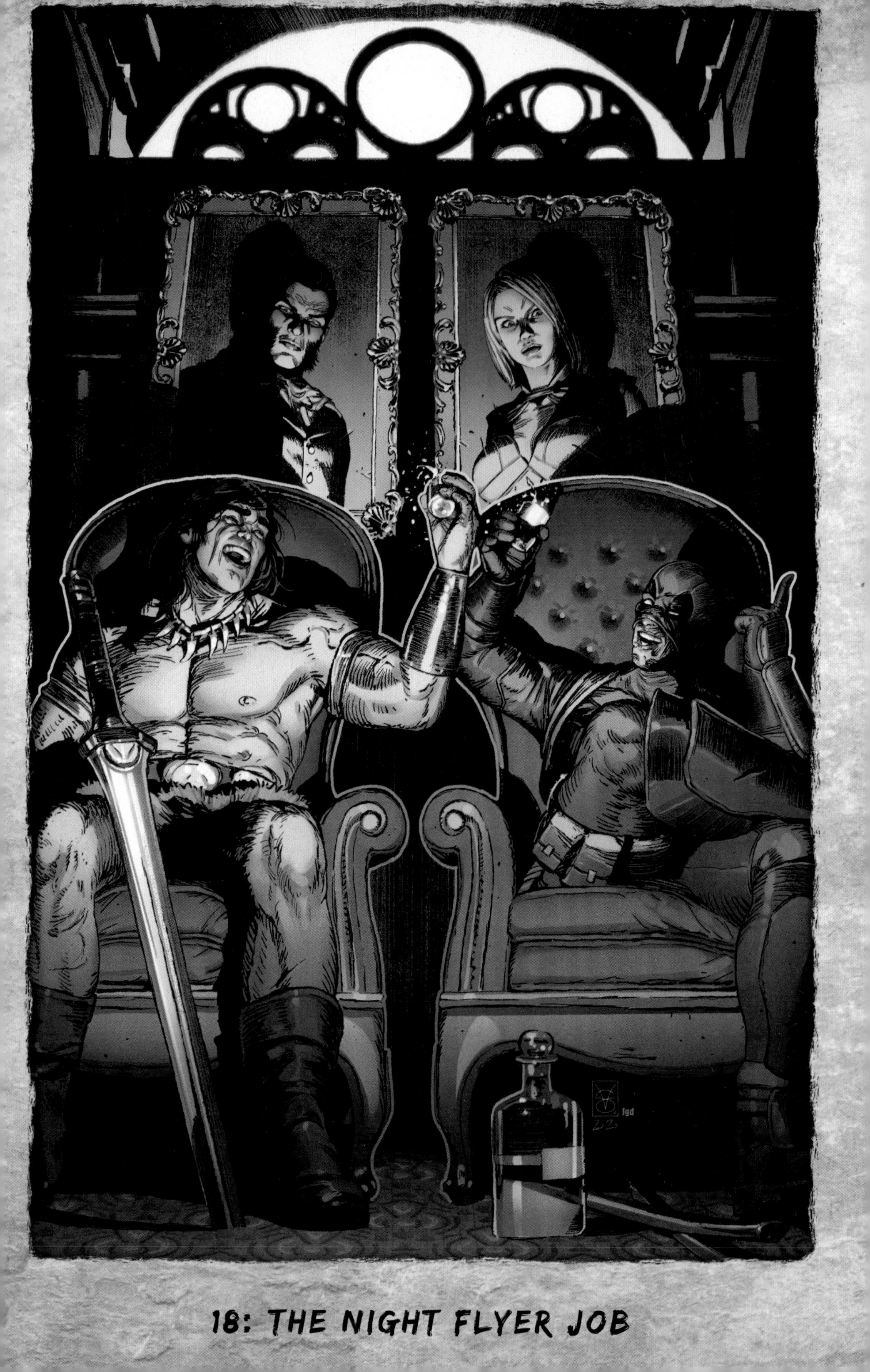

18: THE NIGHT FLYER JOB

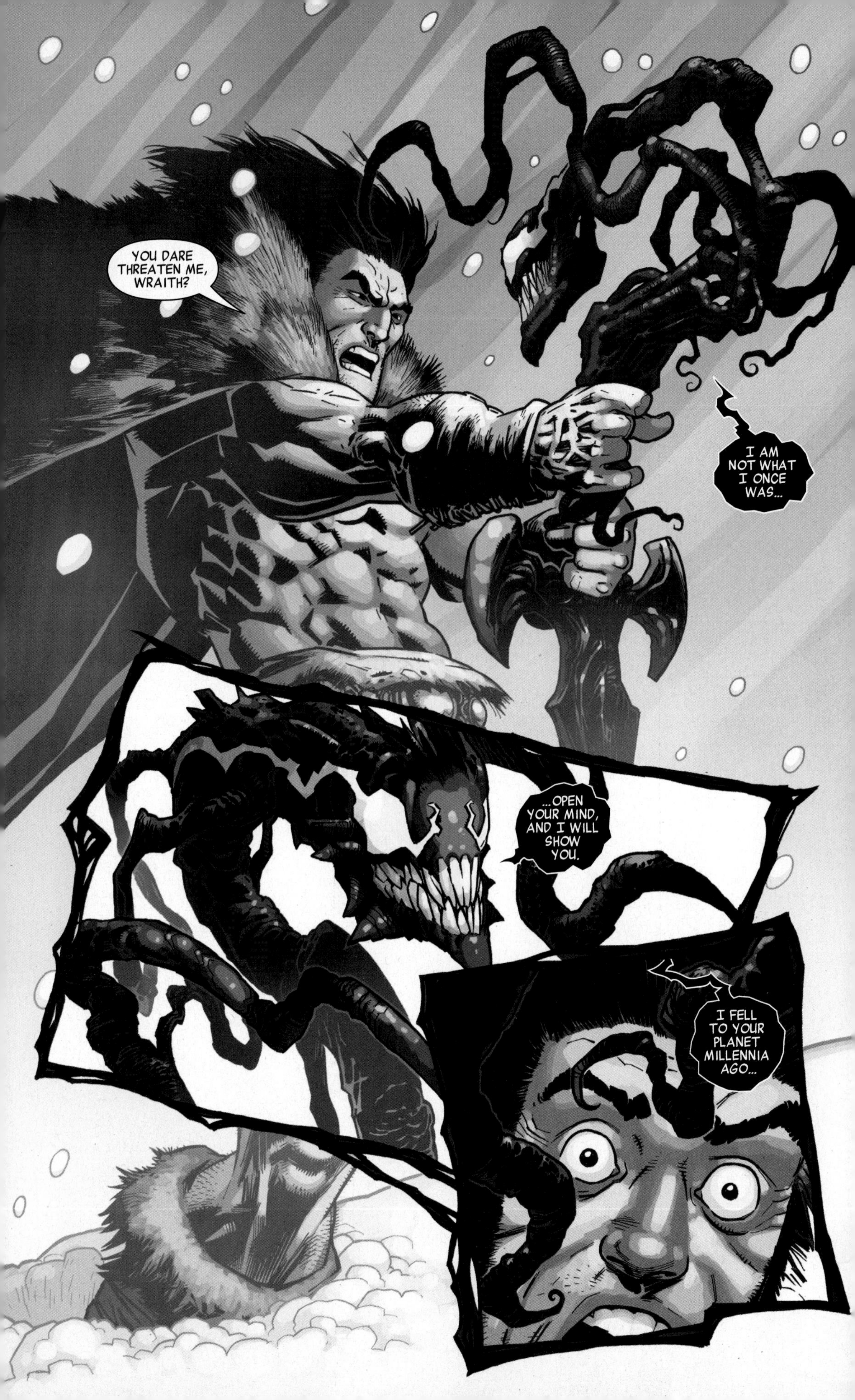
YOU DARE THREATEN ME, WRAITH?
I AM NOT WHAT I ONCE WAS...
...OPEN YOUR MIND, AND I WILL SHOW YOU.
I FELL TO YOUR PLANET MILLENNIA AGO...

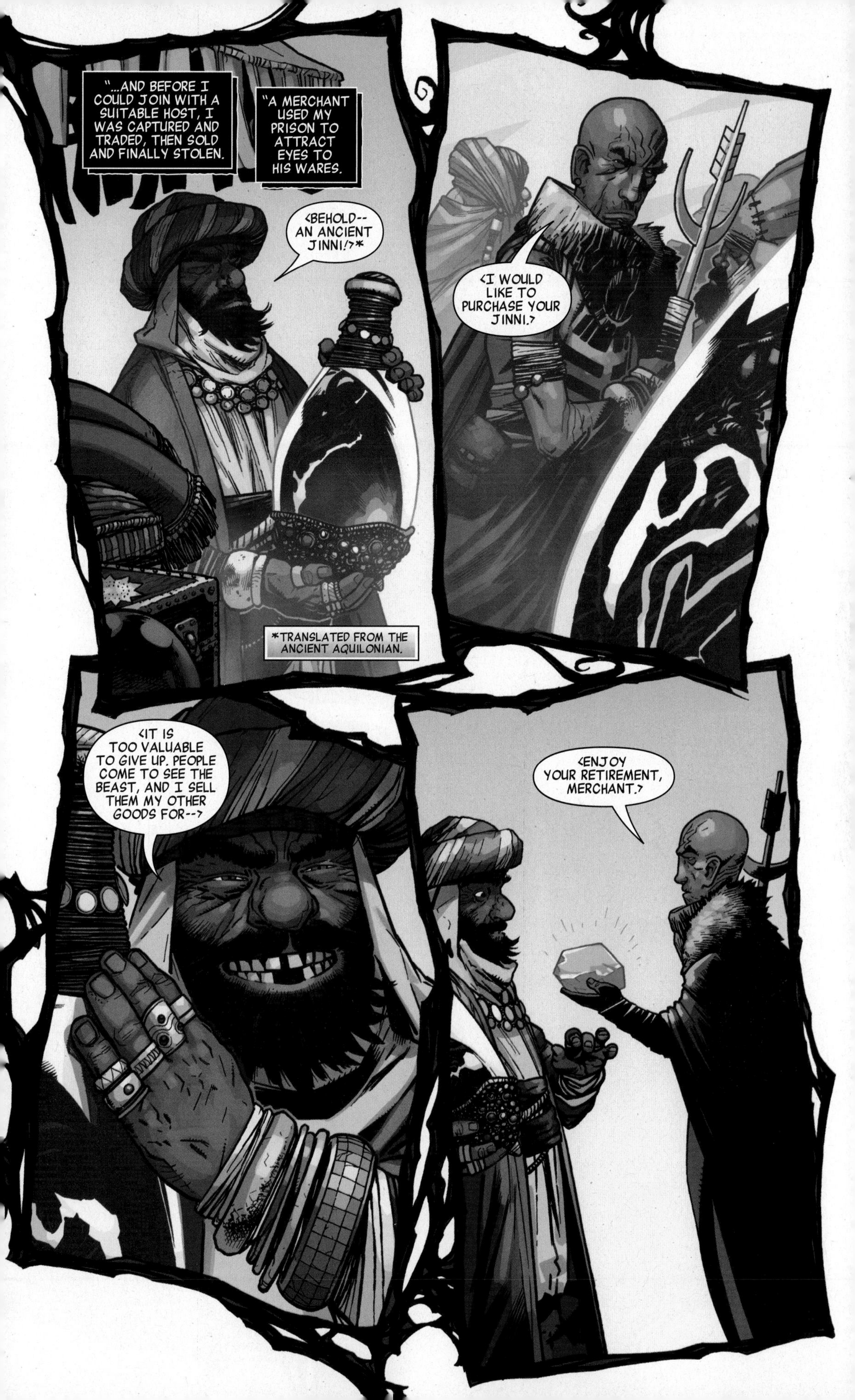
"...AND BEFORE I COULD JOIN WITH A SUITABLE HOST, I WAS CAPTURED AND TRADED, THEN SOLD AND FINALLY STOLEN.
"A MERCHANT USED MY PRISON TO ATTRACT EYES TO HIS WARES.
<BEHOLD-- AN ANCIENT JINNI!>*
*TRANSLATED FROM THE ANCIENT AQUILONIAN.
<I WOULD LIKE TO PURCHASE YOUR JINNI.>
<IT IS TOO VALUABLE TO GIVE UP. PEOPLE COME TO SEE THE BEAST, AND I SELL THEM MY OTHER GOODS FOR-->
<ENJOY YOUR RETIREMENT, MERCHANT.>

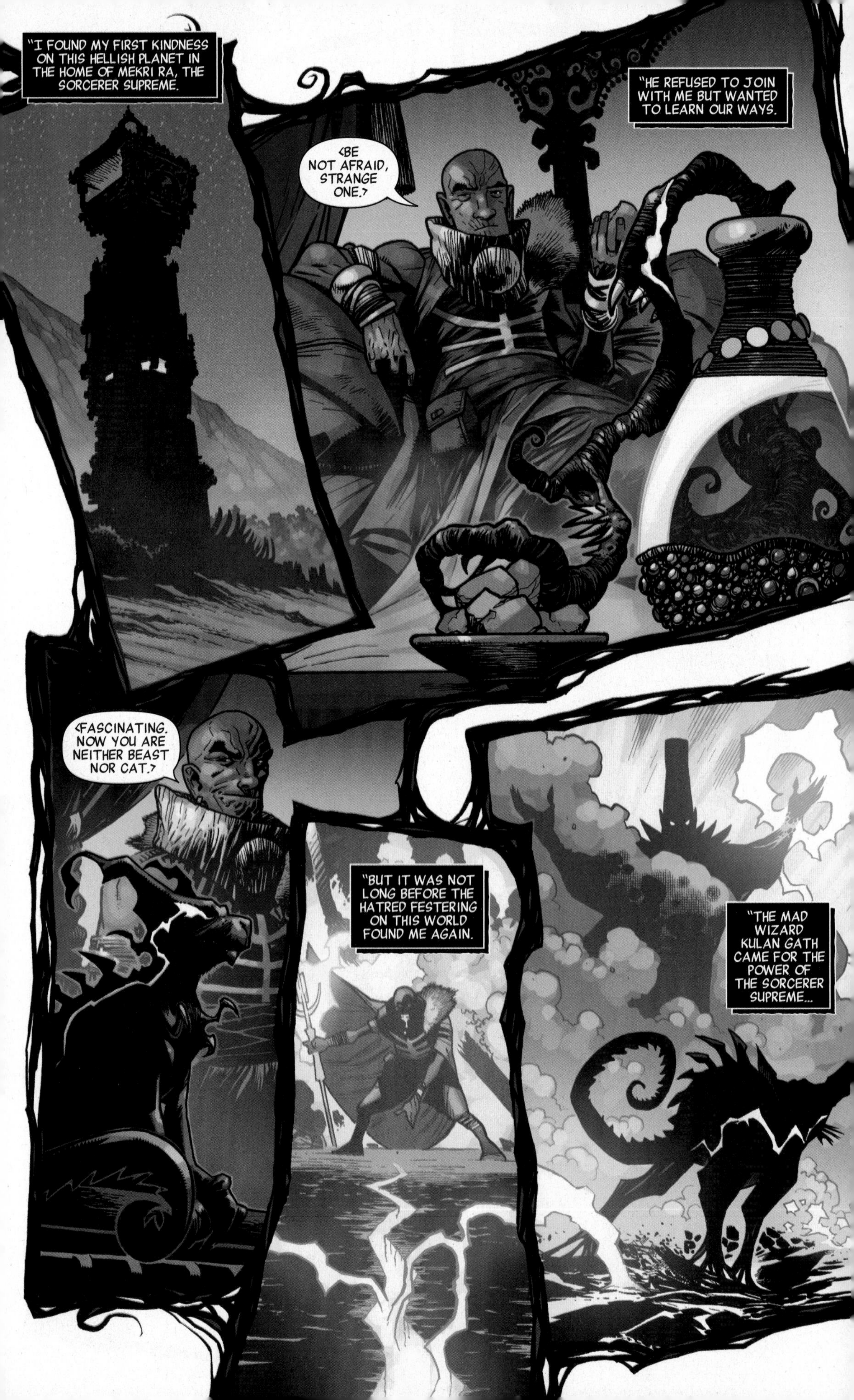
"I FOUND MY FIRST KINDNESS ON THIS HELLISH PLANET IN THE HOME OF MEKRI RA, THE SORCERER SUPREME.
"HE REFUSED TO JOIN WITH ME BUT WANTED TO LEARN OUR WAYS.
<BE NOT AFRAID, STRANGE ONE.>
<FASCINATING. NOW YOU ARE NEITHER BEAST NOR CAT.>
"BUT IT WAS NOT LONG BEFORE THE HATRED FESTERING ON THIS WORLD FOUND ME AGAIN.
"THE MAD WIZARD KULAN GATH CAME FOR THE POWER OF THE SORCERER SUPREME...

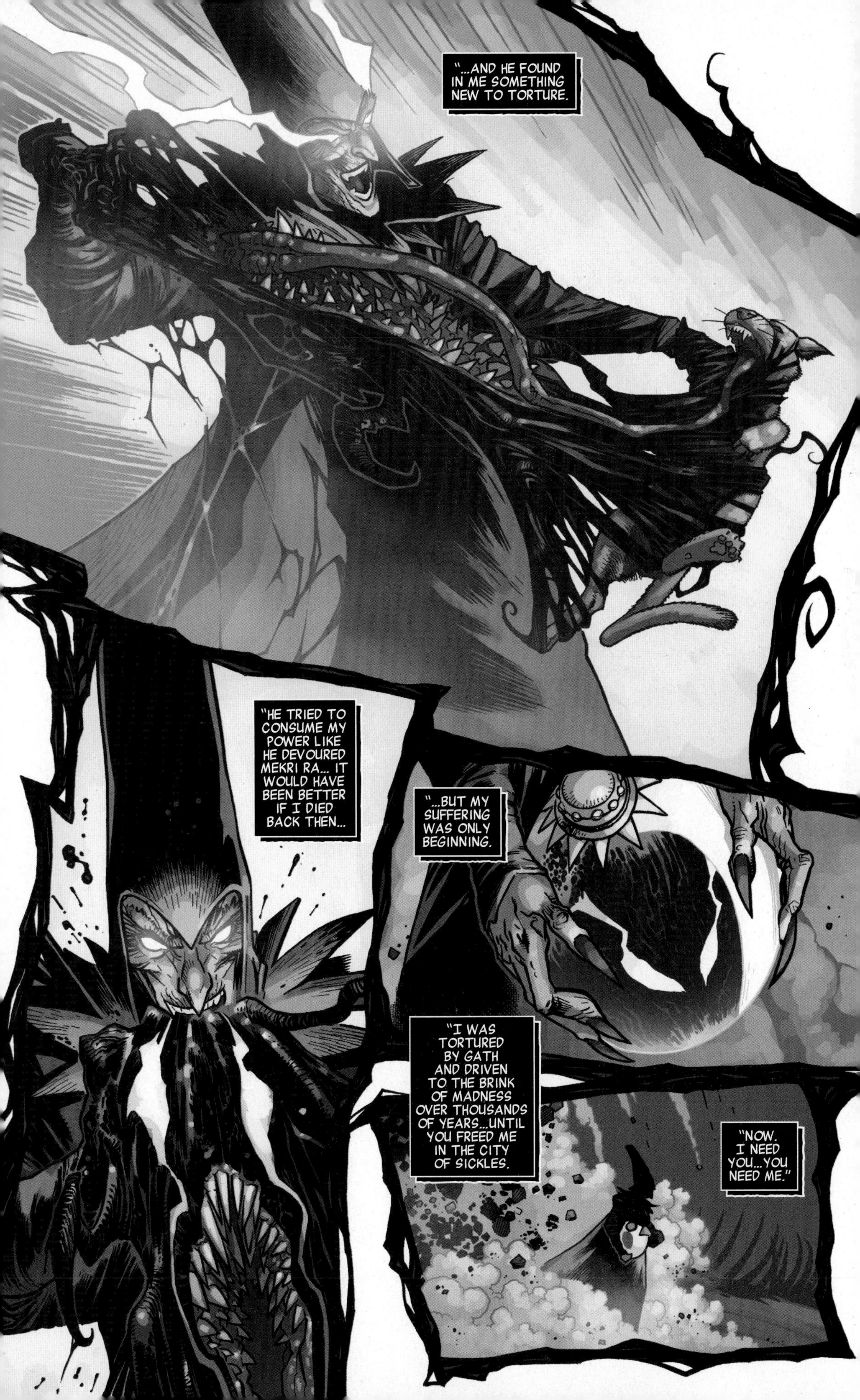
"...AND HE FOUND IN ME SOMETHING NEW TO TORTURE.
"HE TRIED TO CONSUME MY POWER LIKE HE DEVOURED MEKRI RA... IT WOULD HAVE BEEN BETTER IF I DIED BACK THEN...
"...BUT MY SUFFERING WAS ONLY BEGINNING.
"I WAS TORTURED BY GATH AND DRIVEN TO THE BRINK OF MADNESS OVER THOUSANDS OF YEARS...UNTIL YOU FREED ME IN THE CITY OF SICKLES.
"NOW. I NEED YOU...YOU NEED ME."

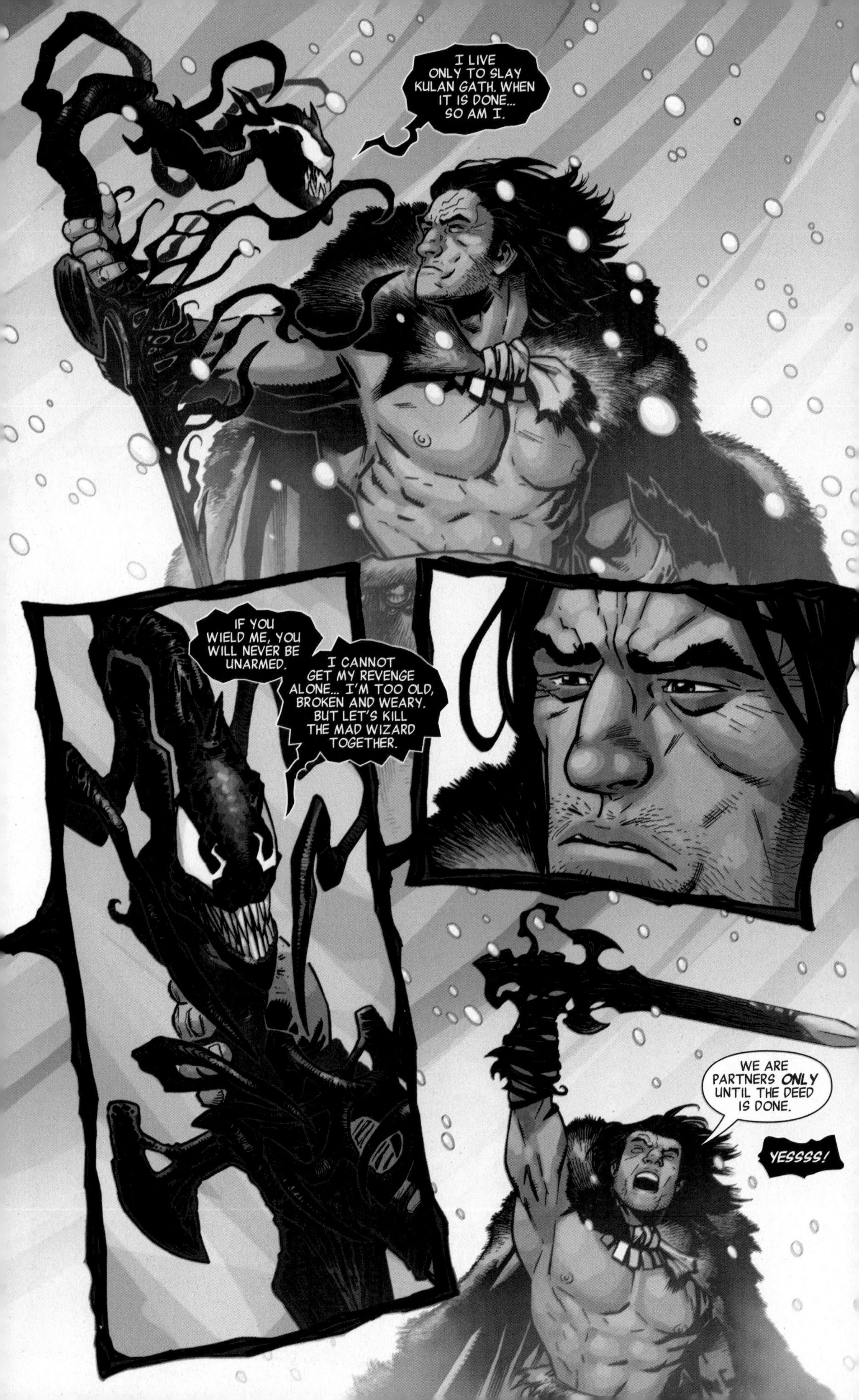

I LIVE ONLY TO SLAY KULAN GATH. WHEN IT IS DONE... SO AM I.
IF YOU WIELD ME, YOU WILL NEVER BE UNARMED.
I CANNOT GET MY REVENGE ALONE... I'M TOO OLD, BROKEN AND WEARY. BUT LET'S KILL THE MAD WIZARD TOGETHER.
WE ARE PARTNERS ONLY UNTIL THE DEED IS DONE.
YESSSS!

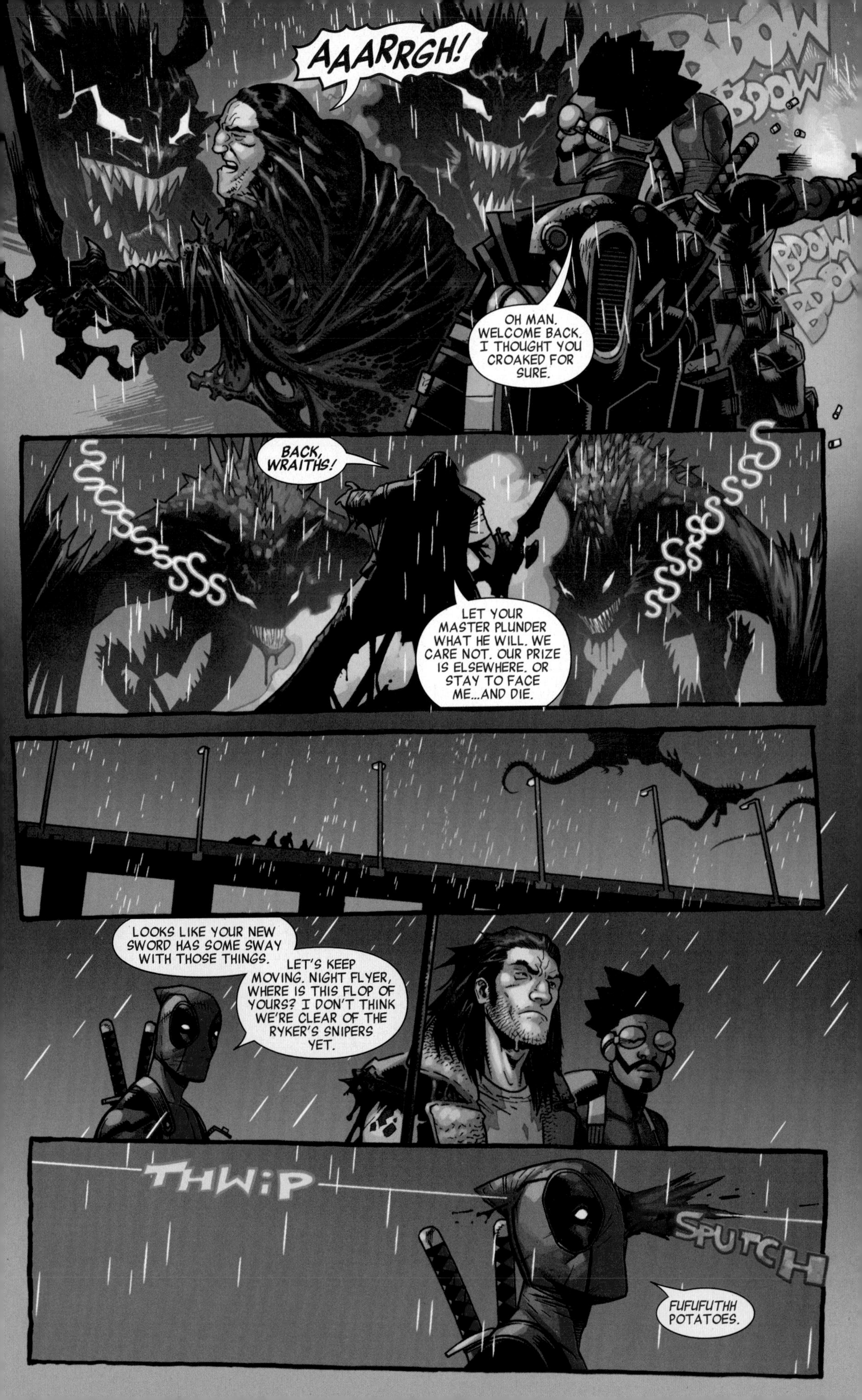

AAARRGH!
BDOW
BDOW
OH MAN. WELCOME BACK. I THOUGHT YOU CROAKED FOR SURE.
BDOW
BDOW
BACK, WRAITHS!
SSSSSSSSS
SSSSSSSS
LET YOUR MASTER PLUNDER WHAT HE WILL. WE CARE NOT. OUR PRIZE IS ELSEWHERE. OR STAY TO FACE ME...AND DIE.
LOOKS LIKE YOUR NEW SWORD HAS SOME SWAY WITH THOSE THINGS.
LET'S KEEP MOVING. NIGHT FLYER, WHERE IS THIS FLOP OF YOURS? I DON'T THINK WE'RE CLEAR OF THE RYKER'S SNIPERS YET.
THWiP
SPUTCH
FUFUFUTHH POTATOES.

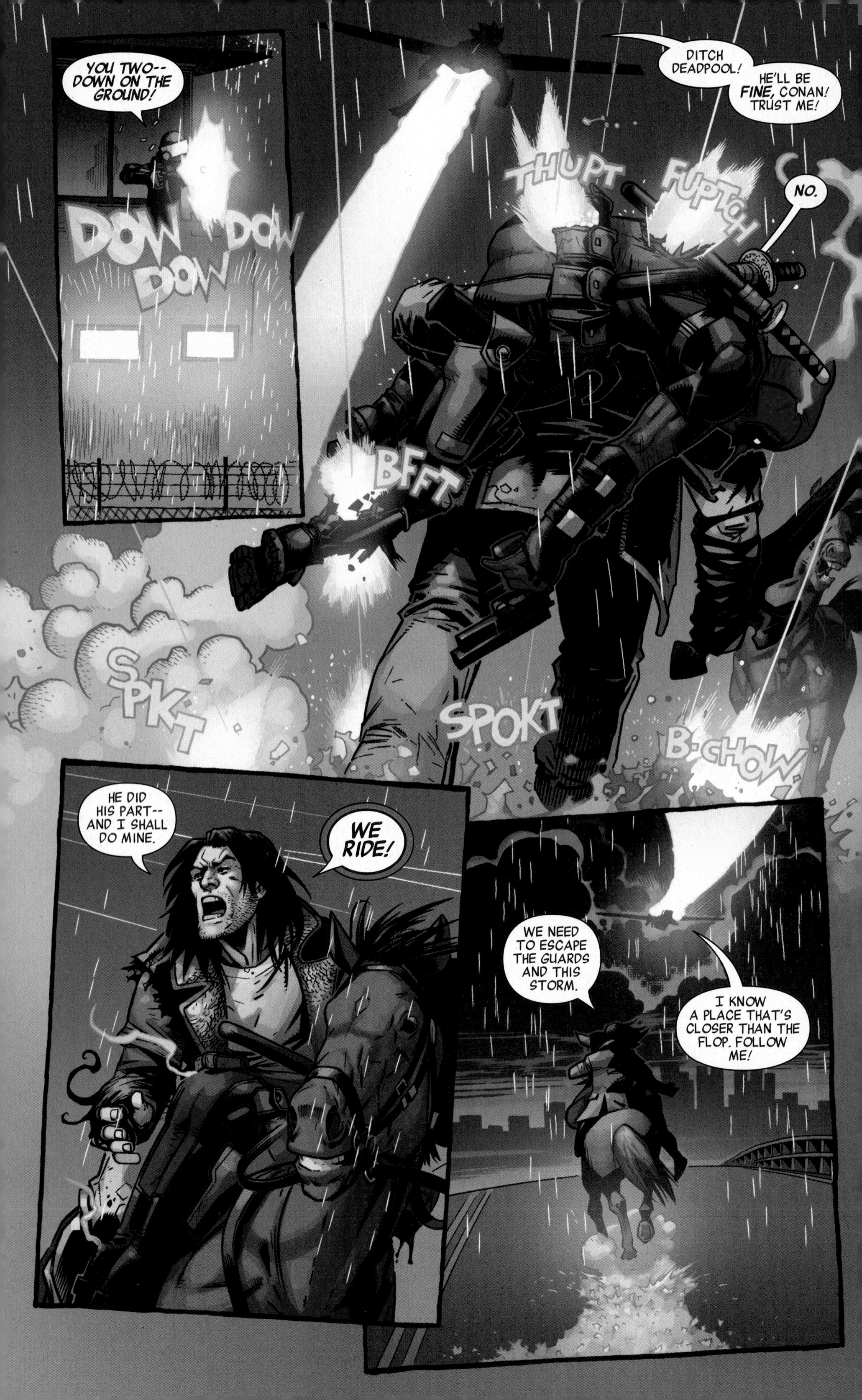

YOU TWO-- DOWN ON THE GROUND!
DOW DOW DOW
DITCH DEADPOOL!
HE'LL BE FINE, CONAN! TRUST ME!
THUPT
FUPTCH
NO.
BFFT
SPKT
SPOKT
B-CHOW
HE DID HIS PART-- AND I SHALL DO MINE.
WE RIDE!
WE NEED TO ESCAPE THE GUARDS AND THIS STORM.
I KNOW A PLACE THAT'S CLOSER THAN THE FLOP. FOLLOW ME!

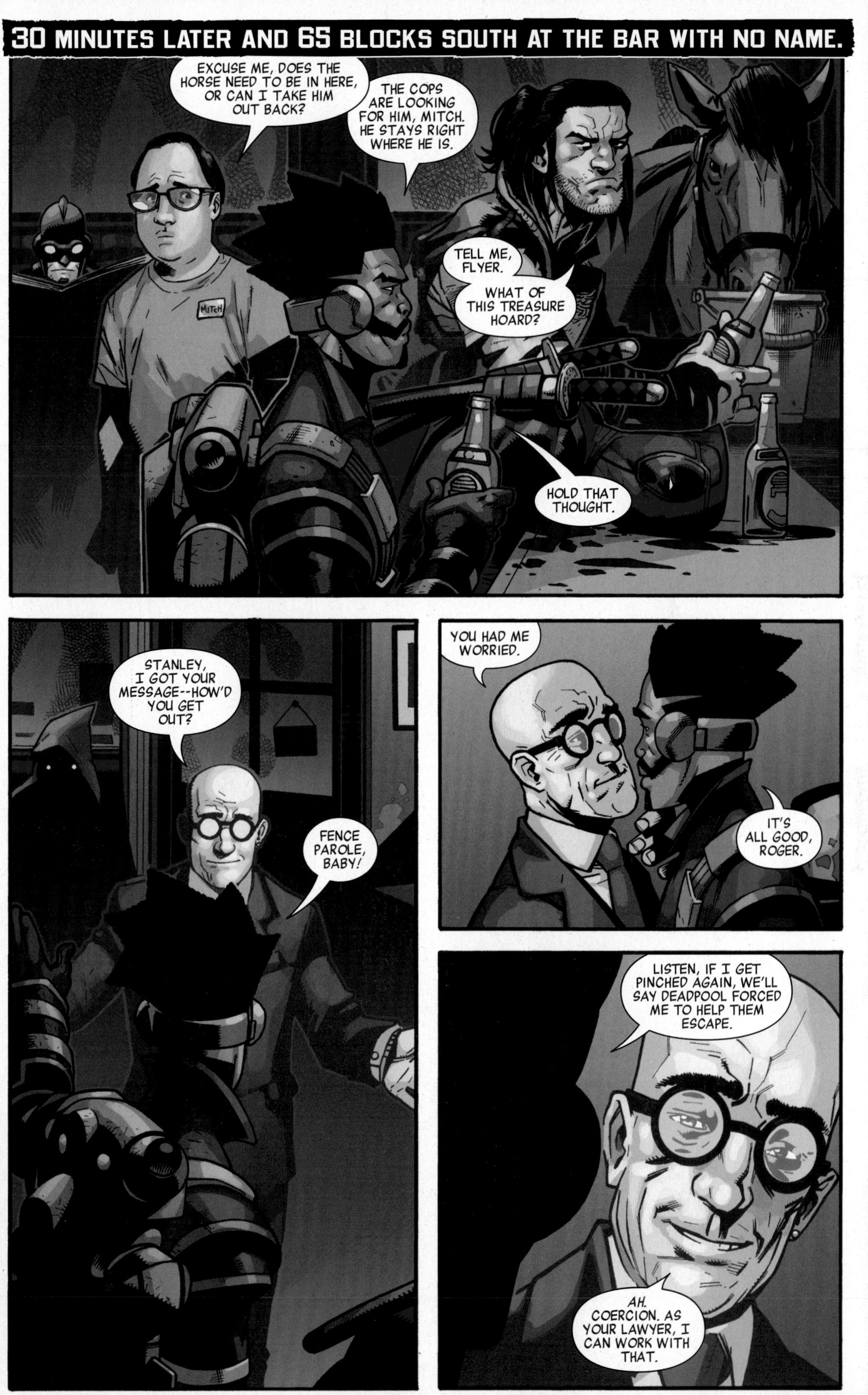
30 MINUTES LATER AND 65 BLOCKS SOUTH AT THE BAR WITH NO NAME.
EXCUSE ME, DOES THE HORSE NEED TO BE IN HERE, OR CAN I TAKE HIM OUT BACK?
THE COPS ARE LOOKING FOR HIM, MITCH. HE STAYS RIGHT WHERE HE IS.
MITCH
TELL ME, FLYER.
WHAT OF THIS TREASURE HOARD?
HOLD THAT THOUGHT.
STANLEY, I GOT YOUR MESSAGE--HOW'D YOU GET OUT?
FENCE PAROLE, BABY!
YOU HAD ME WORRIED.
IT'S ALL GOOD, ROGER.
LISTEN, IF I GET PINCHED AGAIN, WE'LL SAY DEADPOOL FORCED ME TO HELP THEM ESCAPE.
AH. COERCION. AS YOUR LAWYER, I CAN WORK WITH THAT.

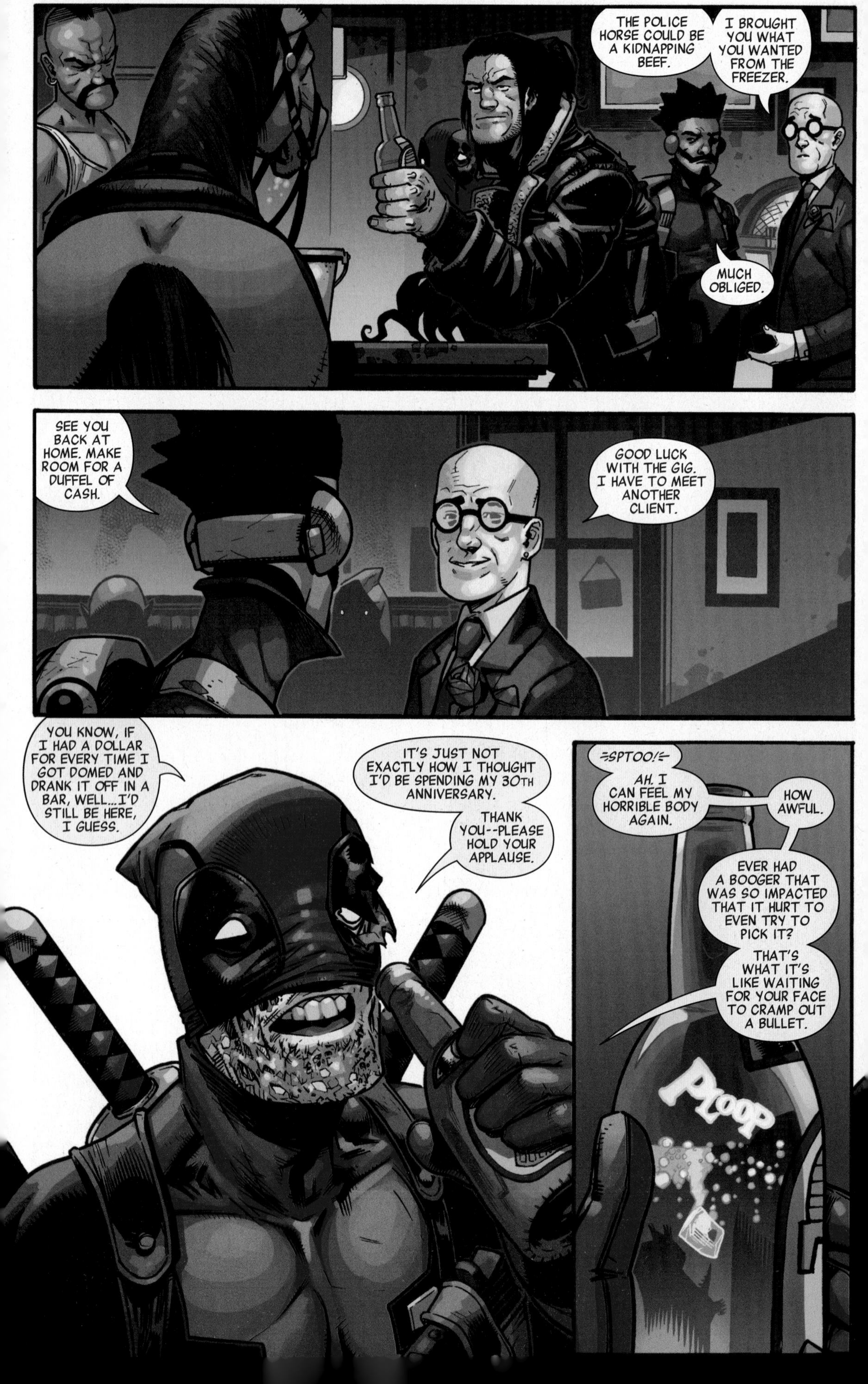
THE POLICE HORSE COULD BE A KIDNAPPING BEEF.
I BROUGHT YOU WHAT YOU WANTED FROM THE FREEZER.
MUCH OBLIGED.
SEE YOU BACK AT HOME. MAKE ROOM FOR A DUFFEL OF CASH.
GOOD LUCK WITH THE GIG. I HAVE TO MEET ANOTHER CLIENT.
YOU KNOW, IF I HAD A DOLLAR FOR EVERY TIME I GOT DOMED AND DRANK IT OFF IN A BAR, WELL...I'D STILL BE HERE, I GUESS.
IT'S JUST NOT EXACTLY HOW I THOUGHT I'D BE SPENDING MY 30TH ANNIVERSARY.
THANK YOU--PLEASE HOLD YOUR APPLAUSE.
SPTOO!
AH. I CAN FEEL MY HORRIBLE BODY AGAIN.
HOW AWFUL.
EVER HAD A BOOGER THAT WAS SO IMPACTED THAT IT HURT TO EVEN TRY TO PICK IT?
THAT'S WHAT IT'S LIKE WAITING FOR YOUR FACE TO CRAMP OUT A BULLET.
PLOOP

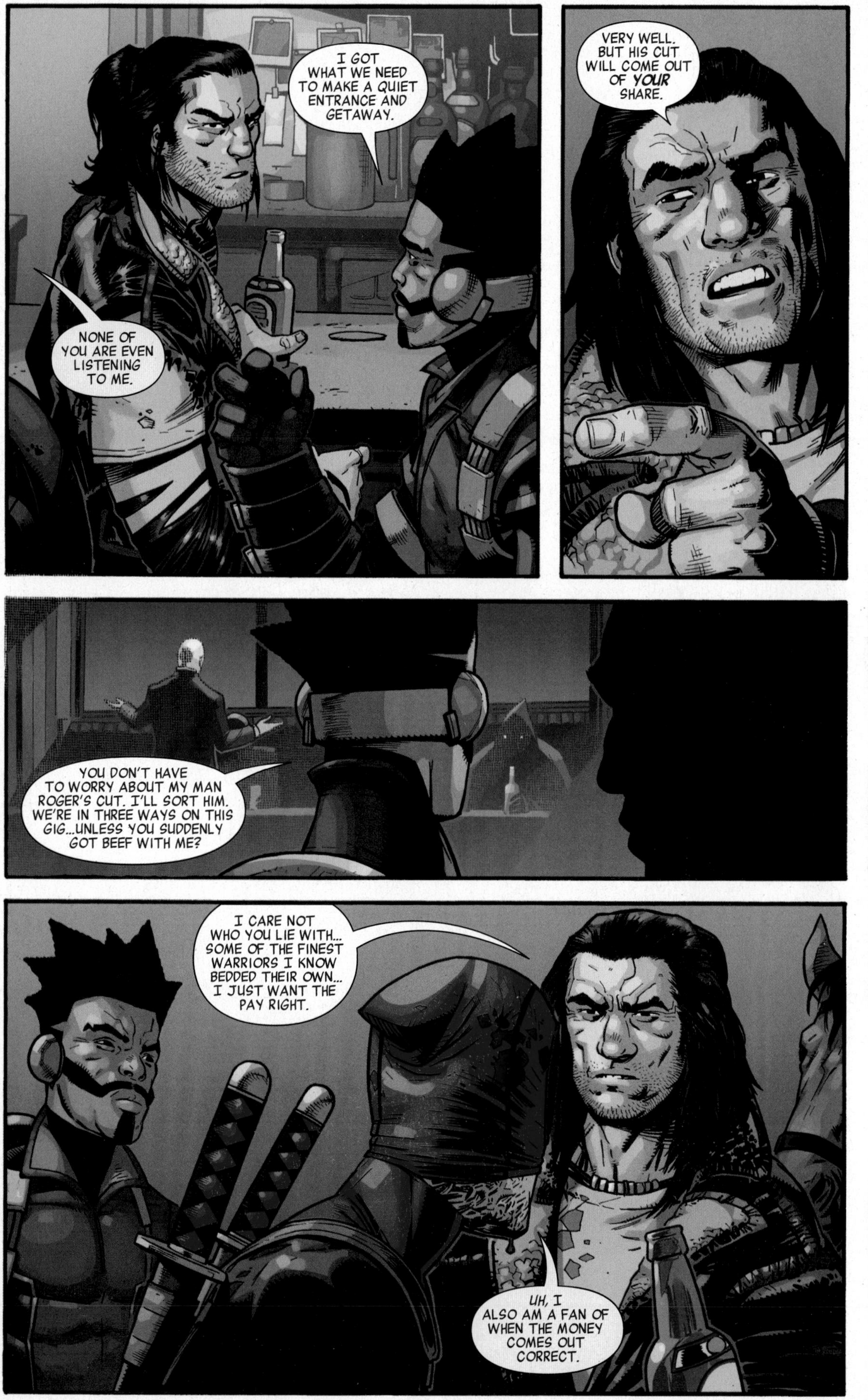
I GOT WHAT WE NEED TO MAKE A QUIET ENTRANCE AND GETAWAY.
NONE OF YOU ARE EVEN LISTENING TO ME.
VERY WELL. BUT HIS CUT WILL COME OUT OF *YOUR* SHARE.
YOU DON'T HAVE TO WORRY ABOUT MY MAN ROGER'S CUT. I'LL SORT HIM. WE'RE IN THREE WAYS ON THIS GIG...UNLESS YOU SUDDENLY GOT BEEF WITH ME?
I CARE NOT WHO YOU LIE WITH... SOME OF THE FINEST WARRIORS I KNOW BEDDED THEIR OWN... I JUST WANT THE PAY RIGHT.
UH, I ALSO AM A FAN OF WHEN THE MONEY COMES OUT CORRECT.

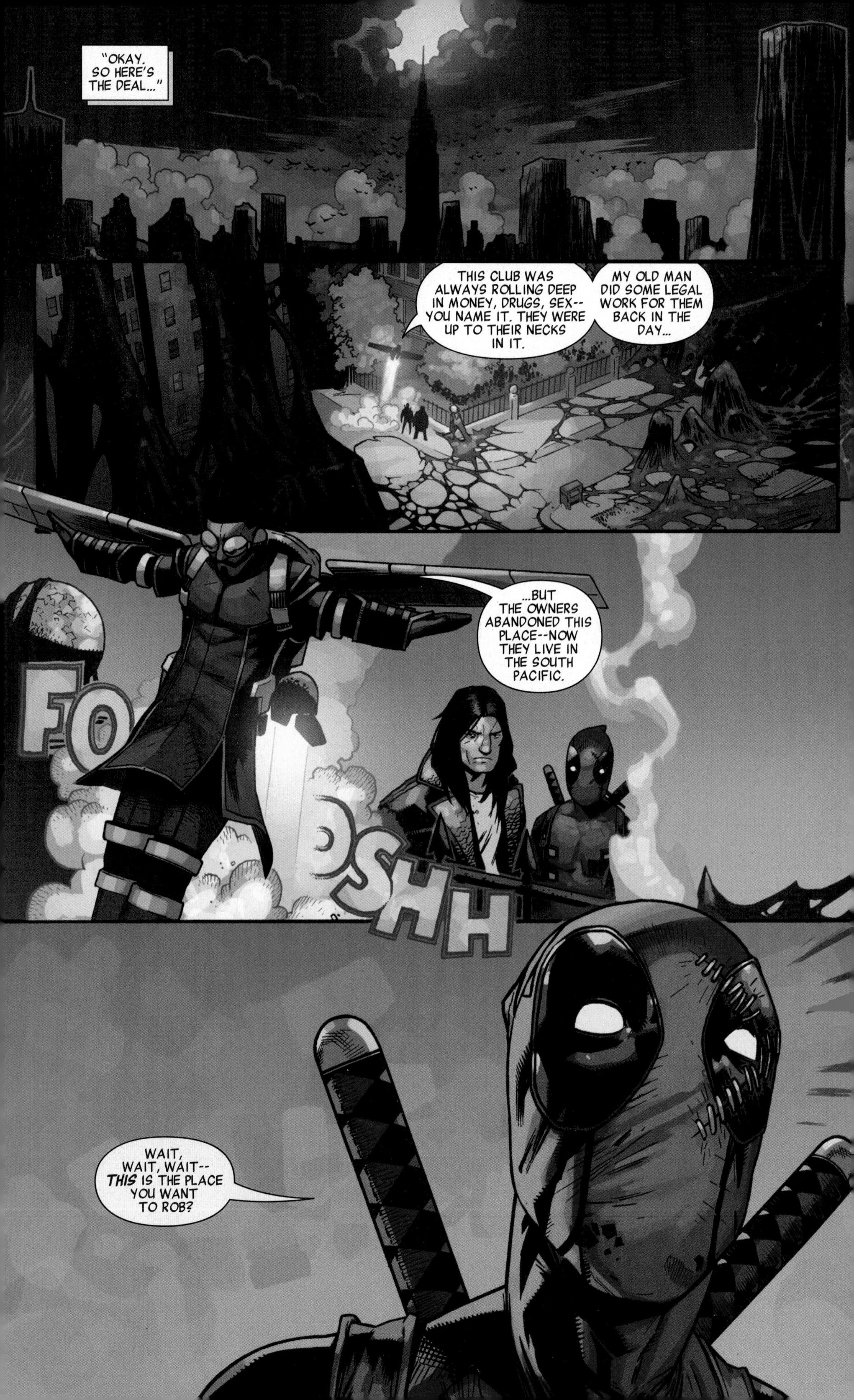
"OKAY. SO HERE'S THE DEAL..."
THIS CLUB WAS ALWAYS ROLLING DEEP IN MONEY, DRUGS, SEX-- YOU NAME IT. THEY WERE UP TO THEIR NECKS IN IT.
MY OLD MAN DID SOME LEGAL WORK FOR THEM BACK IN THE DAY...
...BUT THE OWNERS ABANDONED THIS PLACE--NOW THEY LIVE IN THE SOUTH PACIFIC.
FOOSHH
WAIT, WAIT, WAIT-- *THIS* IS THE PLACE YOU WANT TO ROB?

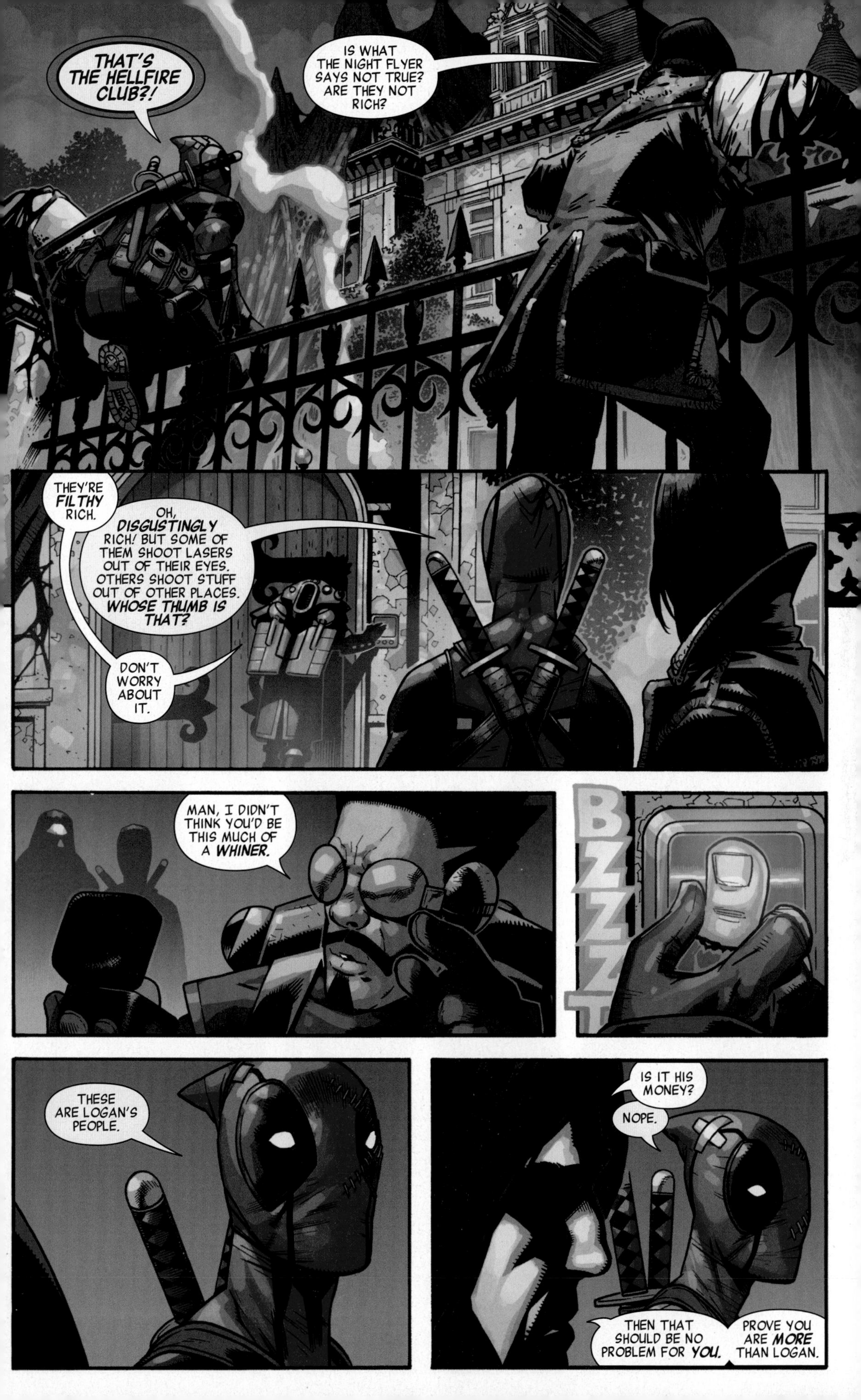
THAT'S THE HELLFIRE CLUB?!
IS WHAT THE NIGHT FLYER SAYS NOT TRUE? ARE THEY NOT RICH?
THEY'RE FILTHY RICH.
OH, DISGUSTINGLY RICH! BUT SOME OF THEM SHOOT LASERS OUT OF THEIR EYES. OTHERS SHOOT STUFF OUT OF OTHER PLACES. WHOSE THUMB IS THAT?
DON'T WORRY ABOUT IT.
MAN, I DIDN'T THINK YOU'D BE THIS MUCH OF A WHINER.
BZZZT
THESE ARE LOGAN'S PEOPLE.
IS IT HIS MONEY?
NOPE.
THEN THAT SHOULD BE NO PROBLEM FOR YOU.
PROVE YOU ARE MORE THAN LOGAN.

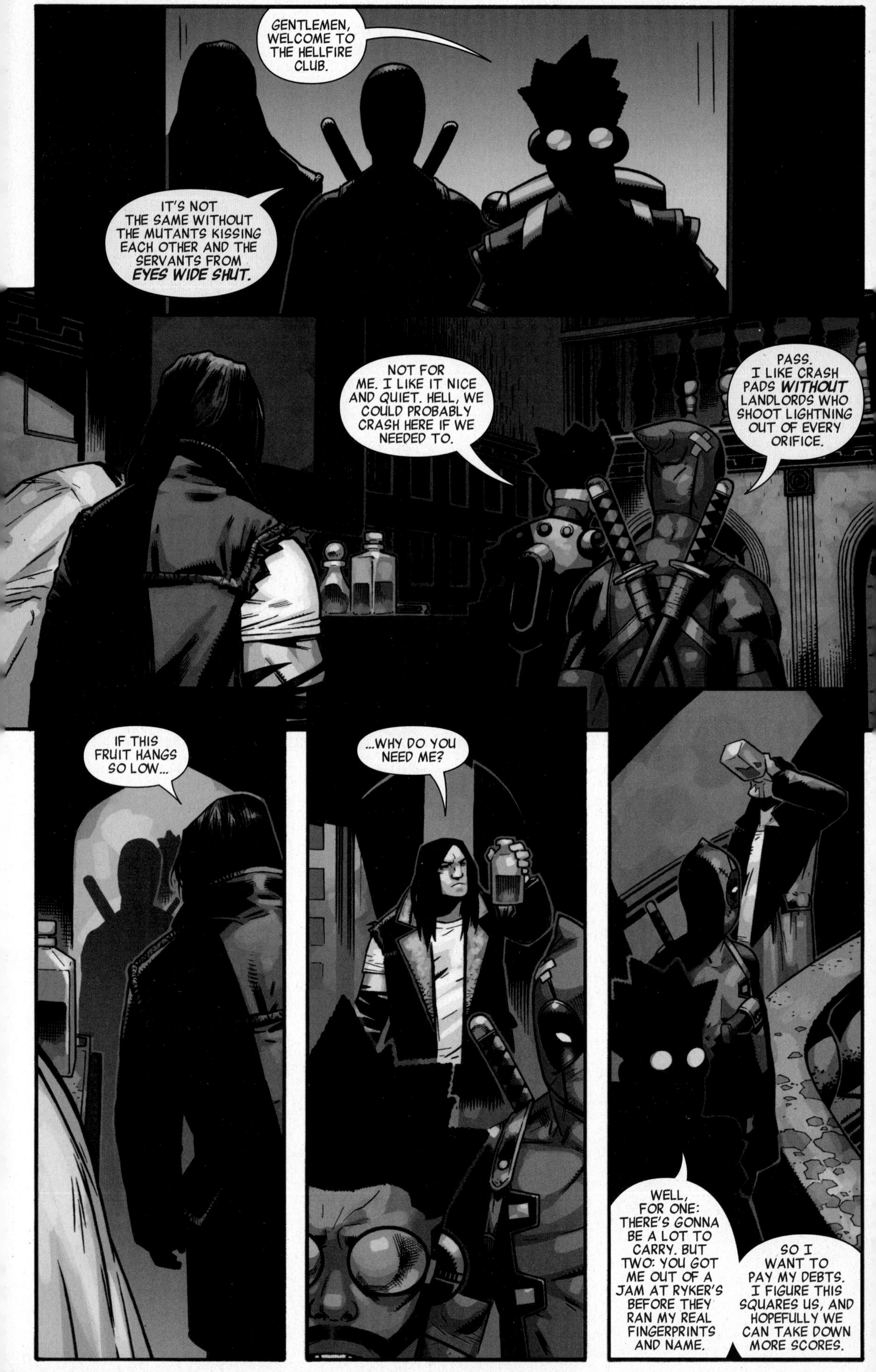
GENTLEMEN, WELCOME TO THE HELLFIRE CLUB.
IT'S NOT THE SAME WITHOUT THE MUTANTS KISSING EACH OTHER AND THE SERVANTS FROM **EYES WIDE SHUT.**
NOT FOR ME. I LIKE IT NICE AND QUIET. HELL, WE COULD PROBABLY CRASH HERE IF WE NEEDED TO.
PASS. I LIKE CRASH PADS **WITHOUT** LANDLORDS WHO SHOOT LIGHTNING OUT OF EVERY ORIFICE.
IF THIS FRUIT HANGS SO LOW...
...WHY DO YOU NEED ME?
WELL, FOR ONE: THERE'S GONNA BE A LOT TO CARRY. BUT TWO: YOU GOT ME OUT OF A JAM AT RYKER'S BEFORE THEY RAN MY REAL FINGERPRINTS AND NAME.
SO I WANT TO PAY MY DEBTS. I FIGURE THIS SQUARES US, AND HOPEFULLY WE CAN TAKE DOWN MORE SCORES.

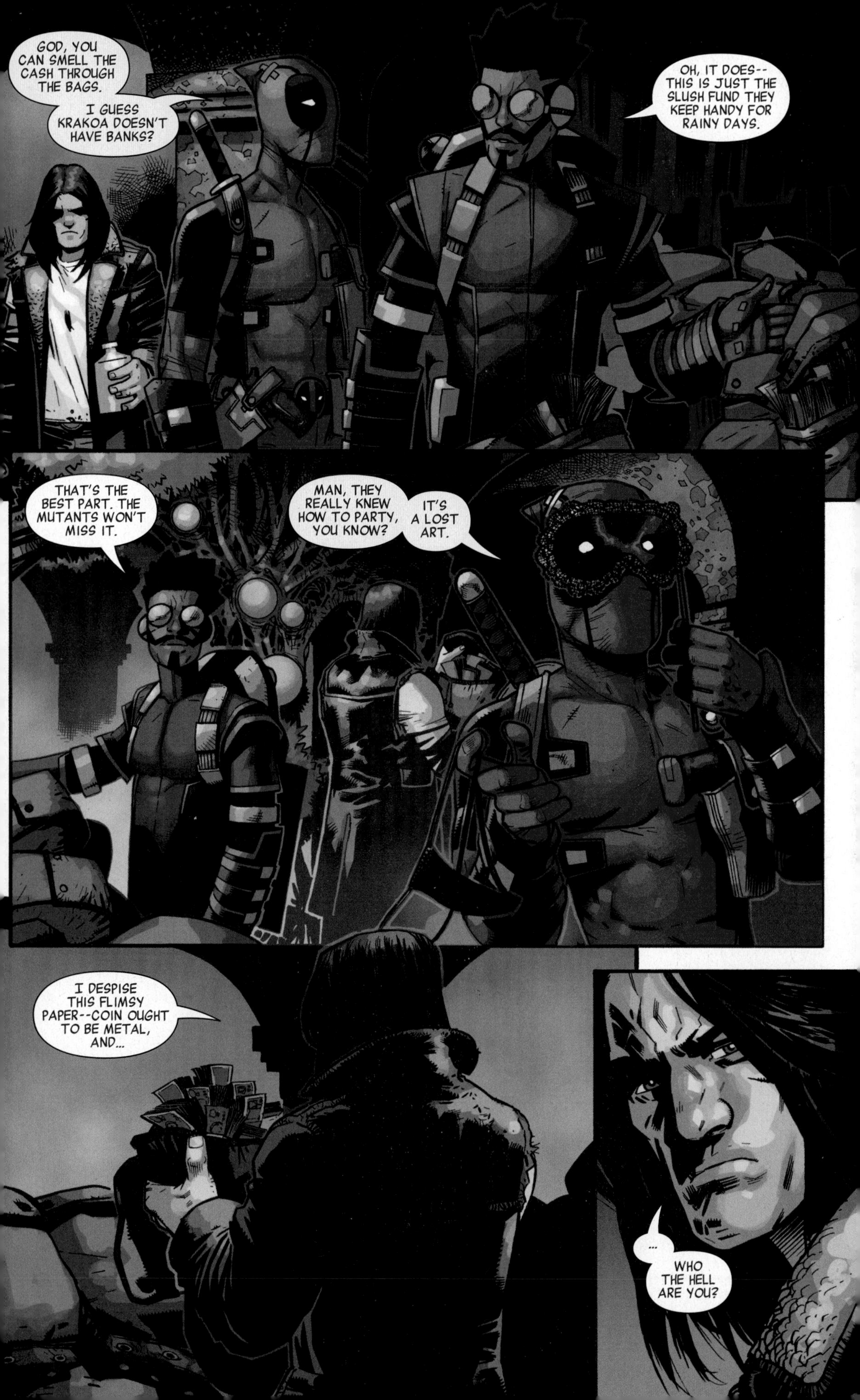
GOD, YOU CAN SMELL THE CASH THROUGH THE BAGS.
I GUESS KRAKOA DOESN'T HAVE BANKS?
OH, IT DOES-- THIS IS JUST THE SLUSH FUND THEY KEEP HANDY FOR RAINY DAYS.
THAT'S THE BEST PART. THE MUTANTS WON'T MISS IT.
MAN, THEY REALLY KNEW HOW TO PARTY, YOU KNOW?
IT'S A LOST ART.
I DESPISE THIS FLIMSY PAPER--COIN OUGHT TO BE METAL, AND...
...
WHO THE HELL ARE YOU?

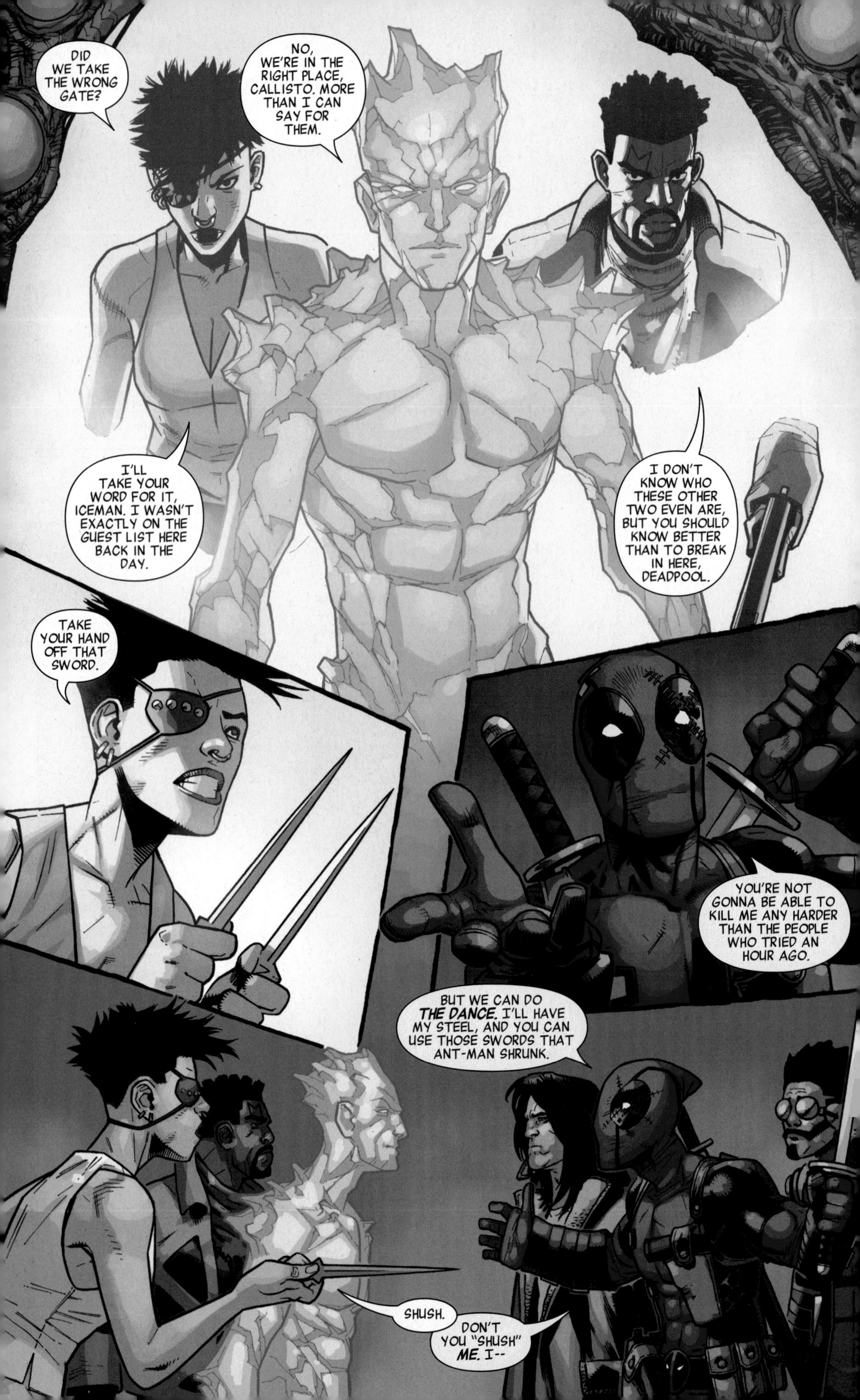
DID WE TAKE THE WRONG GATE?
NO, WE'RE IN THE RIGHT PLACE, CALLISTO. MORE THAN I CAN SAY FOR THEM.
I'LL TAKE YOUR WORD FOR IT, ICEMAN. I WASN'T EXACTLY ON THE GUEST LIST HERE BACK IN THE DAY.
I DON'T KNOW WHO THESE OTHER TWO EVEN ARE, BUT YOU SHOULD KNOW BETTER THAN TO BREAK IN HERE, DEADPOOL.
TAKE YOUR HAND OFF THAT SWORD.
YOU'RE NOT GONNA BE ABLE TO KILL ME ANY HARDER THAN THE PEOPLE WHO TRIED AN HOUR AGO.
BUT WE CAN DO ***THE DANCE.*** I'LL HAVE MY STEEL, AND YOU CAN USE THOSE SWORDS THAT ANT-MAN SHRUNK.
SHUSH.
DON'T YOU "SHUSH" ***ME.*** I--

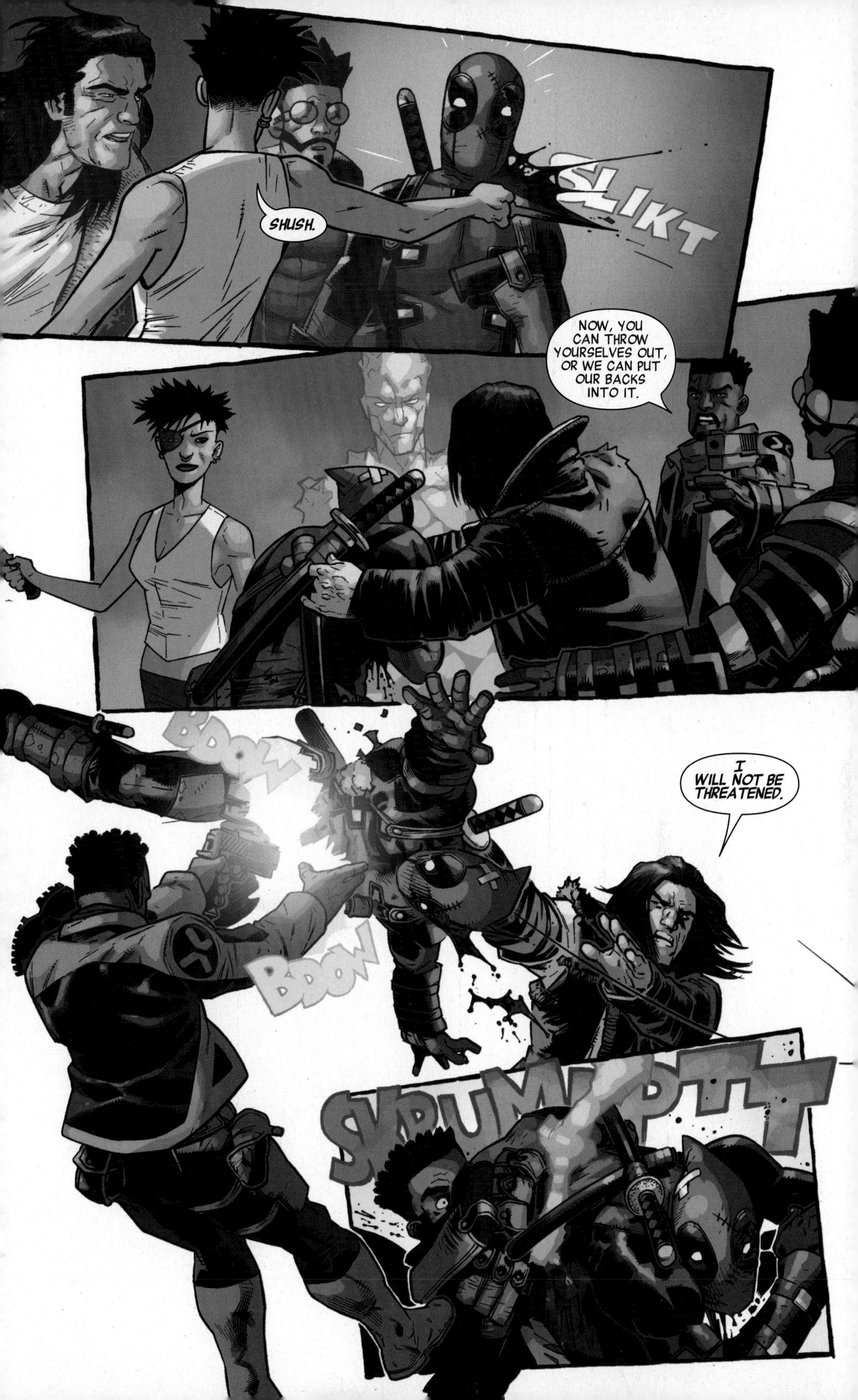

SHUSH.
SLIKT
NOW, YOU CAN THROW YOURSELVES OUT, OR WE CAN PUT OUR BACKS INTO IT.
BDOW
I WILL NOT BE THREATENED.
BDOW
SPUMPTT

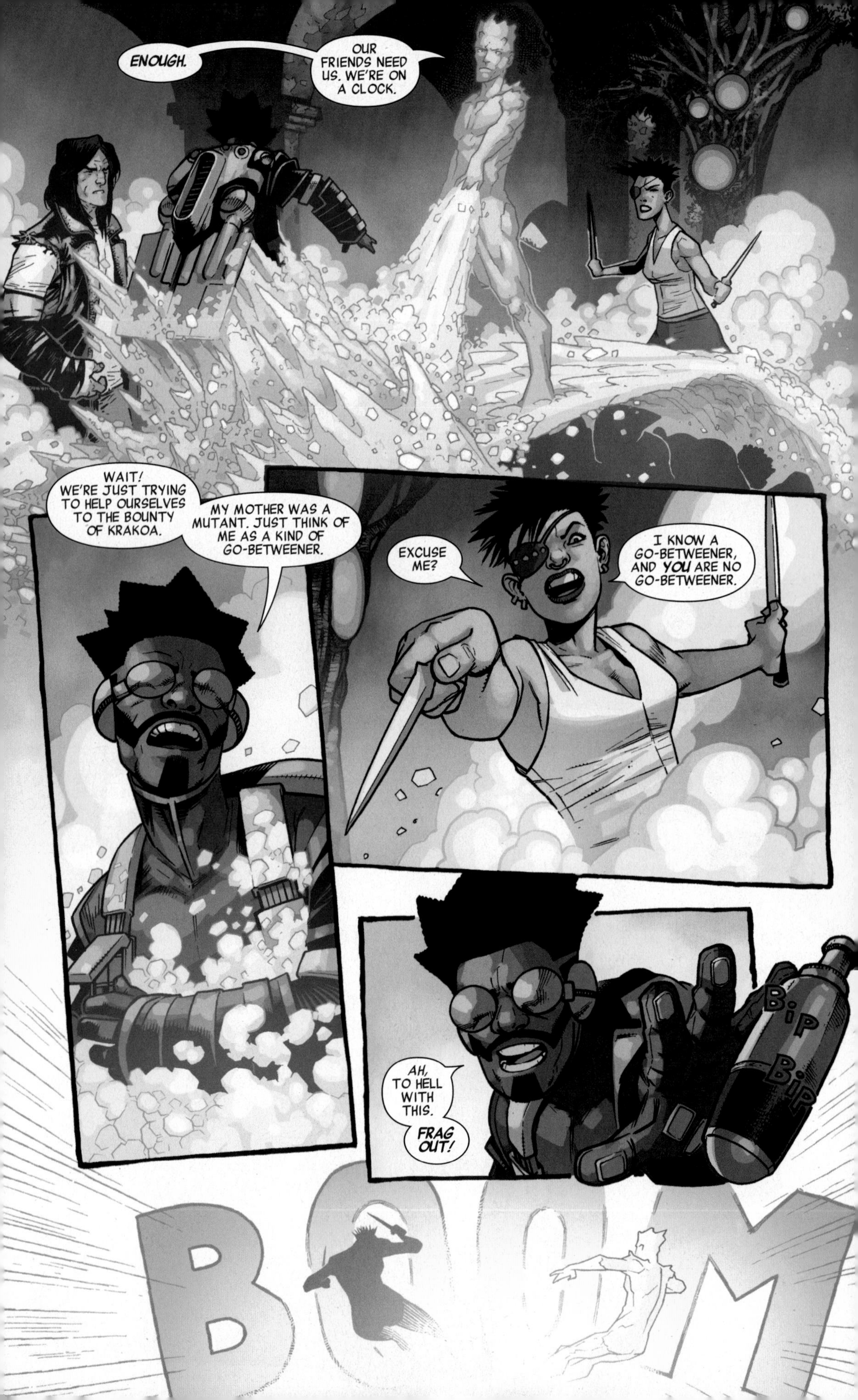
ENOUGH.
OUR FRIENDS NEED US. WE'RE ON A CLOCK.
WAIT! WE'RE JUST TRYING TO HELP OURSELVES TO THE BOUNTY OF KRAKOA.
MY MOTHER WAS A MUTANT. JUST THINK OF ME AS A KIND OF GO-BETWEENER.
EXCUSE ME?
I KNOW A GO-BETWEENER, AND YOU ARE NO GO-BETWEENER.
AH, TO HELL WITH THIS.
FRAG OUT!
BIP
BIP
BOOM

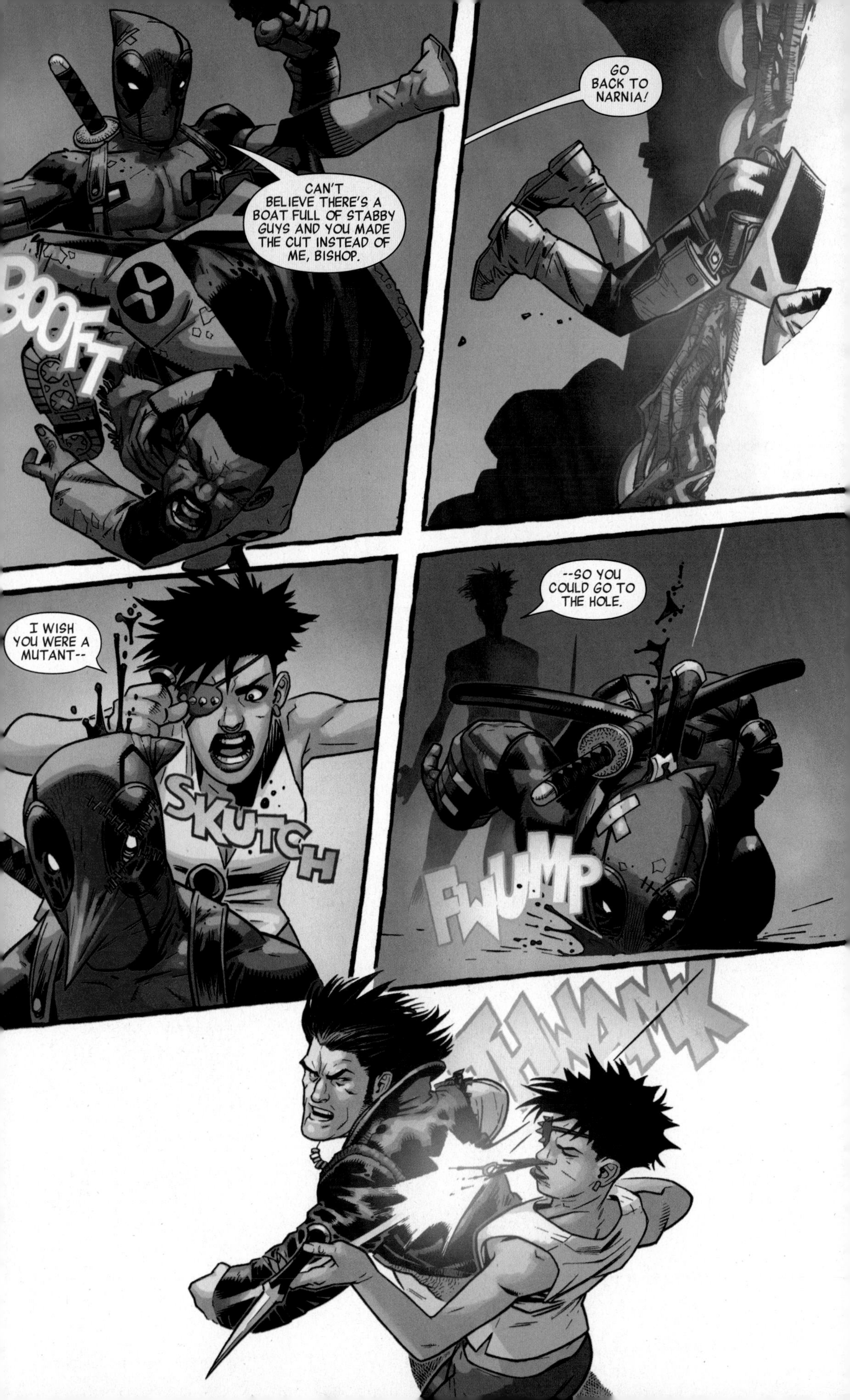
CAN'T BELIEVE THERE'S A BOAT FULL OF STABBY GUYS AND YOU MADE THE CUT INSTEAD OF ME, BISHOP.
BOOFT
GO BACK TO NARNIA!
I WISH YOU WERE A MUTANT--
SKUTCH
--SO YOU COULD GO TO THE HOLE.
FWUMP
THWAK

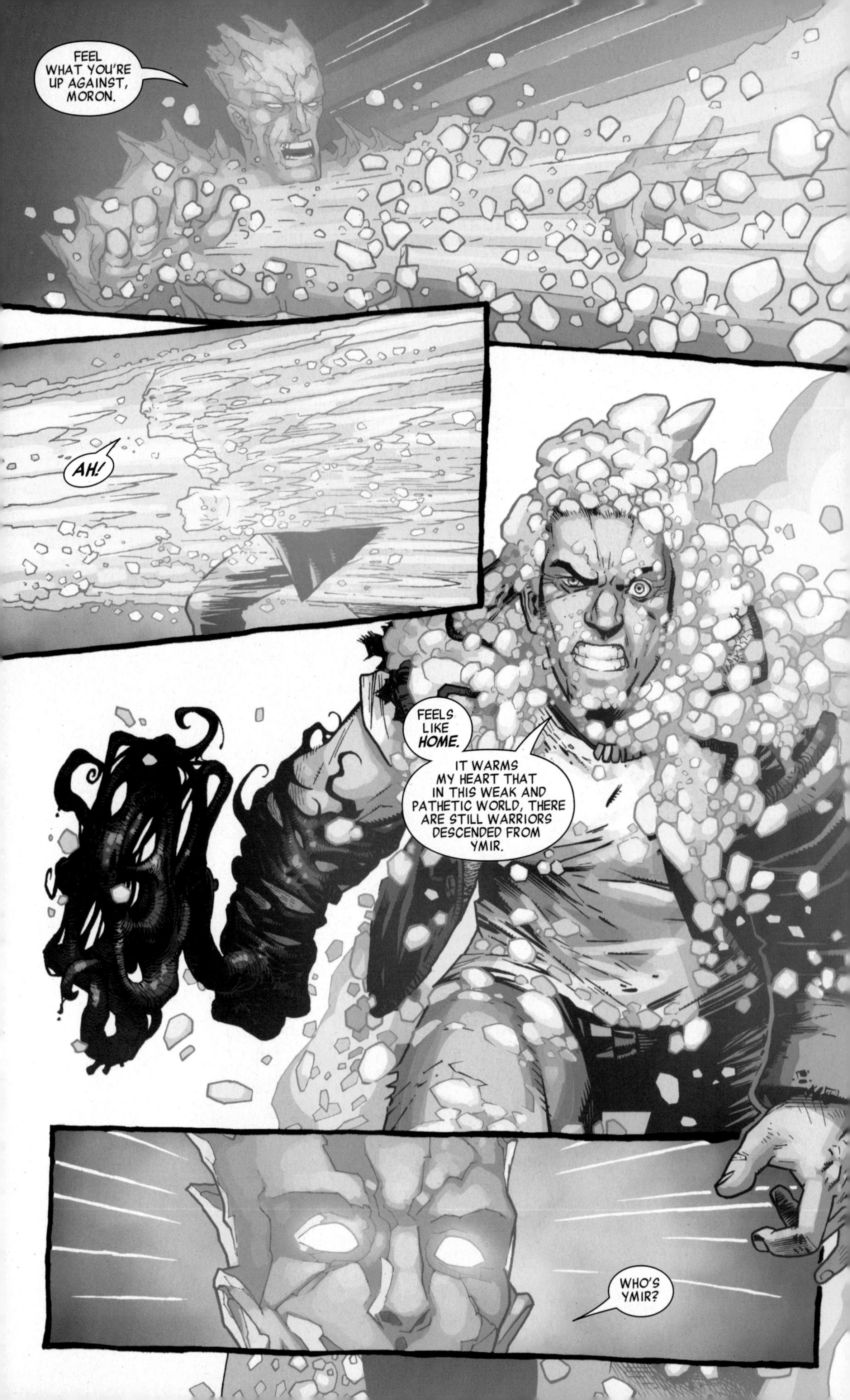
FEEL WHAT YOU'RE UP AGAINST, MORON.
AH!
FEELS LIKE **HOME.**
IT WARMS MY HEART THAT IN THIS WEAK AND PATHETIC WORLD, THERE ARE STILL WARRIORS DESCENDED FROM YMIR.
WHO'S YMIR?

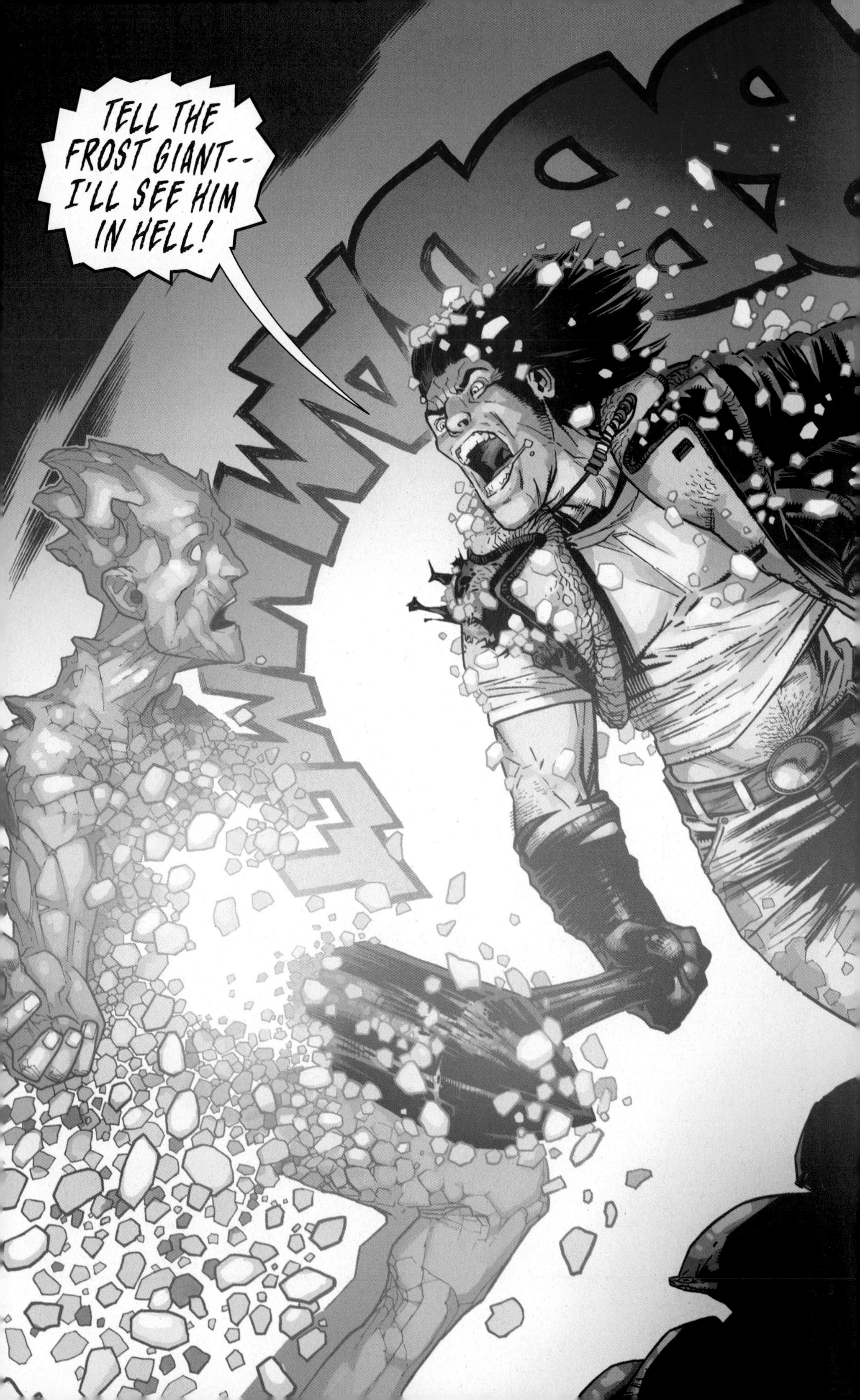
TELL THE FROST GIANT-- I'LL SEE HIM IN HELL!

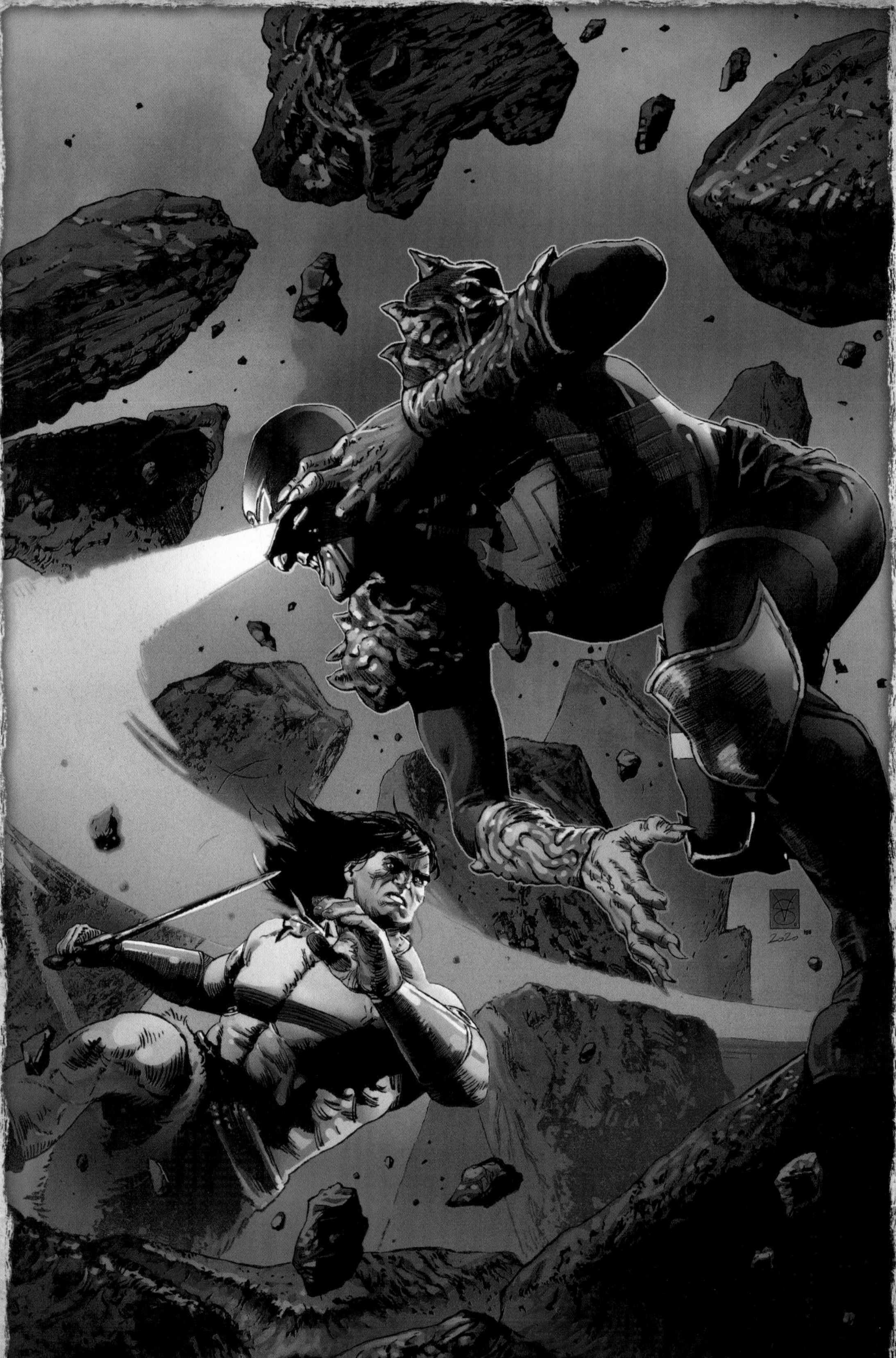

19: THE SON OF YMIR

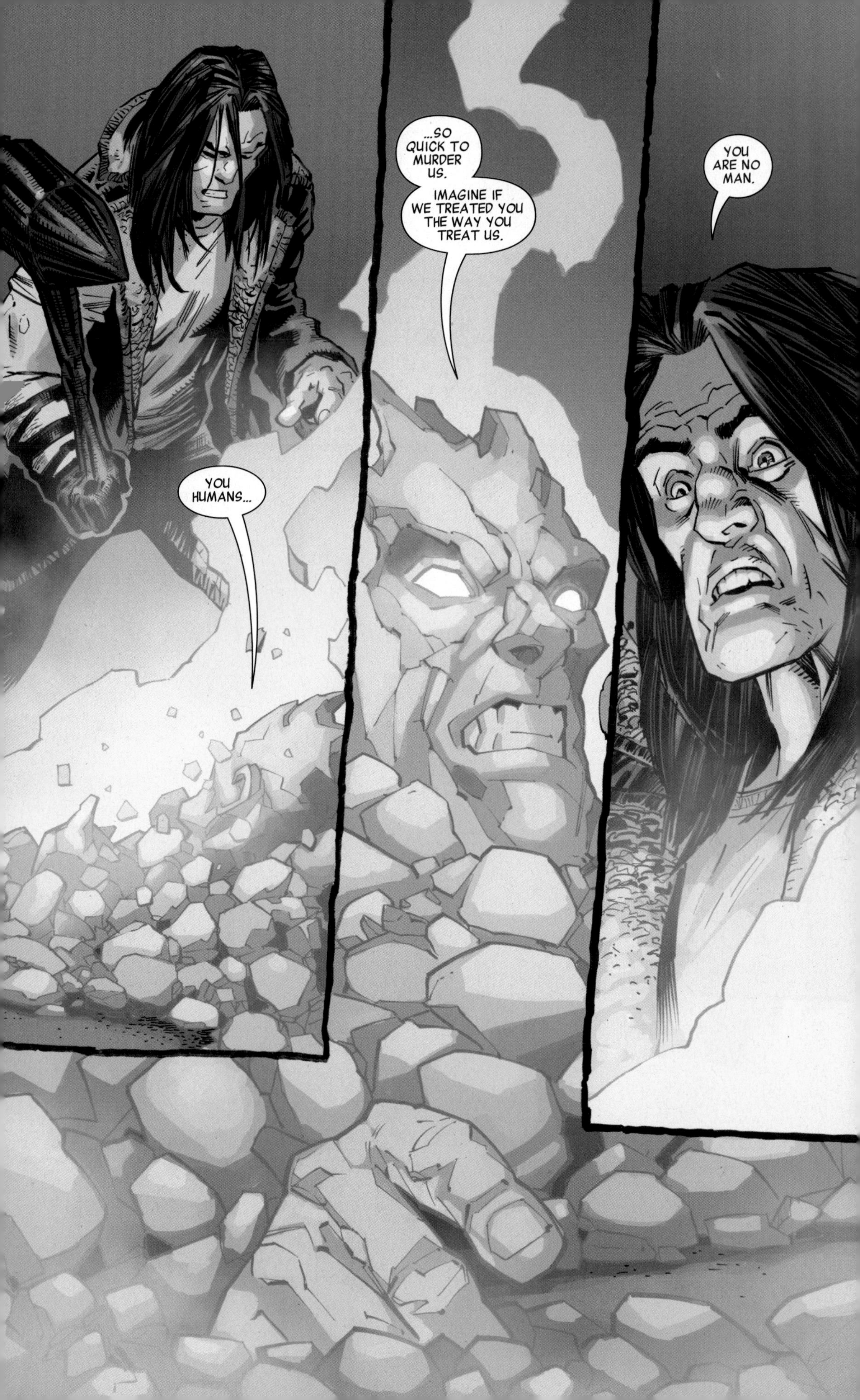
YOU HUMANS...
...SO QUICK TO MURDER US.
IMAGINE IF WE TREATED YOU THE WAY YOU TREAT US.
YOU ARE NO MAN.

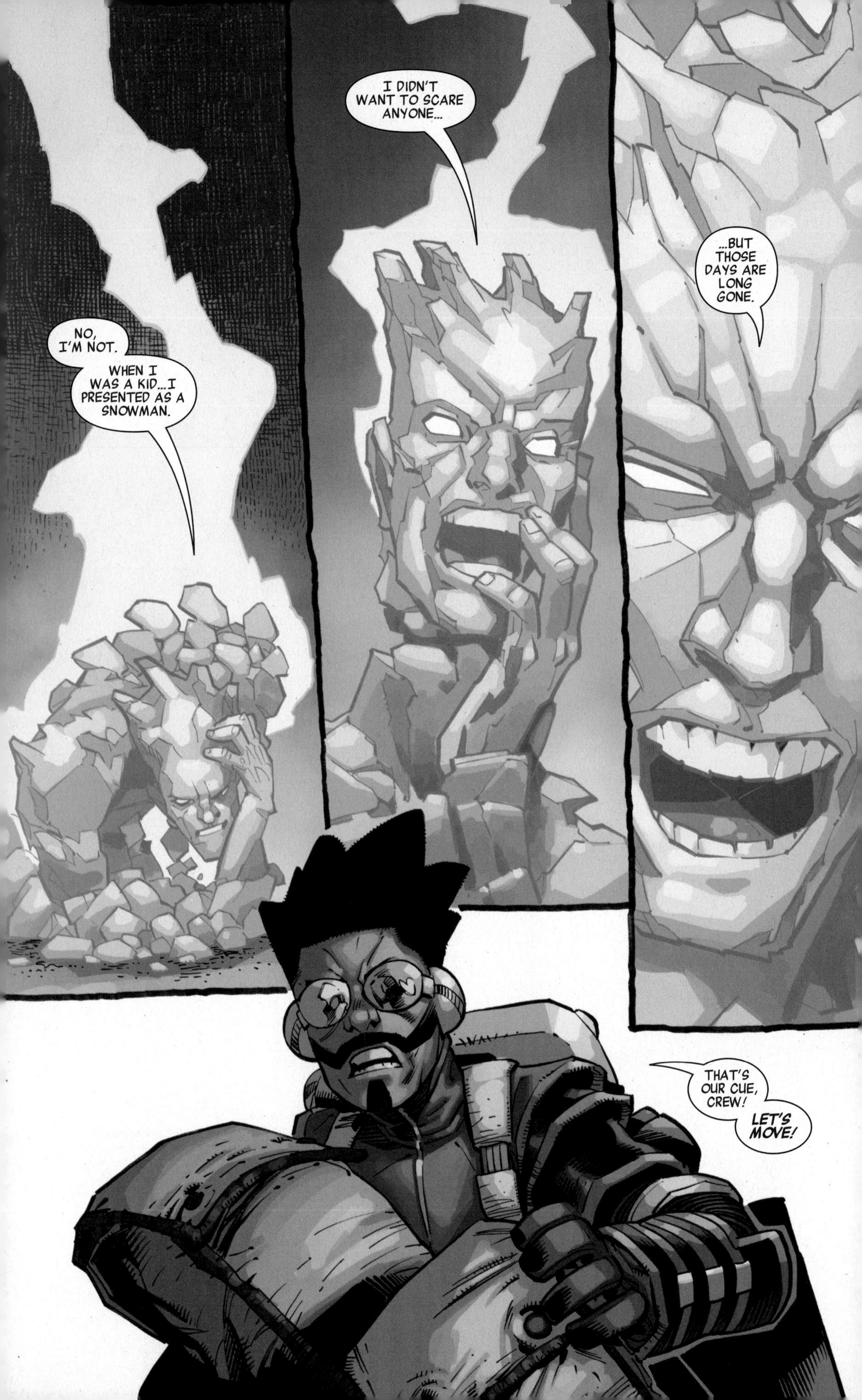
NO, I'M NOT.
WHEN I WAS A KID...I PRESENTED AS A SNOWMAN.
I DIDN'T WANT TO SCARE ANYONE...
...BUT THOSE DAYS ARE LONG GONE.
THAT'S OUR CUE, CREW!
LET'S MOVE!

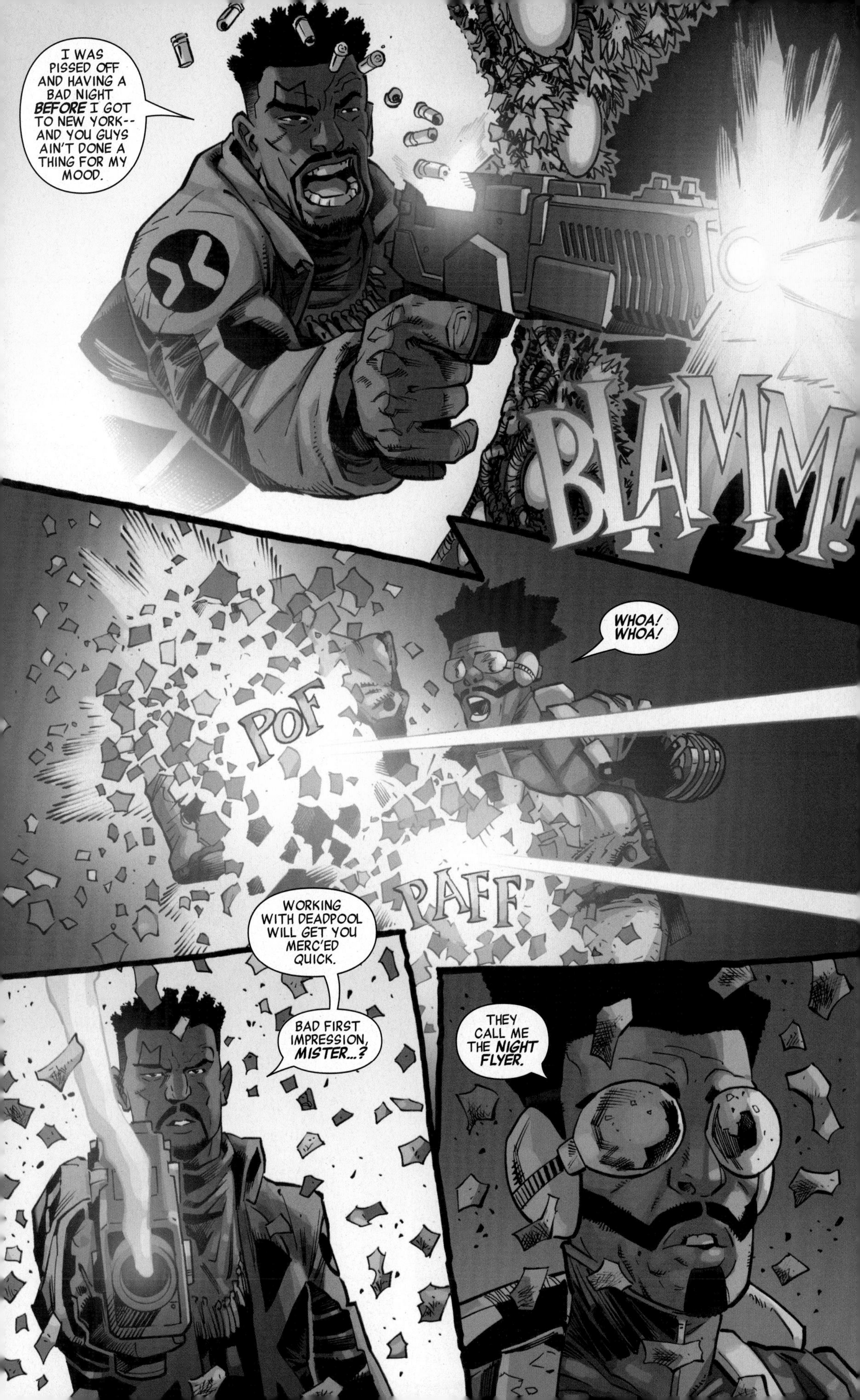
I WAS PISSED OFF AND HAVING A BAD NIGHT *BEFORE* I GOT TO NEW YORK-- AND YOU GUYS AIN'T DONE A THING FOR MY MOOD.
BLAMM!
WHOA! WHOA!
POF
PAFF
WORKING WITH DEADPOOL WILL GET YOU MERC'ED QUICK.
BAD FIRST IMPRESSION, *MISTER...?*
THEY CALL ME THE *NIGHT FLYER.*

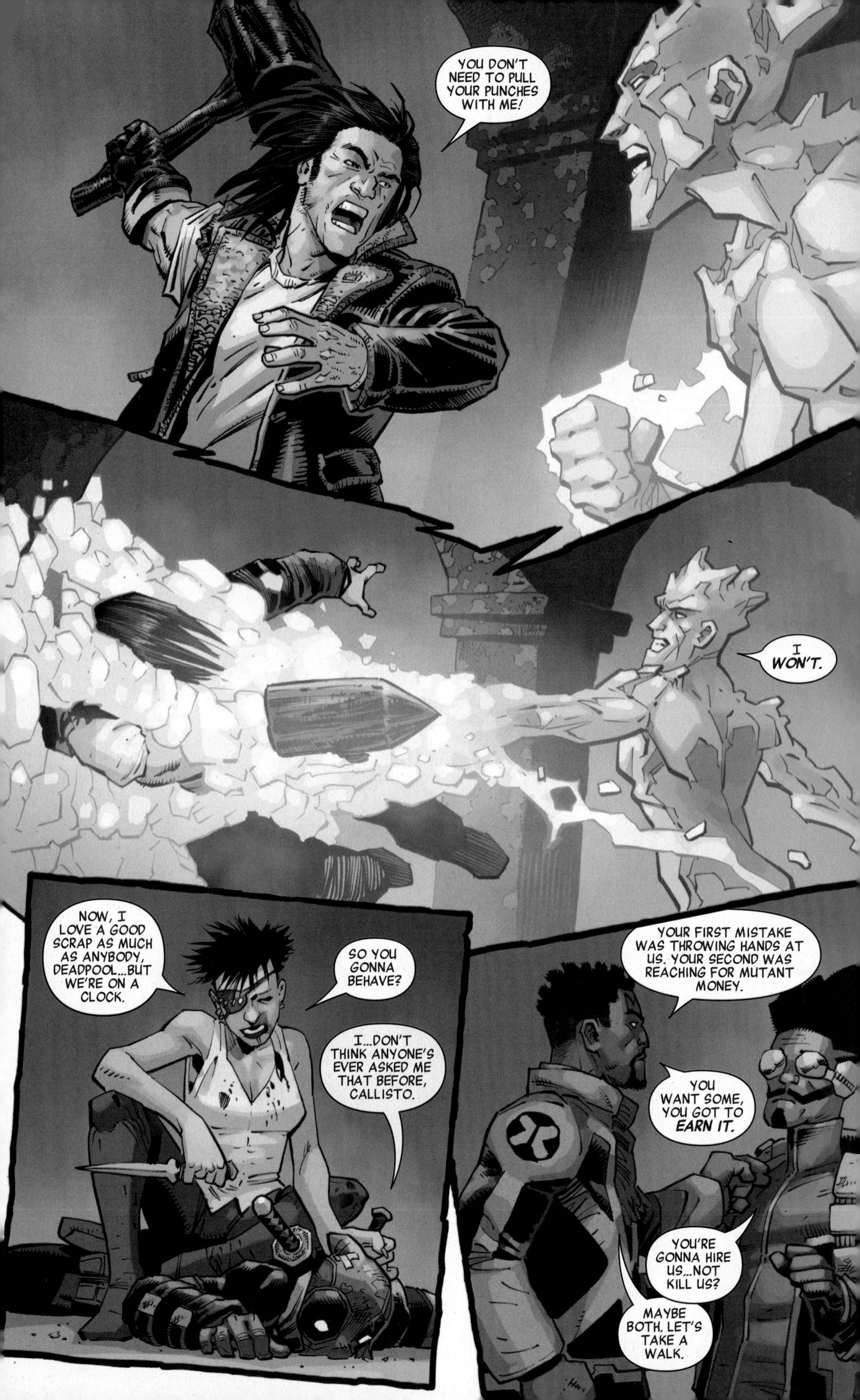
YOU DON'T NEED TO PULL YOUR PUNCHES WITH ME!
I WON'T.
NOW, I LOVE A GOOD SCRAP AS MUCH AS ANYBODY, DEADPOOL...BUT WE'RE ON A CLOCK.
SO YOU GONNA BEHAVE?
I...DON'T THINK ANYONE'S EVER ASKED ME THAT BEFORE, CALLISTO.
YOUR FIRST MISTAKE WAS THROWING HANDS AT US. YOUR SECOND WAS REACHING FOR MUTANT MONEY.
YOU WANT SOME, YOU GOT TO EARN IT.
YOU'RE GONNA HIRE US...NOT KILL US?
MAYBE BOTH. LET'S TAKE A WALK.

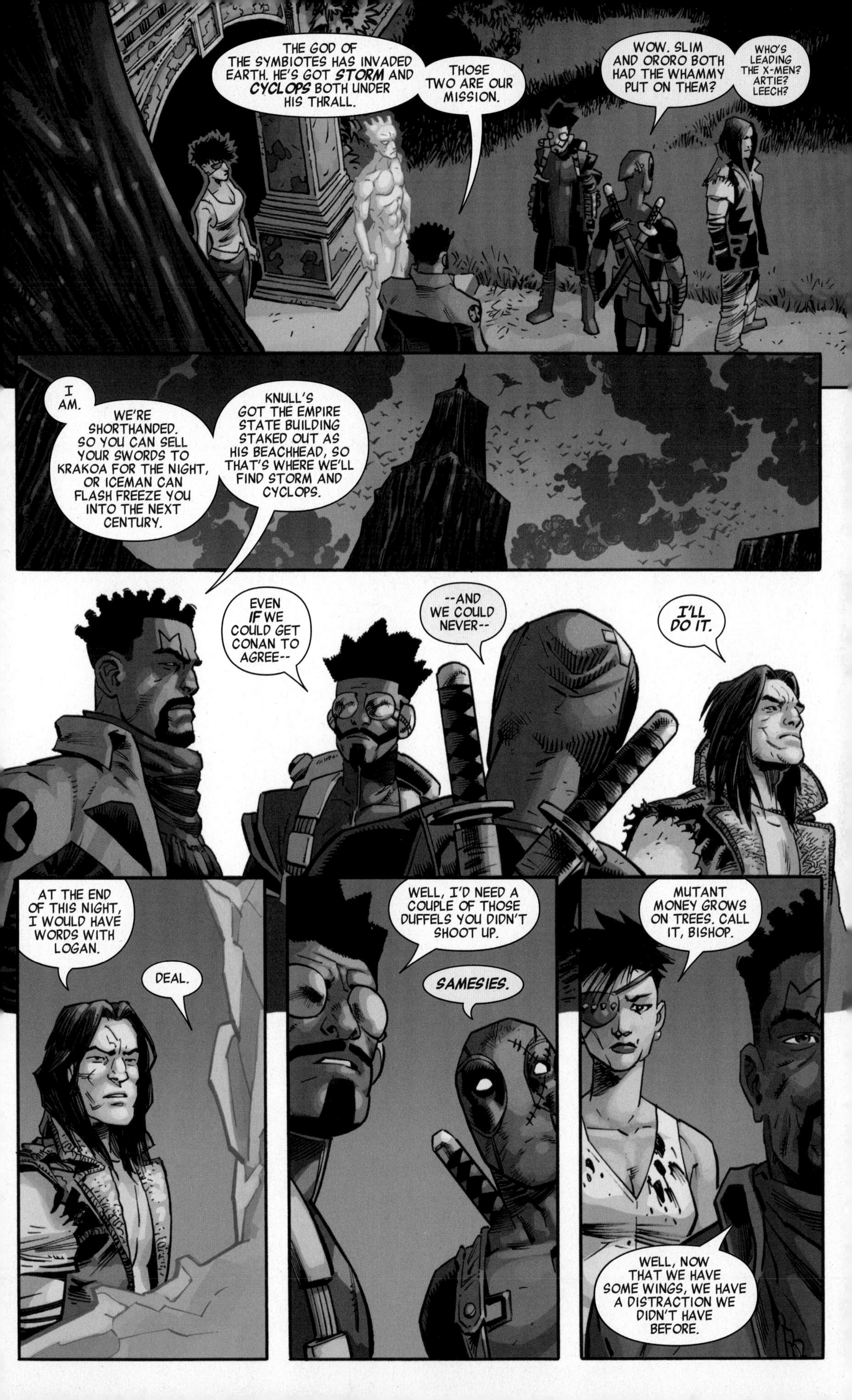
THE GOD OF THE SYMBIOTES HAS INVADED EARTH. HE'S GOT STORM AND CYCLOPS BOTH UNDER HIS THRALL.
THOSE TWO ARE OUR MISSION.
WOW. SLIM AND ORORO BOTH HAD THE WHAMMY PUT ON THEM?
WHO'S LEADING THE X-MEN? ARTIE? LEECH?
I AM.
WE'RE SHORTHANDED. SO YOU CAN SELL YOUR SWORDS TO KRAKOA FOR THE NIGHT, OR ICEMAN CAN FLASH FREEZE YOU INTO THE NEXT CENTURY.
KNULL'S GOT THE EMPIRE STATE BUILDING STAKED OUT AS HIS BEACHHEAD, SO THAT'S WHERE WE'LL FIND STORM AND CYCLOPS.
EVEN IF WE COULD GET CONAN TO AGREE--
--AND WE COULD NEVER--
I'LL DO IT.
AT THE END OF THIS NIGHT, I WOULD HAVE WORDS WITH LOGAN.
DEAL.
WELL, I'D NEED A COUPLE OF THOSE DUFFELS YOU DIDN'T SHOOT UP.
SAMESIES.
MUTANT MONEY GROWS ON TREES. CALL IT, BISHOP.
WELL, NOW THAT WE HAVE SOME WINGS, WE HAVE A DISTRACTION WE DIDN'T HAVE BEFORE.

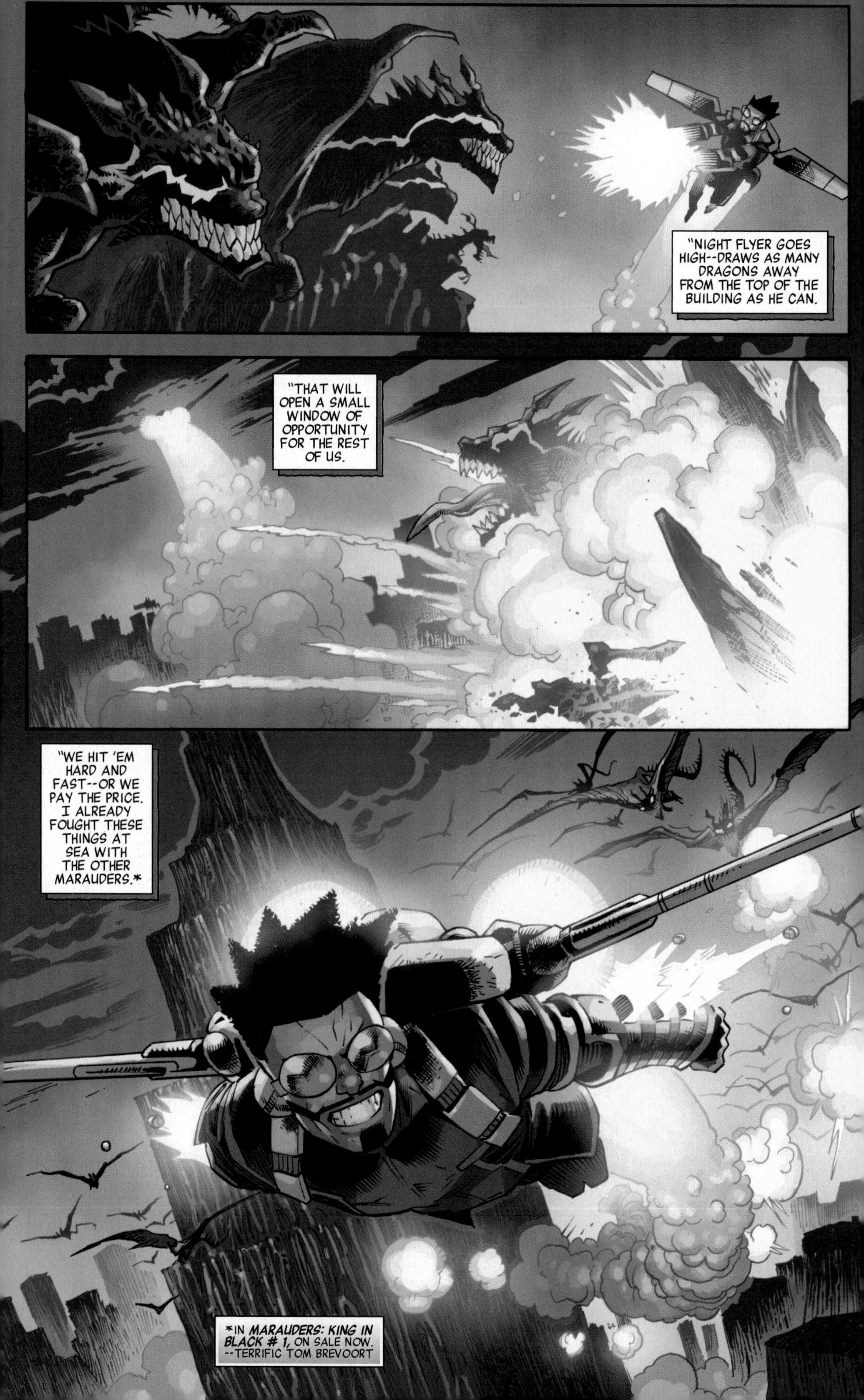
"NIGHT FLYER GOES HIGH--DRAWS AS MANY DRAGONS AWAY FROM THE TOP OF THE BUILDING AS HE CAN.
"THAT WILL OPEN A SMALL WINDOW OF OPPORTUNITY FOR THE REST OF US.
"WE HIT 'EM HARD AND FAST--OR WE PAY THE PRICE. I ALREADY FOUGHT THESE THINGS AT SEA WITH THE OTHER MARAUDERS.*
*IN MARAUDERS: KING IN BLACK # 1, ON SALE NOW. --TERRIFIC TOM BREVOORT

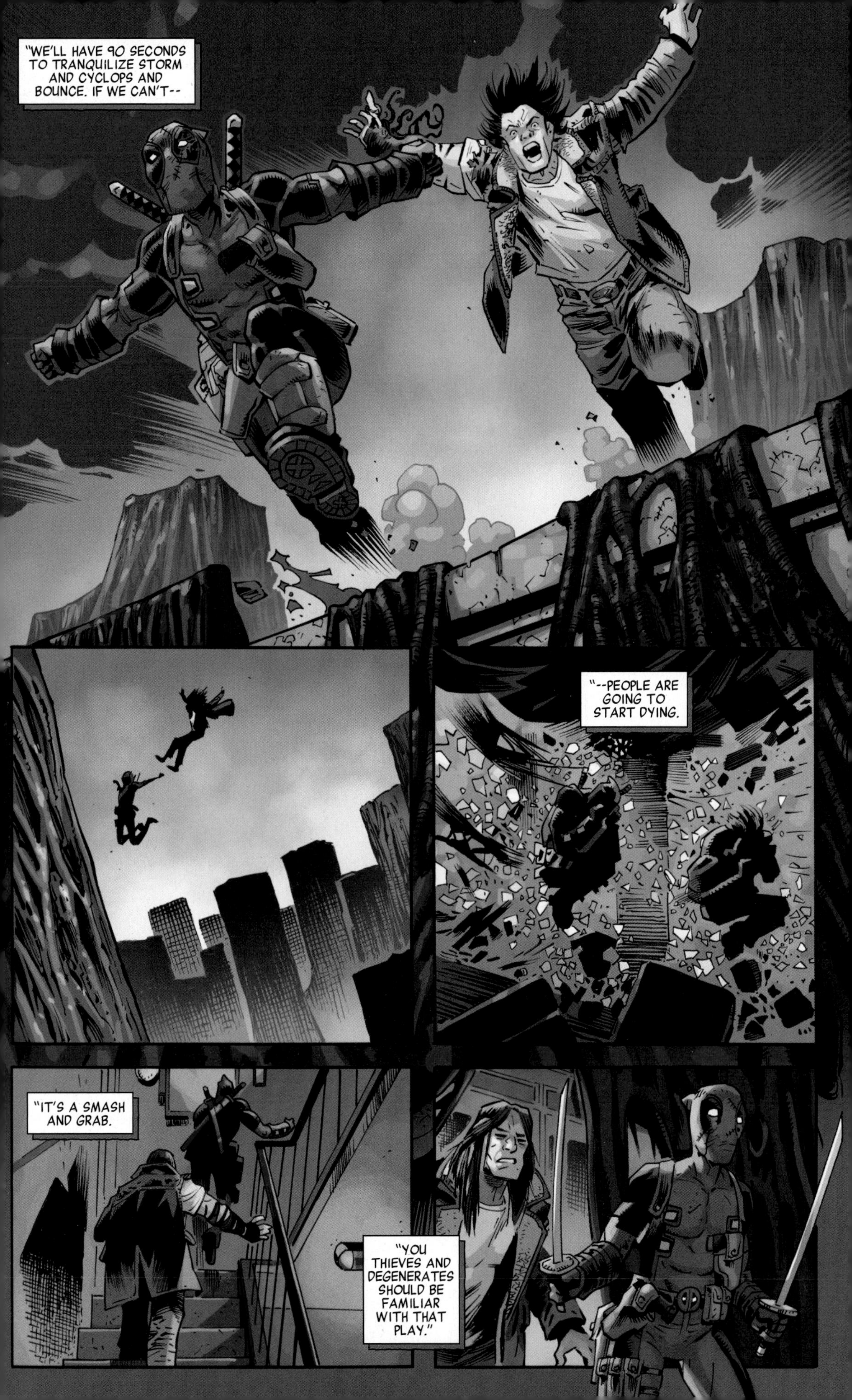
"WE'LL HAVE 90 SECONDS TO TRANQUILIZE STORM AND CYCLOPS AND BOUNCE. IF WE CAN'T--
"--PEOPLE ARE GOING TO START DYING.
"IT'S A SMASH AND GRAB.
"YOU THIEVES AND DEGENERATES SHOULD BE FAMILIAR WITH THAT PLAY."

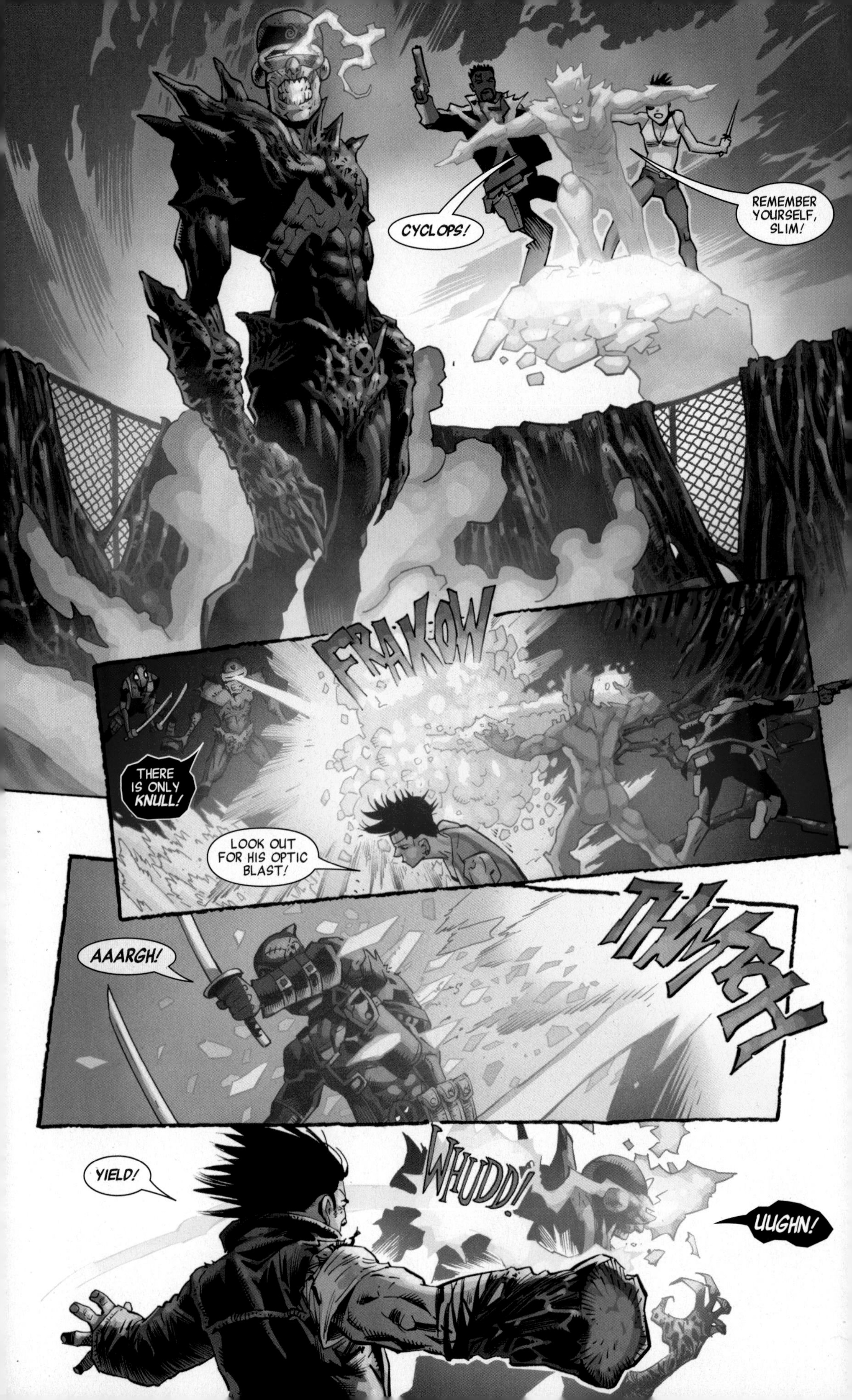
CYCLOPS!
REMEMBER YOURSELF, SLIM!
FRAKOW
THERE IS ONLY KNULL!
LOOK OUT FOR HIS OPTIC BLAST!
THWACH
AAARGH!
YIELD!
WHUDD!
UUGHN!

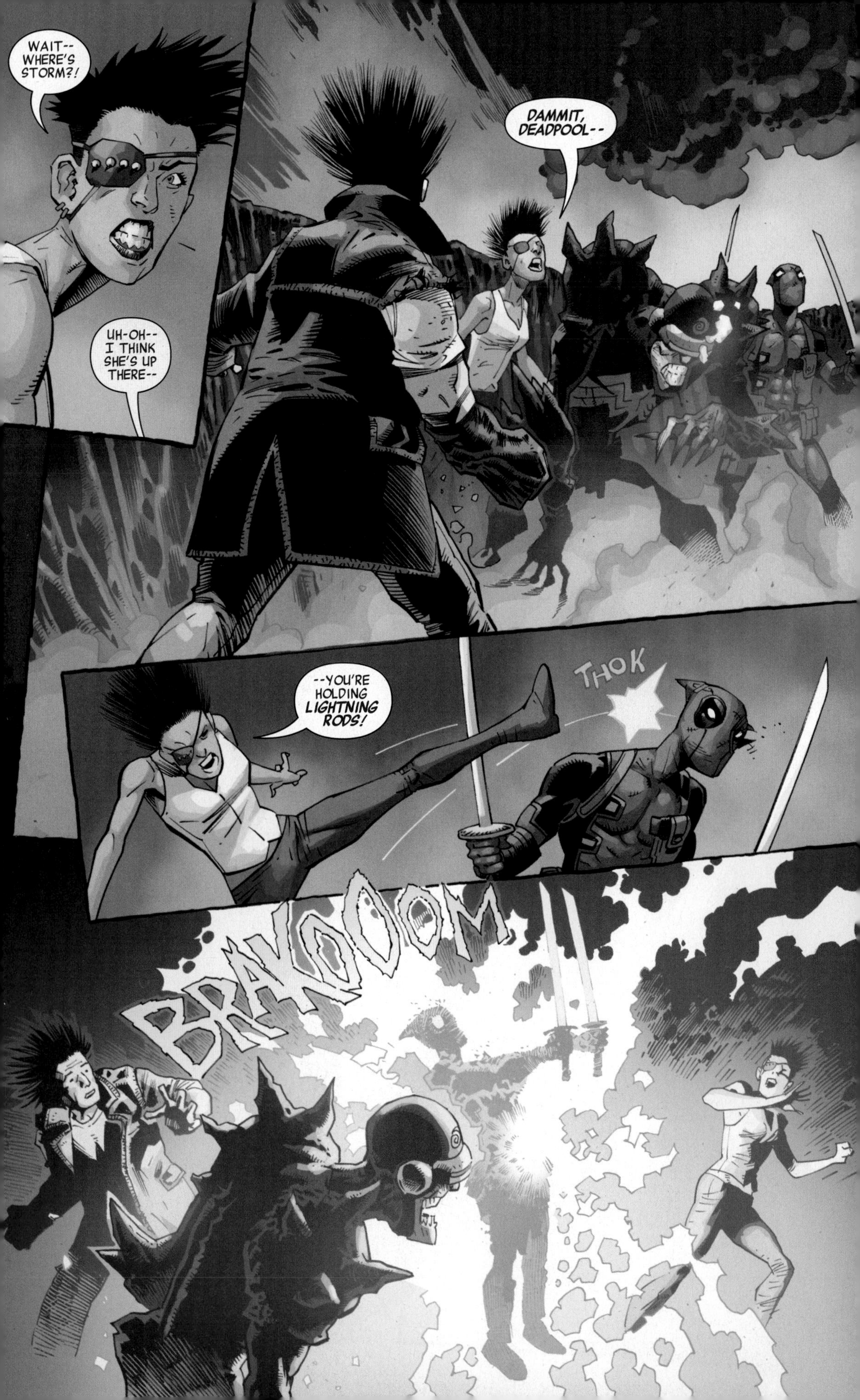
WAIT--
WHERE'S
STORM?!
DAMMIT,
DEADPOOL--
UH-OH--
I THINK
SHE'S UP
THERE--
--YOU'RE
HOLDING
LIGHTNING
RODS!
THOK
BRAKOOOM

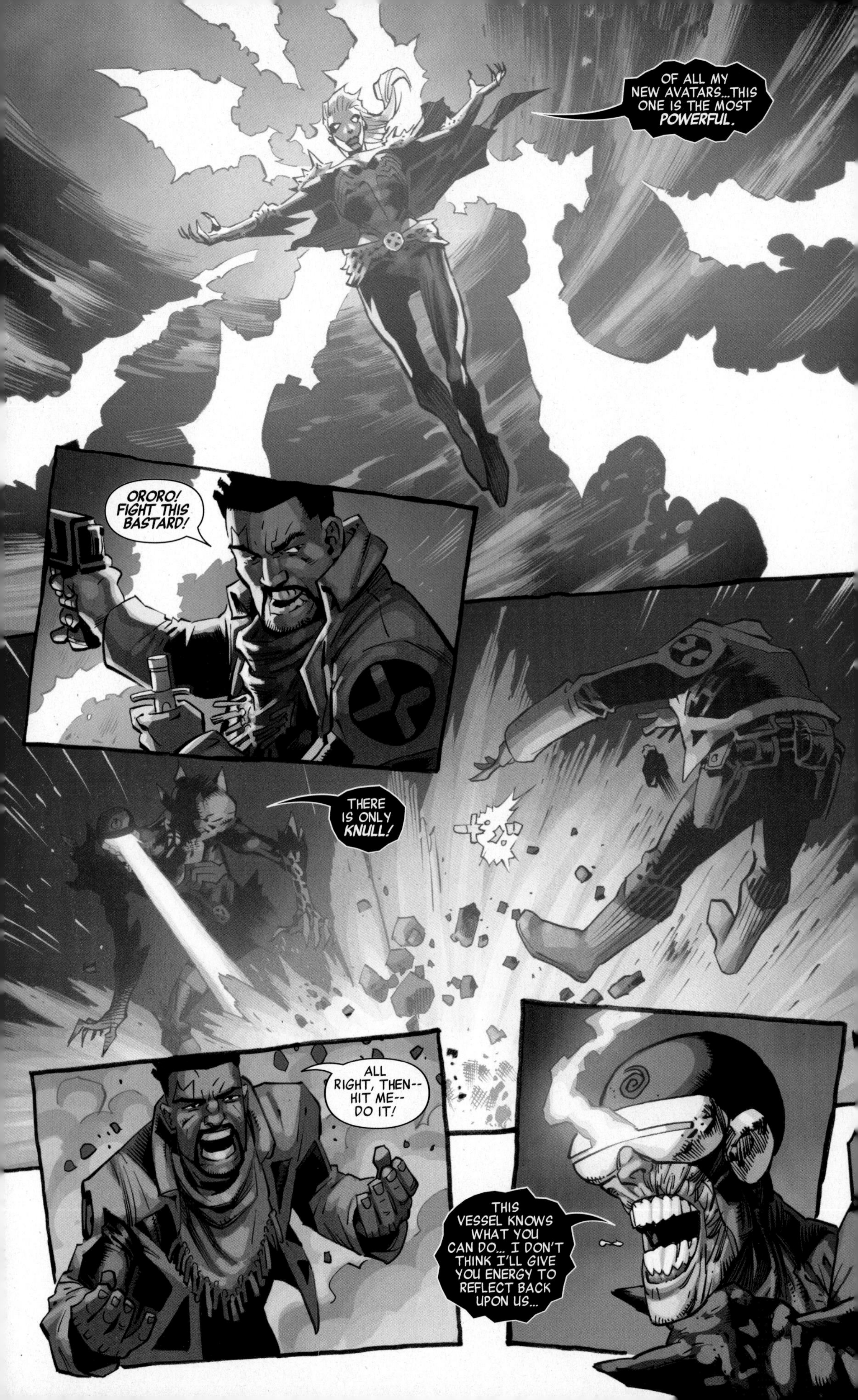
OF ALL MY NEW AVATARS...THIS ONE IS THE MOST POWERFUL.
ORORO! FIGHT THIS BASTARD!
THERE IS ONLY KNULL!
ALL RIGHT, THEN-- HIT ME-- DO IT!
THIS VESSEL KNOWS WHAT YOU CAN DO... I DON'T THINK I'LL GIVE YOU ENERGY TO REFLECT BACK UPON US...

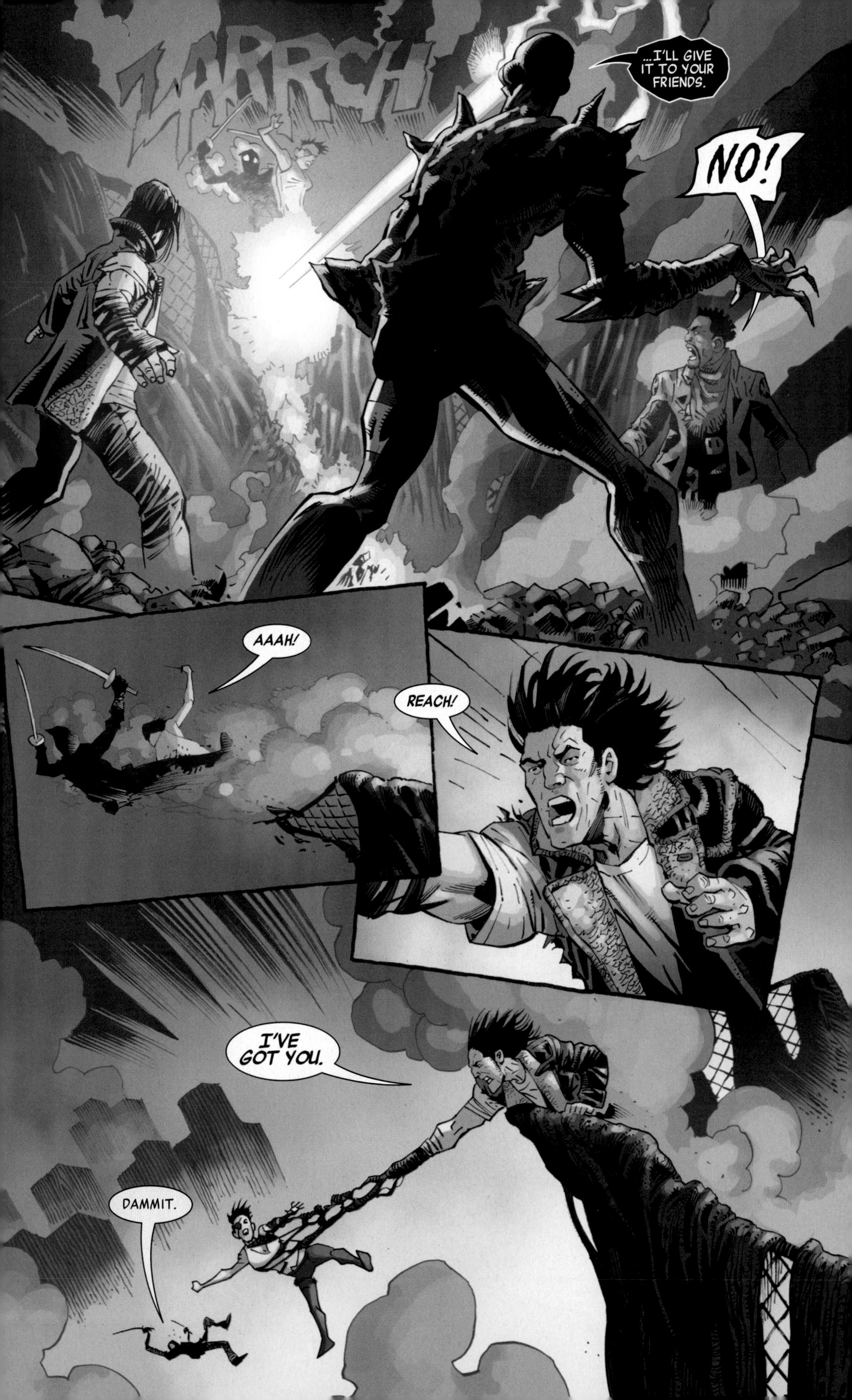
ZARRCH
...I'LL GIVE IT TO YOUR FRIENDS.
NO!
AAAH!
REACH!
I'VE GOT YOU.
DAMMIT.

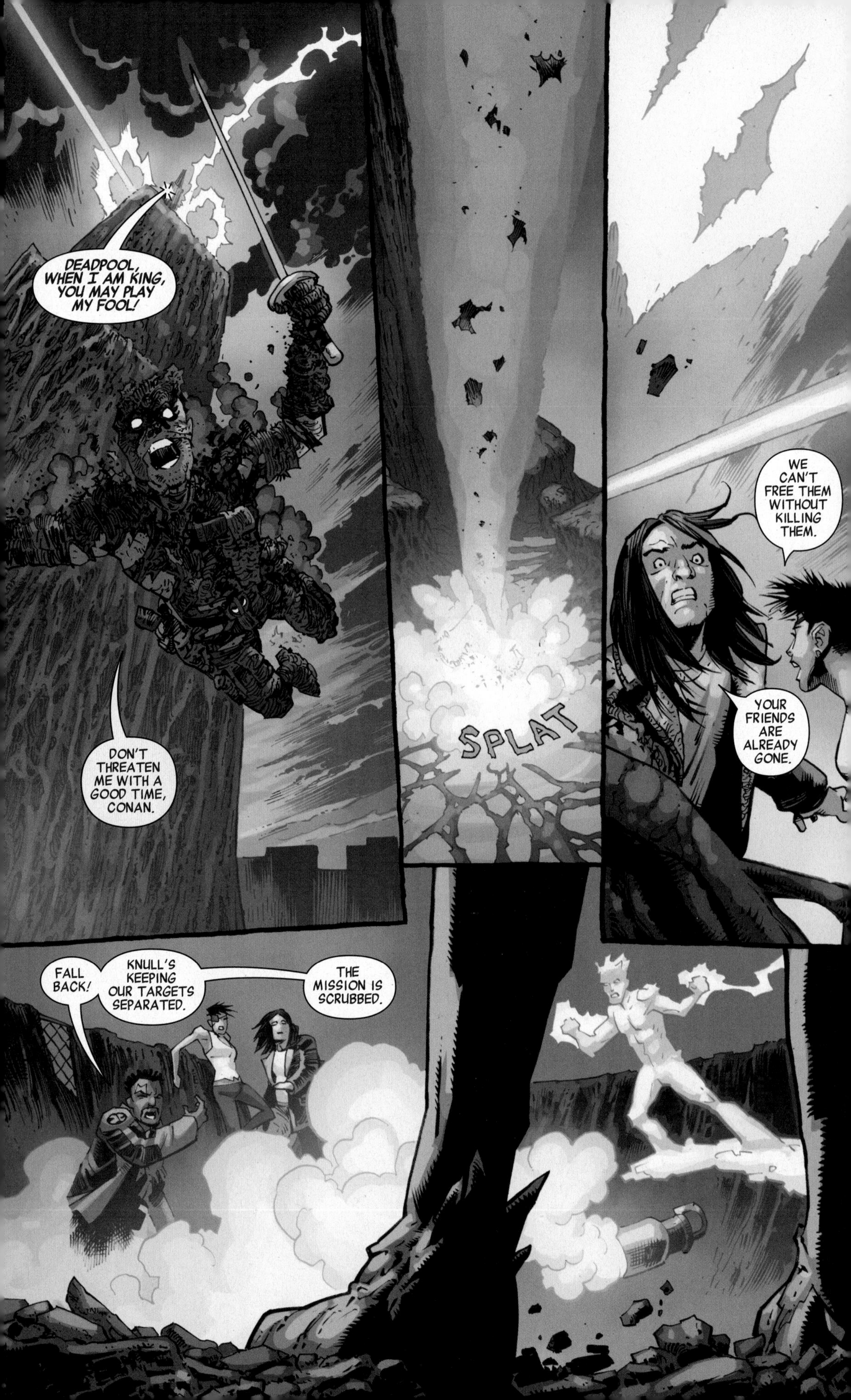
DEADPOOL, WHEN I AM KING, YOU MAY PLAY MY FOOL!
DON'T THREATEN ME WITH A GOOD TIME, CONAN.
SPLAT
WE CAN'T FREE THEM WITHOUT KILLING THEM.
YOUR FRIENDS ARE ALREADY GONE.
FALL BACK!
KNULL'S KEEPING OUR TARGETS SEPARATED.
THE MISSION IS SCRUBBED.

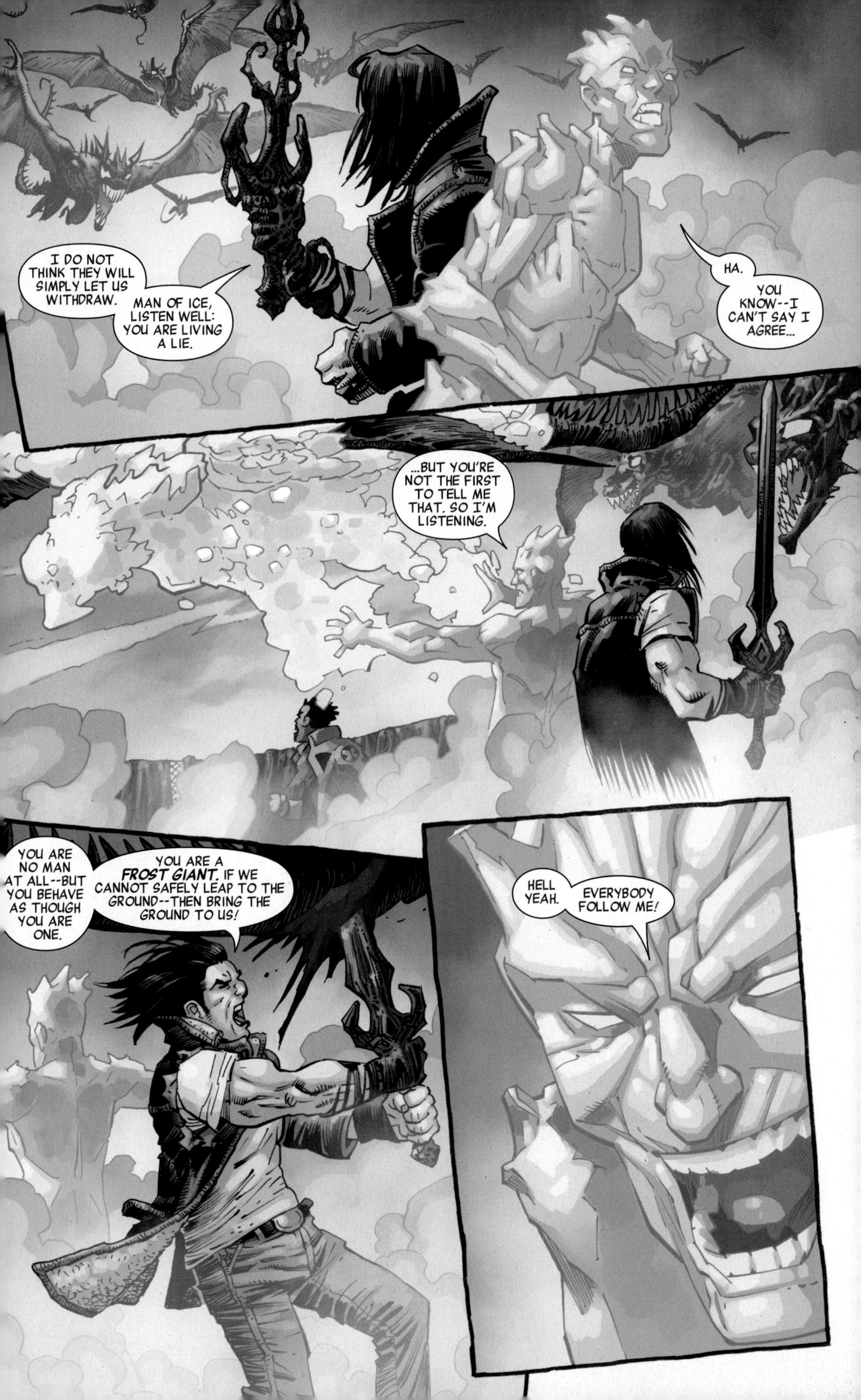
I DO NOT THINK THEY WILL SIMPLY LET US WITHDRAW.
MAN OF ICE, LISTEN WELL: YOU ARE LIVING A LIE.
HA.
YOU KNOW--I CAN'T SAY I AGREE...
...BUT YOU'RE NOT THE FIRST TO TELL ME THAT. SO I'M LISTENING.
YOU ARE NO MAN AT ALL--BUT YOU BEHAVE AS THOUGH YOU ARE ONE.
YOU ARE A FROST GIANT. IF WE CANNOT SAFELY LEAP TO THE GROUND--THEN BRING THE GROUND TO US!
HELL YEAH.
EVERYBODY FOLLOW ME!

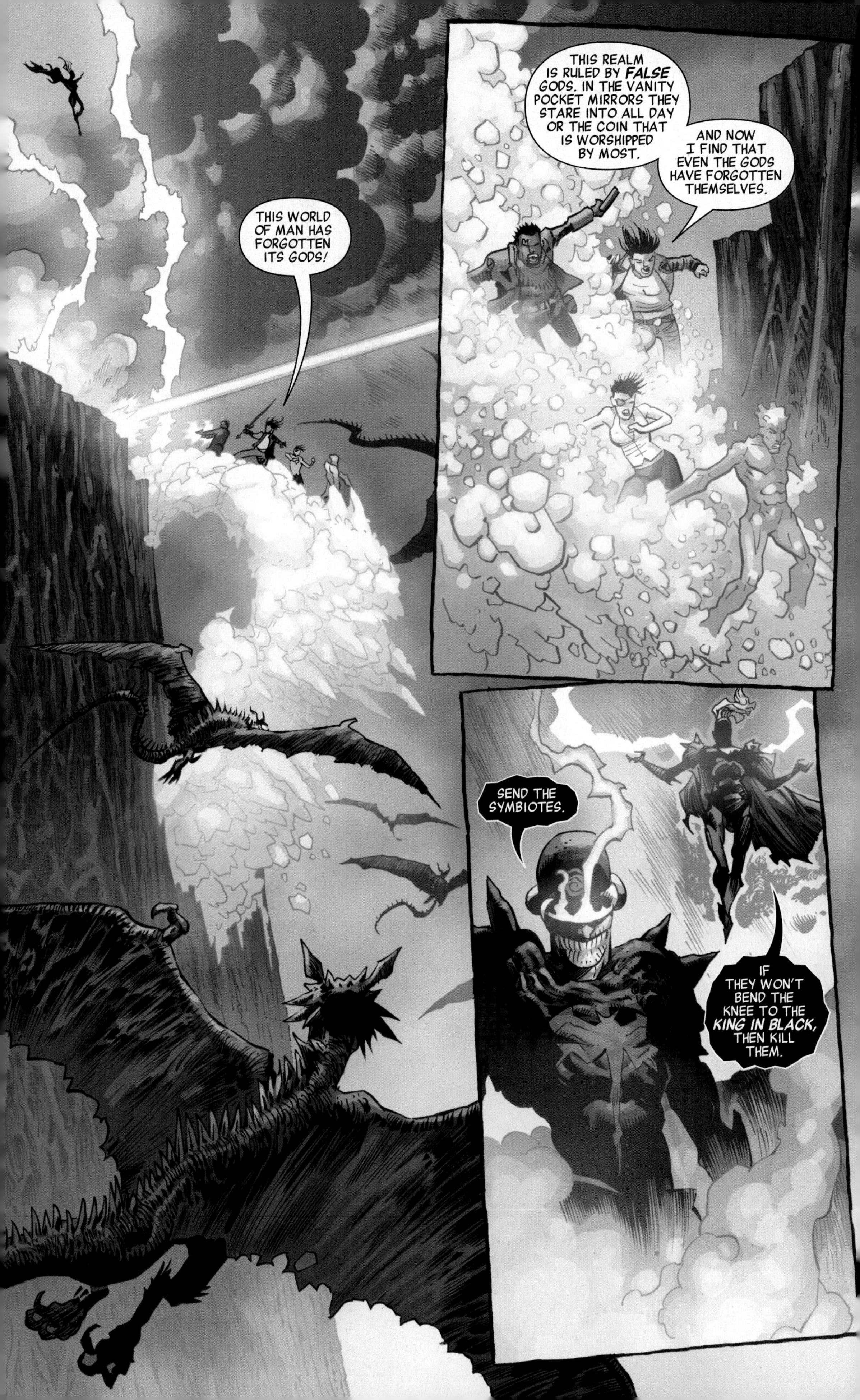
THIS WORLD OF MAN HAS FORGOTTEN ITS GODS!
THIS REALM IS RULED BY FALSE GODS. IN THE VANITY POCKET MIRRORS THEY STARE INTO ALL DAY OR THE COIN THAT IS WORSHIPPED BY MOST.
AND NOW I FIND THAT EVEN THE GODS HAVE FORGOTTEN THEMSELVES.
SEND THE SYMBIOTES.
IF THEY WON'T BEND THE KNEE TO THE KING IN BLACK, THEN KILL THEM.

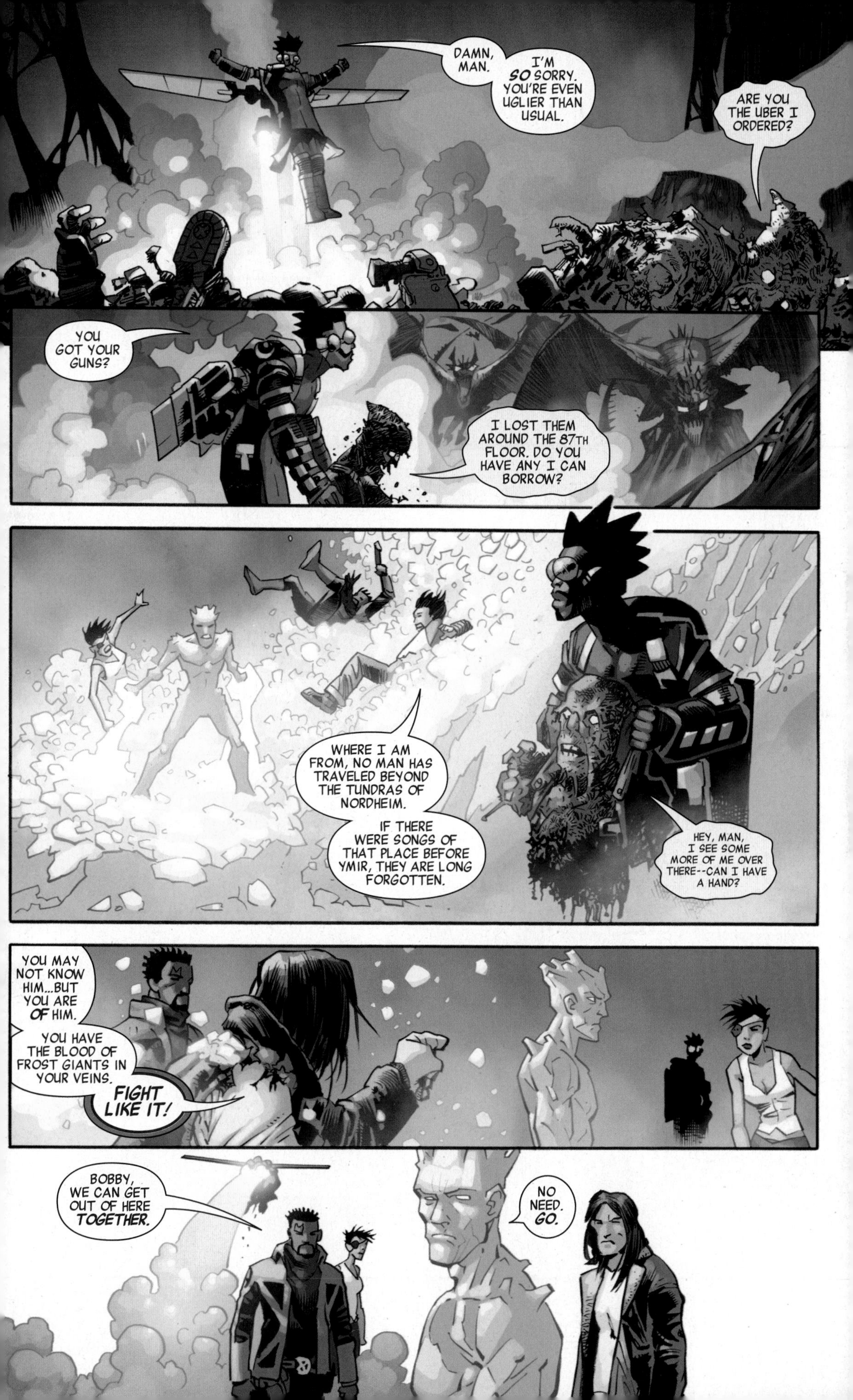
DAMN, MAN.
I'M SO SORRY. YOU'RE EVEN UGLIER THAN USUAL.
ARE YOU THE UBER I ORDERED?
YOU GOT YOUR GUNS?
I LOST THEM AROUND THE 87TH FLOOR. DO YOU HAVE ANY I CAN BORROW?
WHERE I AM FROM, NO MAN HAS TRAVELED BEYOND THE TUNDRAS OF NORDHEIM.
IF THERE WERE SONGS OF THAT PLACE BEFORE YMIR, THEY ARE LONG FORGOTTEN.
HEY, MAN, I SEE SOME MORE OF ME OVER THERE--CAN I HAVE A HAND?
YOU MAY NOT KNOW HIM...BUT YOU ARE OF HIM.
YOU HAVE THE BLOOD OF FROST GIANTS IN YOUR VEINS.
FIGHT LIKE IT!
BOBBY, WE CAN GET OUT OF HERE TOGETHER.
NO NEED. GO.

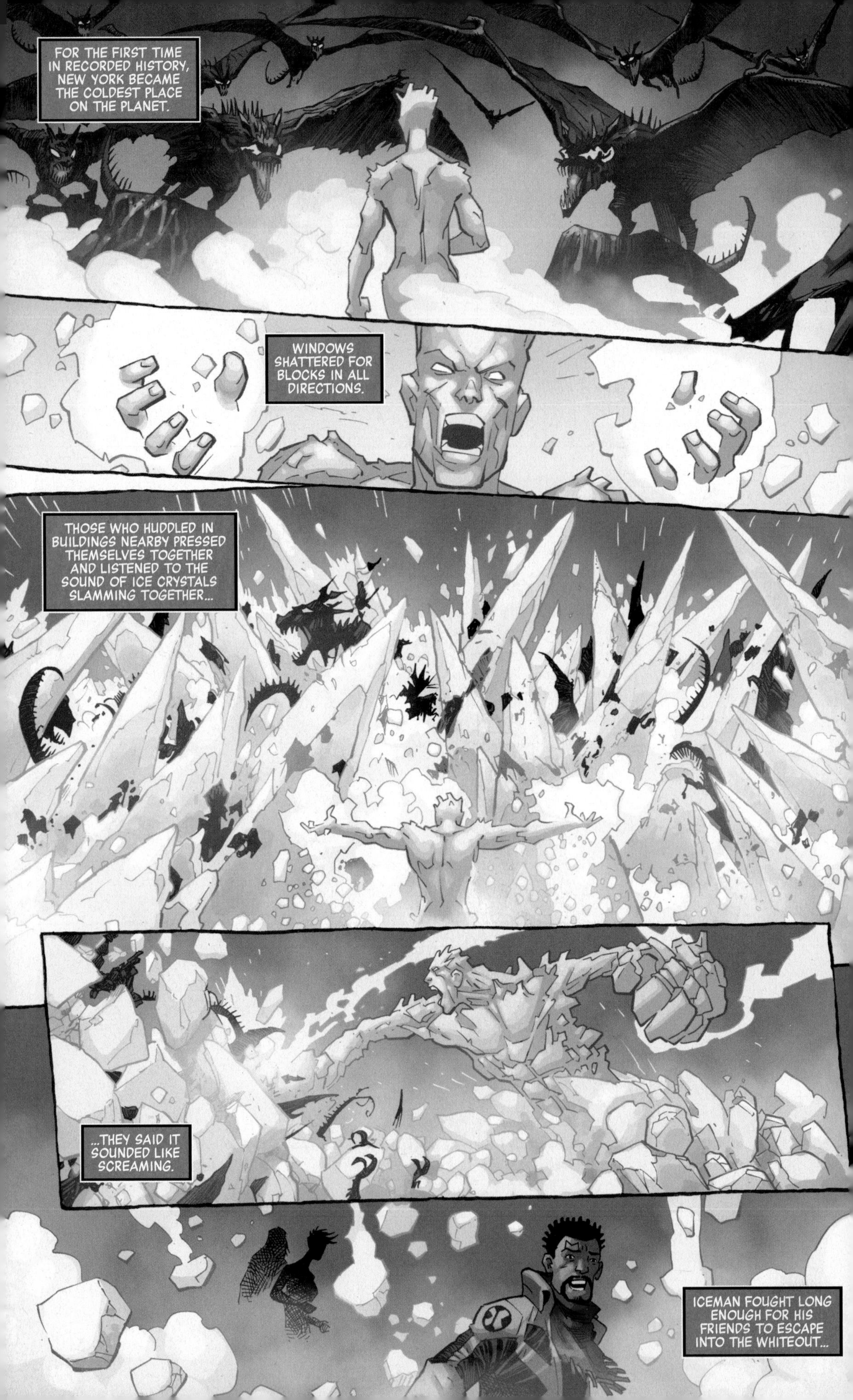
FOR THE FIRST TIME IN RECORDED HISTORY, NEW YORK BECAME THE COLDEST PLACE ON THE PLANET.
WINDOWS SHATTERED FOR BLOCKS IN ALL DIRECTIONS.
THOSE WHO HUDDLED IN BUILDINGS NEARBY PRESSED THEMSELVES TOGETHER AND LISTENED TO THE SOUND OF ICE CRYSTALS SLAMMING TOGETHER...
...THEY SAID IT SOUNDED LIKE SCREAMING.
ICEMAN FOUGHT LONG ENOUGH FOR HIS FRIENDS TO ESCAPE INTO THE WHITEOUT...

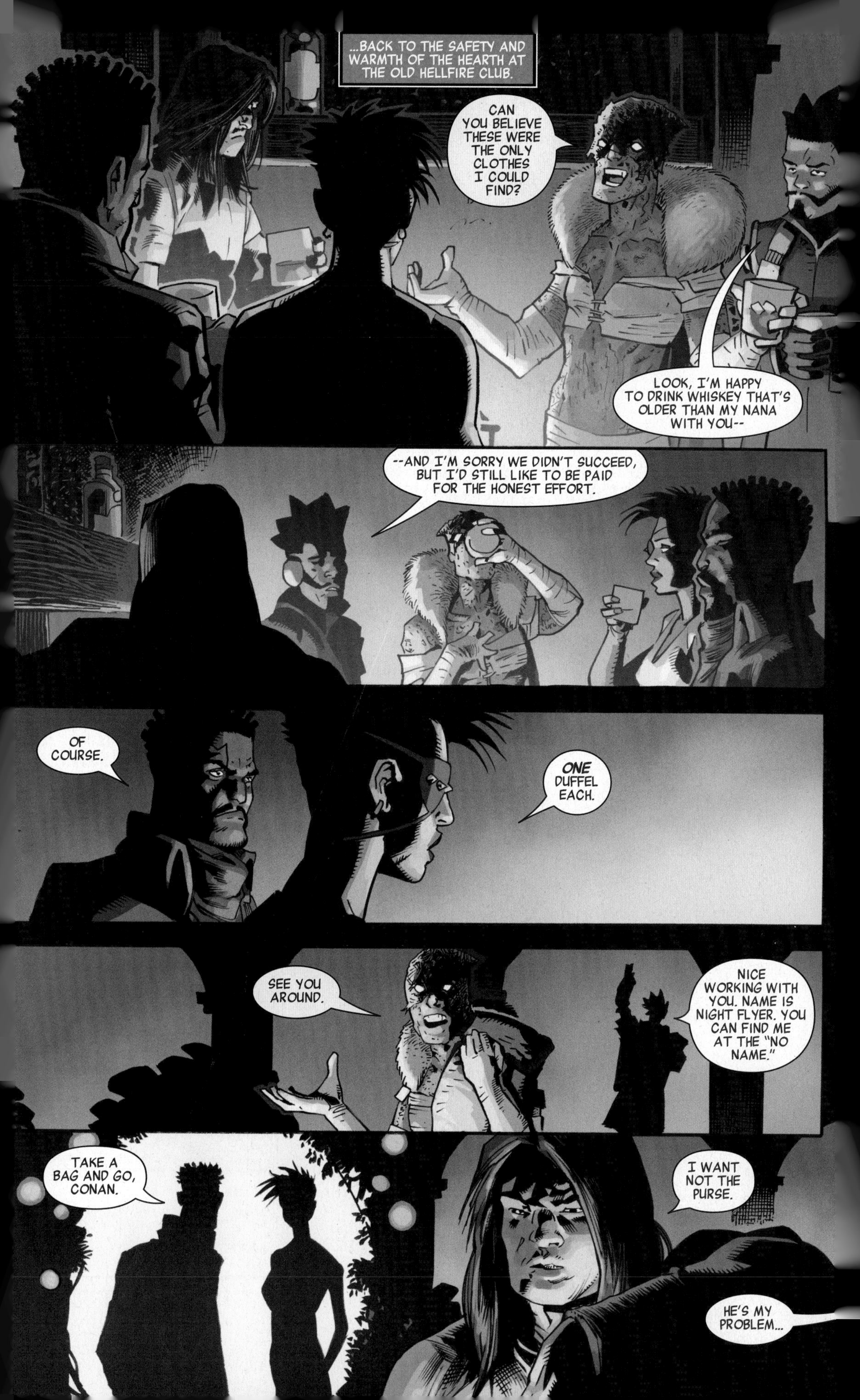
...BACK TO THE SAFETY AND WARMTH OF THE HEARTH AT THE OLD HELLFIRE CLUB.
CAN YOU BELIEVE THESE WERE THE ONLY CLOTHES I COULD FIND?
LOOK, I'M HAPPY TO DRINK WHISKEY THAT'S OLDER THAN MY NANA WITH YOU--
--AND I'M SORRY WE DIDN'T SUCCEED, BUT I'D STILL LIKE TO BE PAID FOR THE HONEST EFFORT.
OF COURSE.
ONE DUFFEL EACH.
SEE YOU AROUND.
NICE WORKING WITH YOU. NAME IS NIGHT FLYER. YOU CAN FIND ME AT THE "NO NAME."
TAKE A BAG AND GO, CONAN.
I WANT NOT THE PURSE.
HE'S MY PROBLEM...

...YOU WANTED ME, CONAN.

YOU GOT ME.

I HAVE TO ASSEMBLE THE CAPTAINS.

LOGAN, BOBBY IS OUT THERE WAGING A ONE-MAN WAR.

NOT FOR LONG.

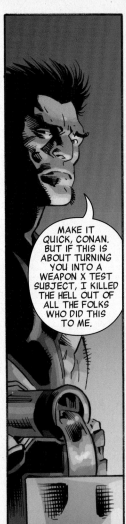

MAKE IT QUICK, CONAN. BUT IF THIS IS ABOUT TURNING YOU INTO A WEAPON X TEST SUBJECT, I KILLED THE HELL OUT OF ALL THE FOLKS WHO DID THIS TO ME.

NO.

OUT OF RESPECT, I WANTED YOU TO KNOW THIS CASTLE IS *MINE* NOW.

I KNOW IT WAS *FORMERLY* CONTROLLED BY YOUR PEOPLE.

TELL ANYONE UPSET ABOUT THIS WHAT I AM CAPABLE OF, AND TELL THEM TO GIVE ME A WIDE BERTH.

YOU BROUGHT ME HERE...TO BROKER A REAL ESTATE DEAL?

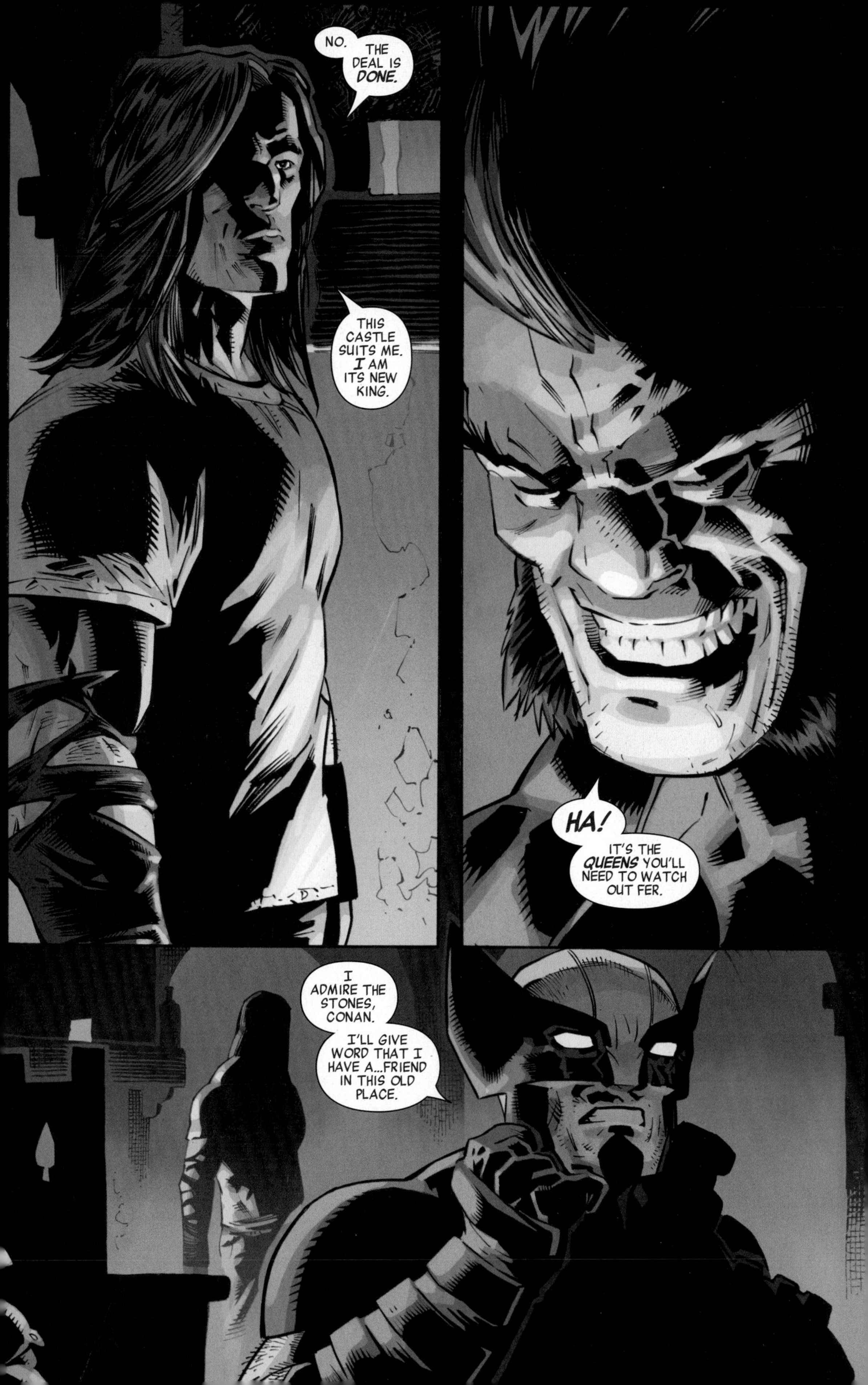
NO.
THE DEAL IS DONE.
THIS CASTLE SUITS ME. I AM ITS NEW KING.
HA!
IT'S THE QUEENS YOU'LL NEED TO WATCH OUT FER.
I ADMIRE THE STONES, CONAN.
I'LL GIVE WORD THAT I HAVE A...FRIEND IN THIS OLD PLACE.

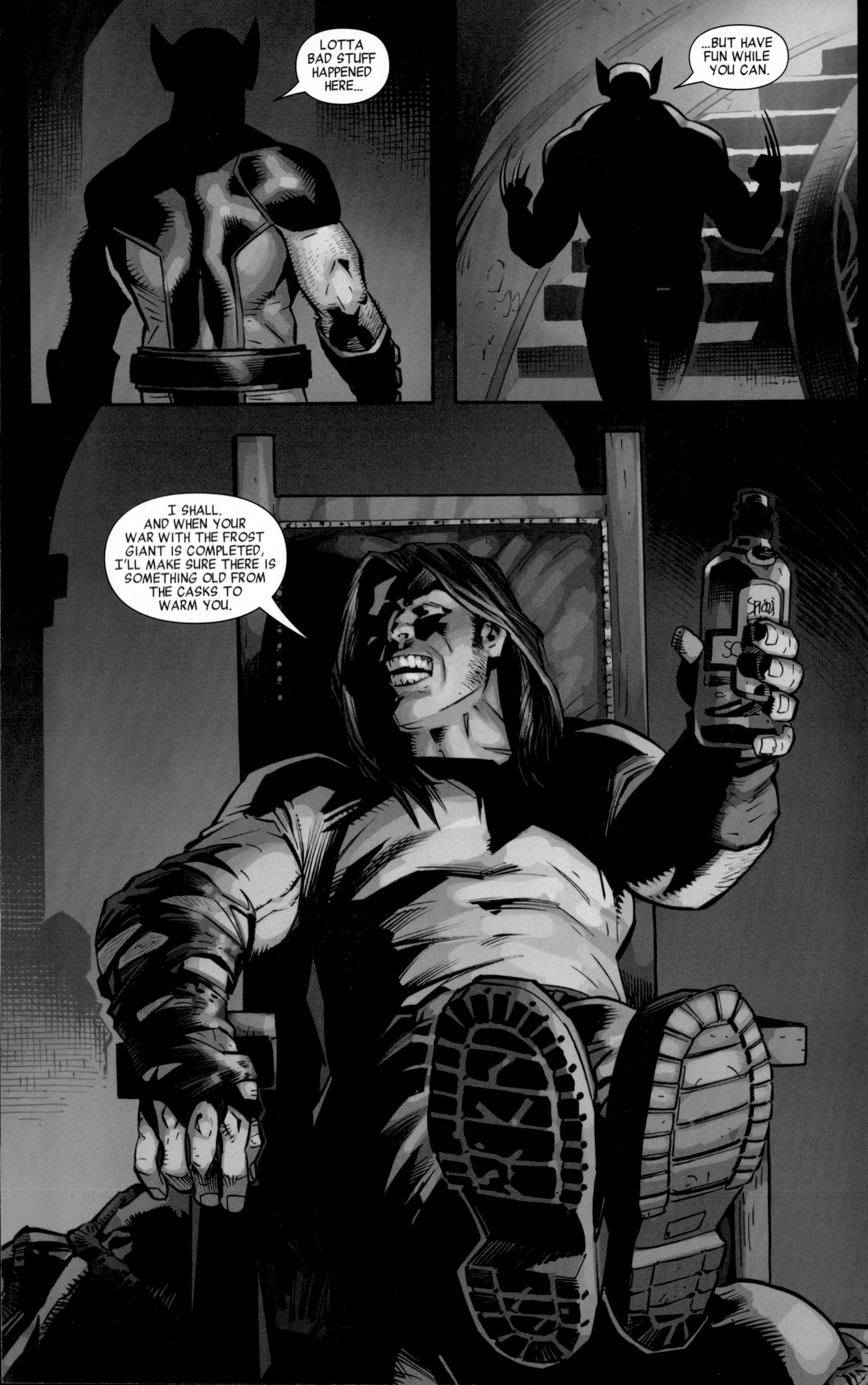
LOTTA BAD STUFF HAPPENED HERE...
...BUT HAVE FUN WHILE YOU CAN.
I SHALL. AND WHEN YOUR WAR WITH THE FROST GIANT IS COMPLETED, I'LL MAKE SURE THERE IS SOMETHING OLD FROM THE CASKS TO WARM YOU.

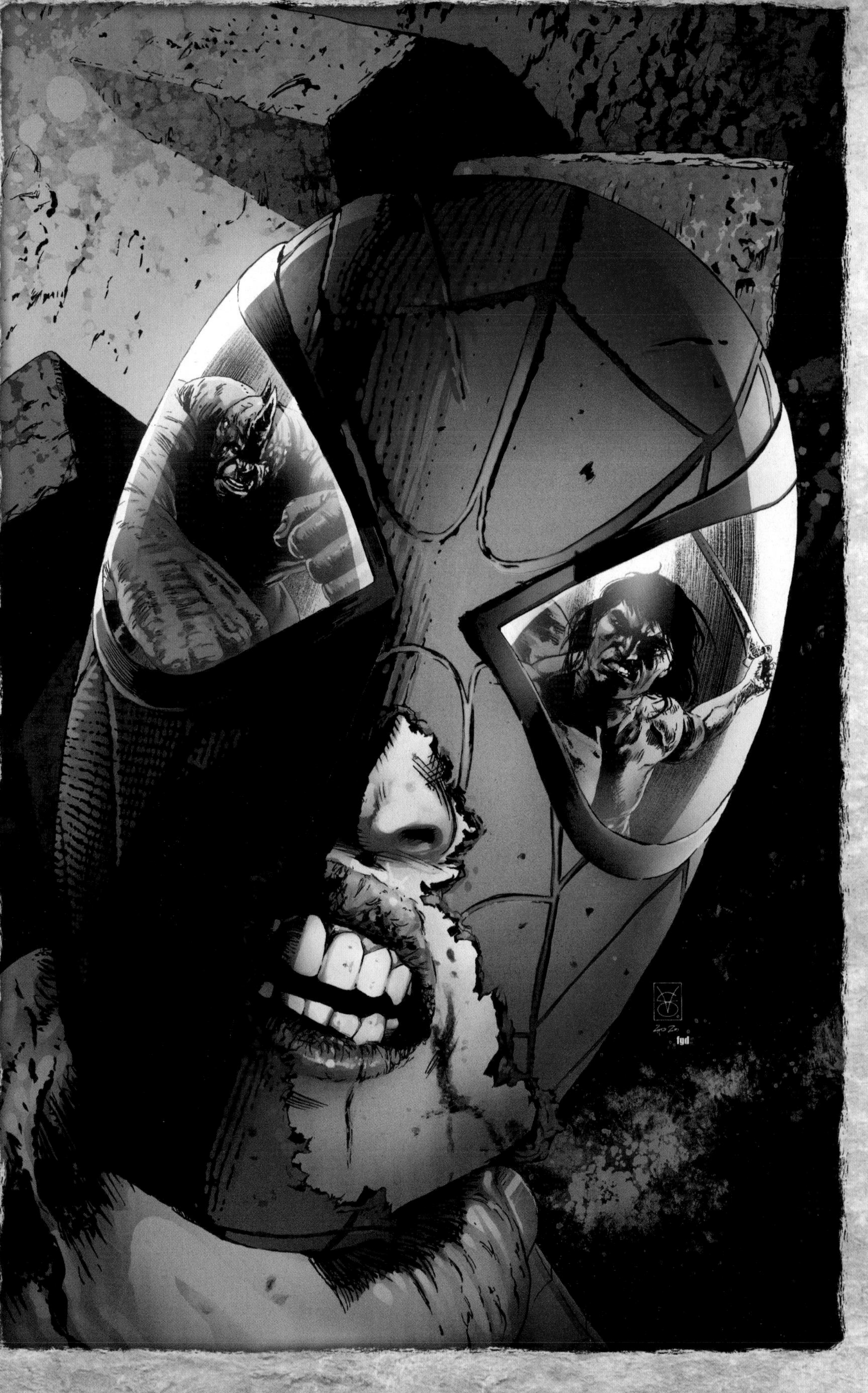

20: THE CLOTHES DO NOT MAKETH THE SPIDER-MAN

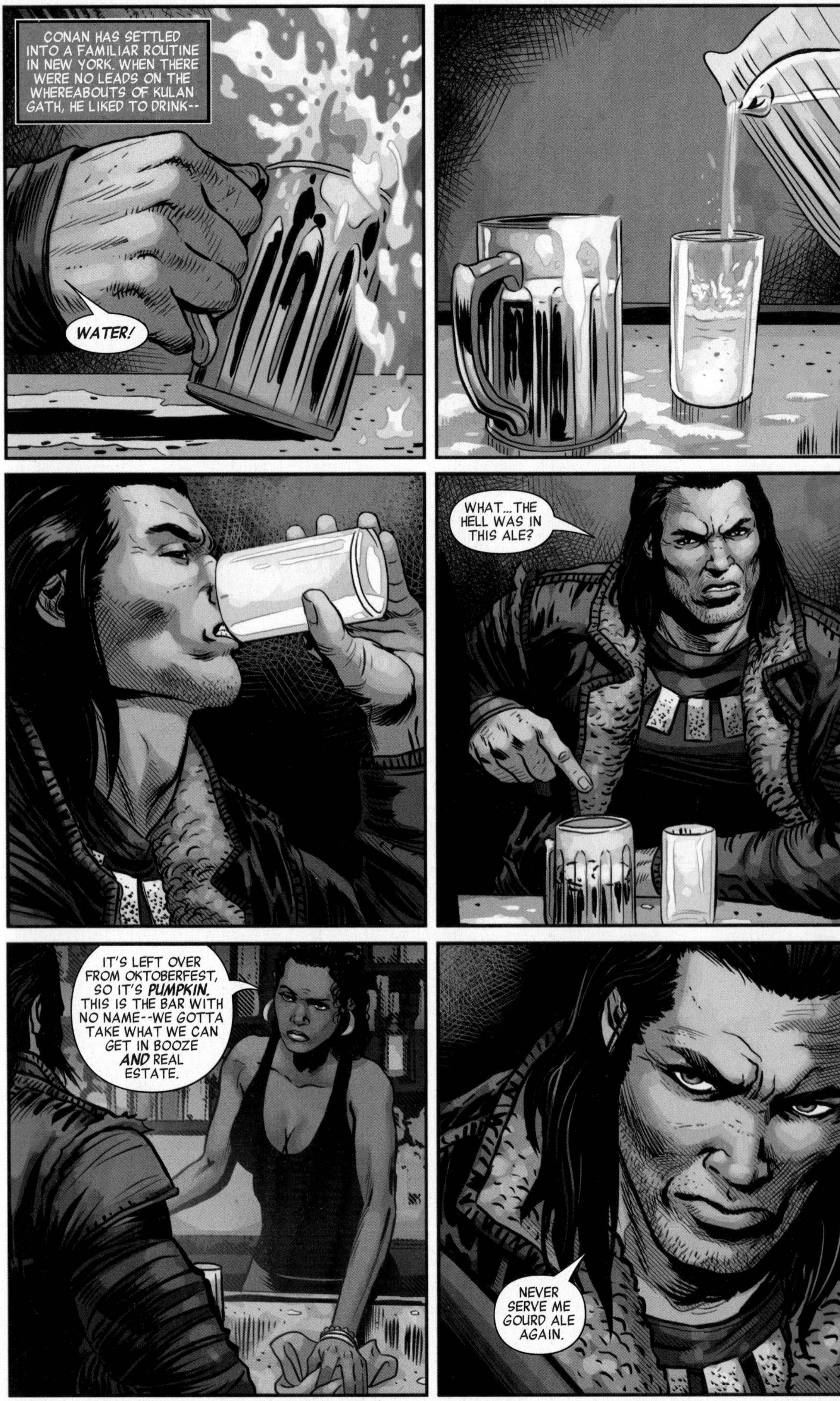
CONAN HAS SETTLED INTO A FAMILIAR ROUTINE IN NEW YORK. WHEN THERE WERE NO LEADS ON THE WHEREABOUTS OF KULAN GATH, HE LIKED TO DRINK--
WATER!
WHAT...THE HELL WAS IN THIS ALE?
IT'S LEFT OVER FROM OKTOBERFEST, SO IT'S PUMPKIN. THIS IS THE BAR WITH NO NAME--WE GOTTA TAKE WHAT WE CAN GET IN BOOZE AND REAL ESTATE.
NEVER SERVE ME GOURD ALE AGAIN.

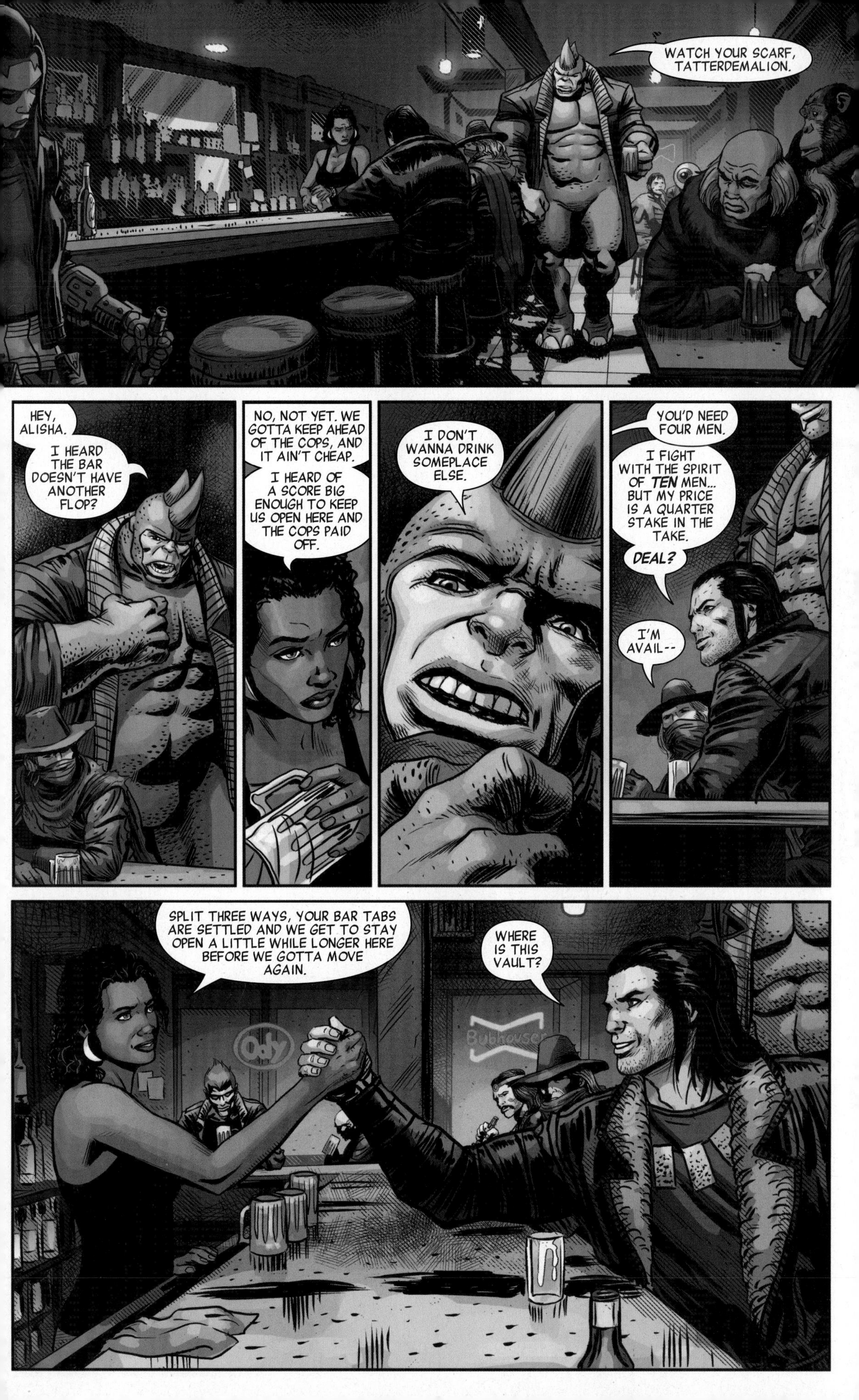
WATCH YOUR SCARF, TATTERDEMALION.
HEY, ALISHA.
I HEARD THE BAR DOESN'T HAVE ANOTHER FLOP?
NO, NOT YET. WE GOTTA KEEP AHEAD OF THE COPS, AND IT AIN'T CHEAP.
I HEARD OF A SCORE BIG ENOUGH TO KEEP US OPEN HERE AND THE COPS PAID OFF.
I DON'T WANNA DRINK SOMEPLACE ELSE.
YOU'D NEED FOUR MEN.
I FIGHT WITH THE SPIRIT OF TEN MEN... BUT MY PRICE IS A QUARTER STAKE IN THE TAKE.
DEAL?
I'M AVAIL--
SPLIT THREE WAYS, YOUR BAR TABS ARE SETTLED AND WE GET TO STAY OPEN A LITTLE WHILE LONGER HERE BEFORE WE GOTTA MOVE AGAIN.
WHERE IS THIS VAULT?

THE JOB CALLED FOR STEALTH, SO CONAN WORE ONE OF THE MANY BLACK SUITS HE FOUND IN HIS NEW CASTLE, THE HELLFIRE CLUB.

CONAN SCOFFED AT THE IDEA OF A MAN LEAVING HIS COIN IN THE CARE OF LESSER MEN. HE MARVELED AT HOW THIS CIVILIZATION HAD ACCOMPLISHED SO MUCH WHILE ATROPHYING IN NEARLY EVERY MEASURE.

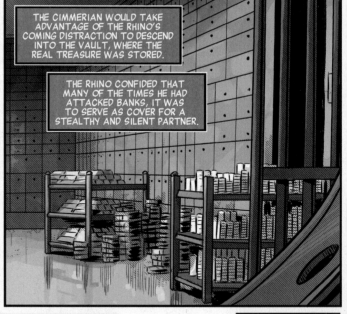

THE CIMMERIAN WOULD TAKE ADVANTAGE OF THE RHINO'S COMING DISTRACTION TO DESCEND INTO THE VAULT, WHERE THE REAL TREASURE WAS STORED.

THE RHINO CONFIDED THAT MANY OF THE TIMES HE HAD ATTACKED BANKS, IT WAS TO SERVE AS COVER FOR A STEALTHY AND SILENT PARTNER.

CONAN'S HEART RATE WAS STEADY, BUT THE SYMBIOTE HE HAD RESCUED FROM KULAN GATH COILED AROUND HIS ARM, READY FOR A FIGHT...

...AND THE RHINO WAS RIGHT ON TIME.

AWRIGHT, YA BUMS--

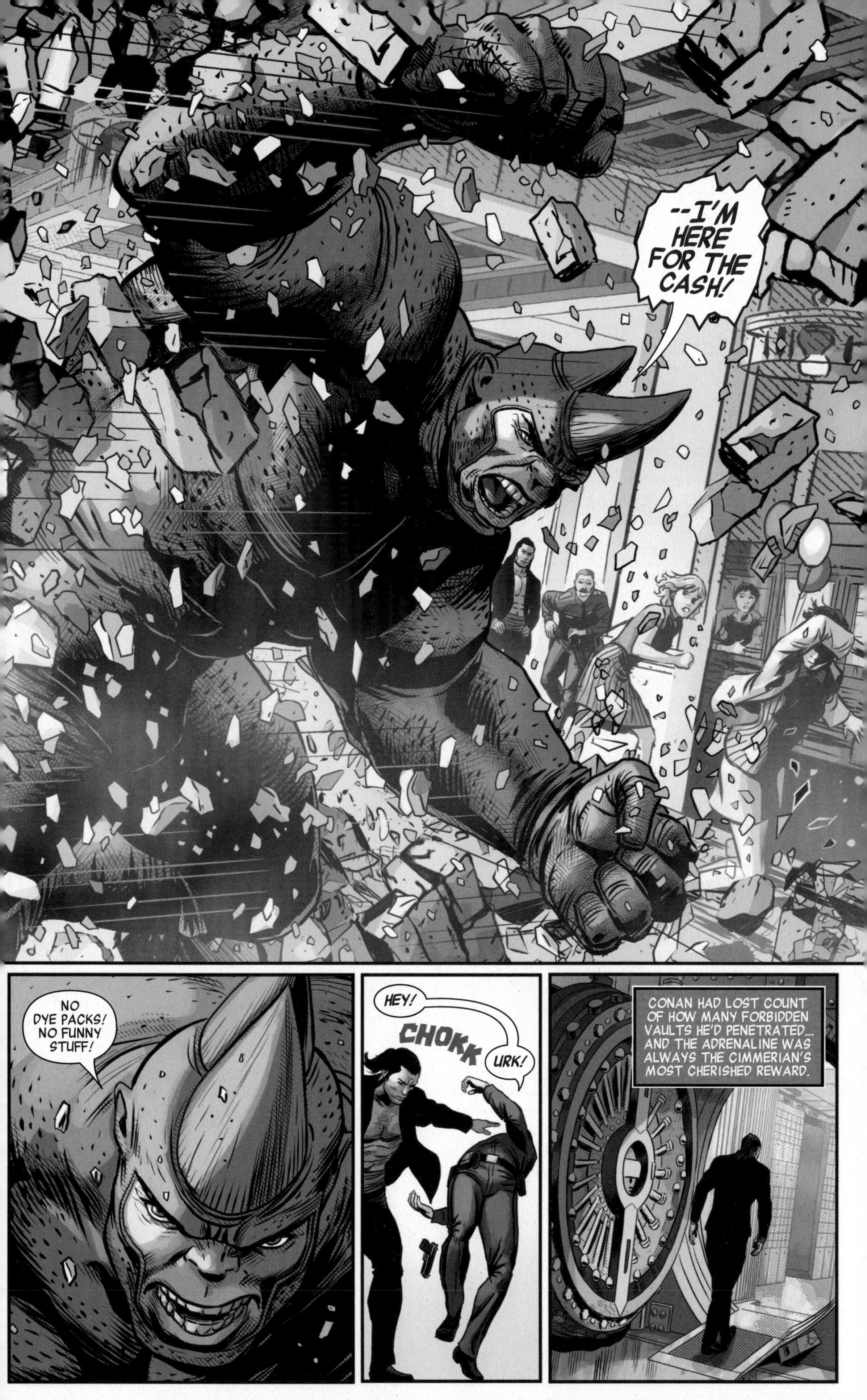
--I'M HERE FOR THE CASH!
NO DYE PACKS! NO FUNNY STUFF!
HEY!
CHOKK
URK!
CONAN HAD LOST COUNT OF HOW MANY FORBIDDEN VAULTS HE'D PENETRATED... AND THE ADRENALINE WAS ALWAYS THE CIMMERIAN'S MOST CHERISHED REWARD.

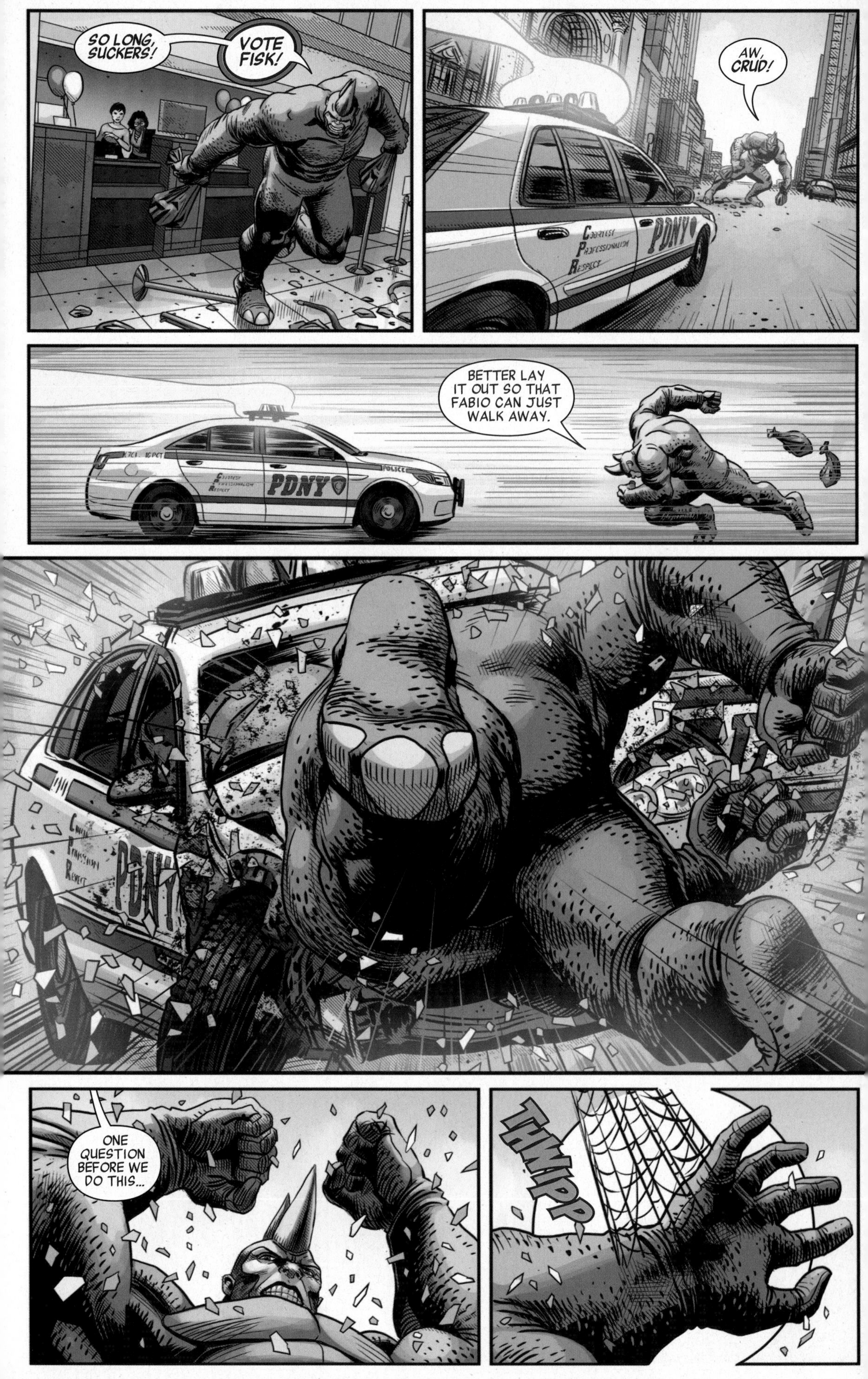

SO LONG, SUCKERS!
VOTE FISK!
AW, CRUD!
BETTER LAY IT OUT SO THAT FABIO CAN JUST WALK AWAY.
PDNY
ONE QUESTION BEFORE WE DO THIS...
THWIPP

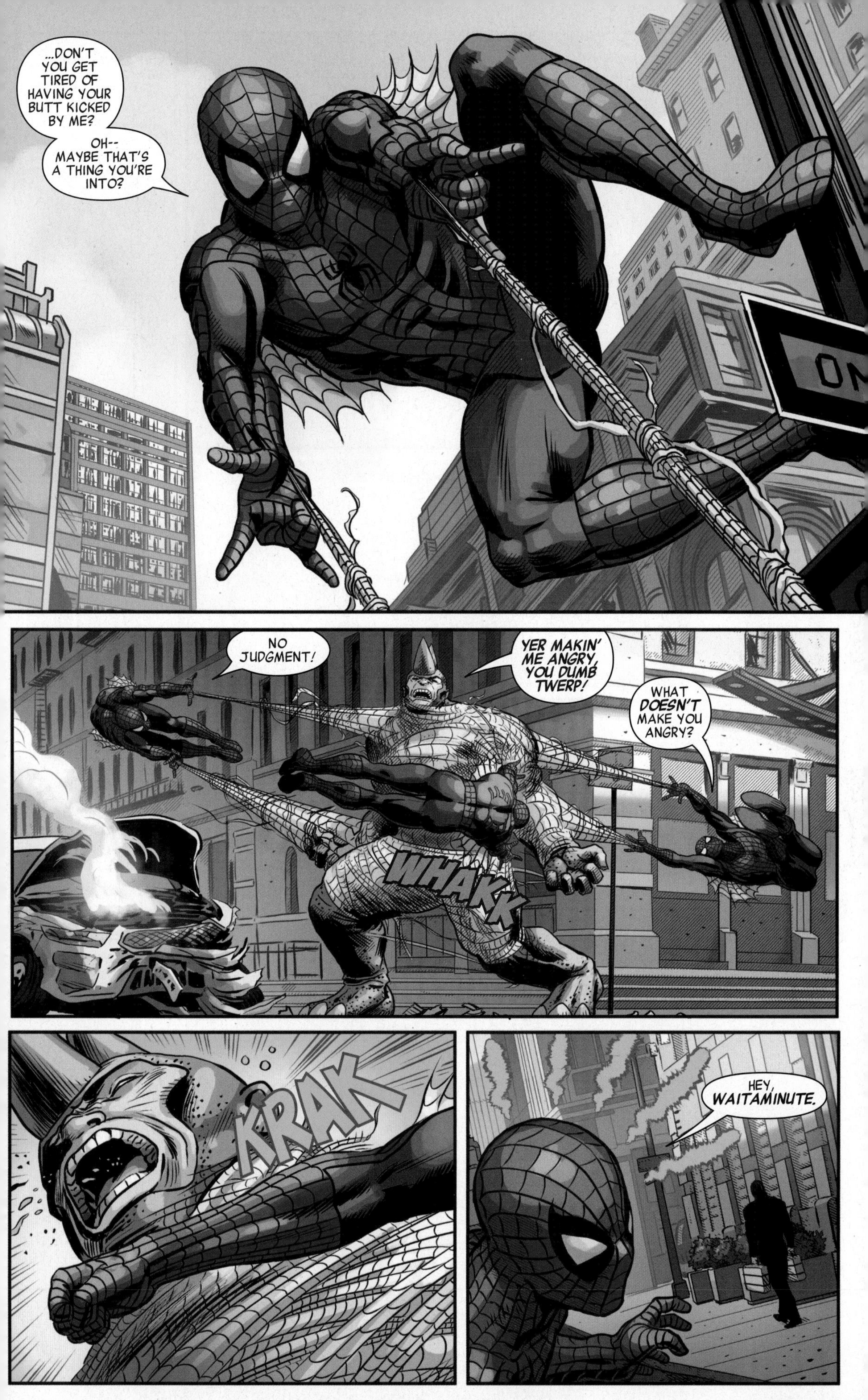

...DON'T YOU GET TIRED OF HAVING YOUR BUTT KICKED BY ME?
OH-- MAYBE THAT'S A THING YOU'RE INTO?
NO JUDGMENT!
YER MAKIN' ME ANGRY, YOU DUMB TWERP!
WHAT DOESN'T MAKE YOU ANGRY?
WHAKK
KRAK
HEY, WAITAMINUTE.

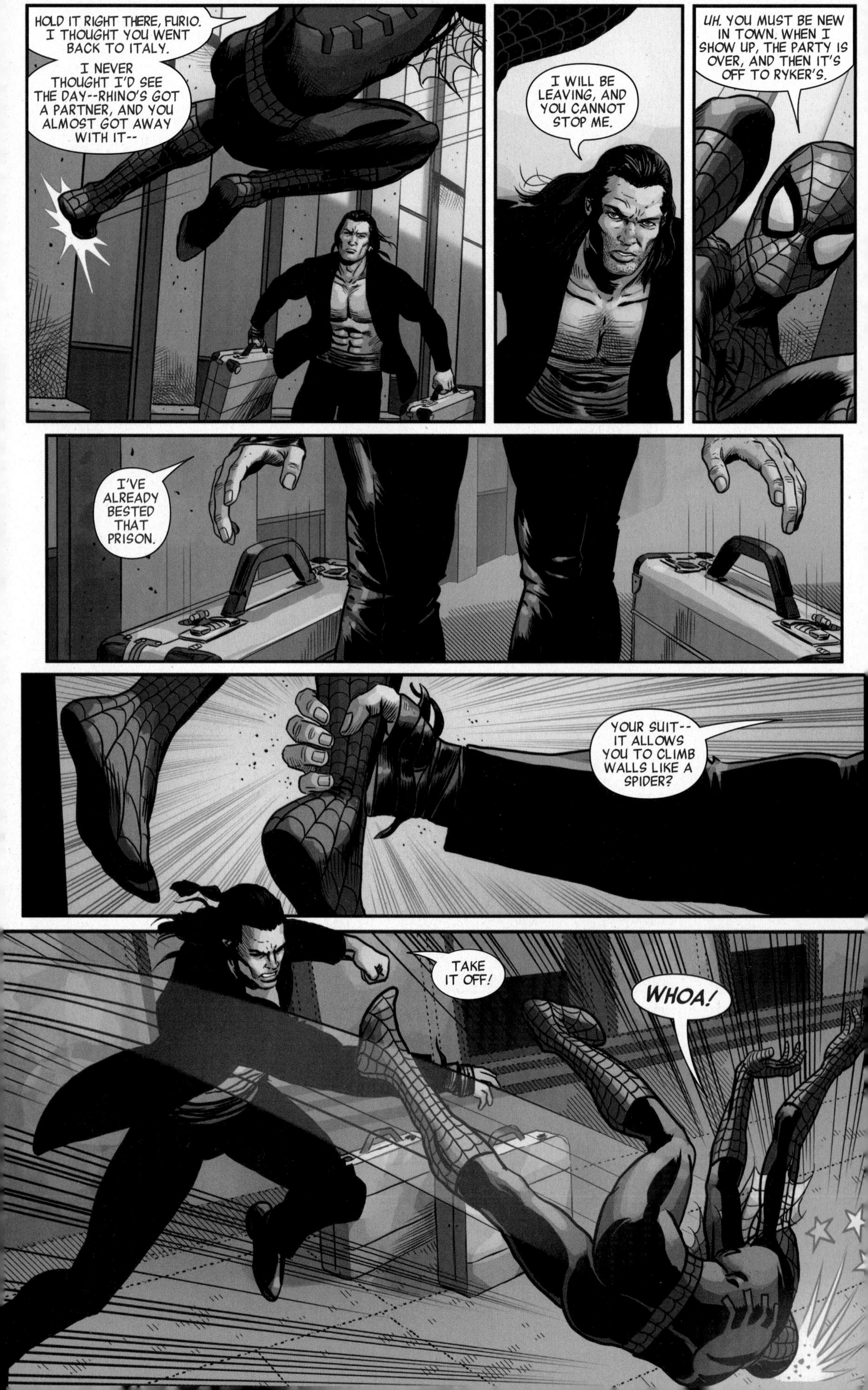
HOLD IT RIGHT THERE, FURIO. I THOUGHT YOU WENT BACK TO ITALY.
I NEVER THOUGHT I'D SEE THE DAY--RHINO'S GOT A PARTNER, AND YOU ALMOST GOT AWAY WITH IT--
I WILL BE LEAVING, AND YOU CANNOT STOP ME.
UH. YOU MUST BE NEW IN TOWN. WHEN I SHOW UP, THE PARTY IS OVER, AND THEN IT'S OFF TO RYKER'S.
I'VE ALREADY BESTED THAT PRISON.
YOUR SUIT-- IT ALLOWS YOU TO CLIMB WALLS LIKE A SPIDER?
TAKE IT OFF!
WHOA!

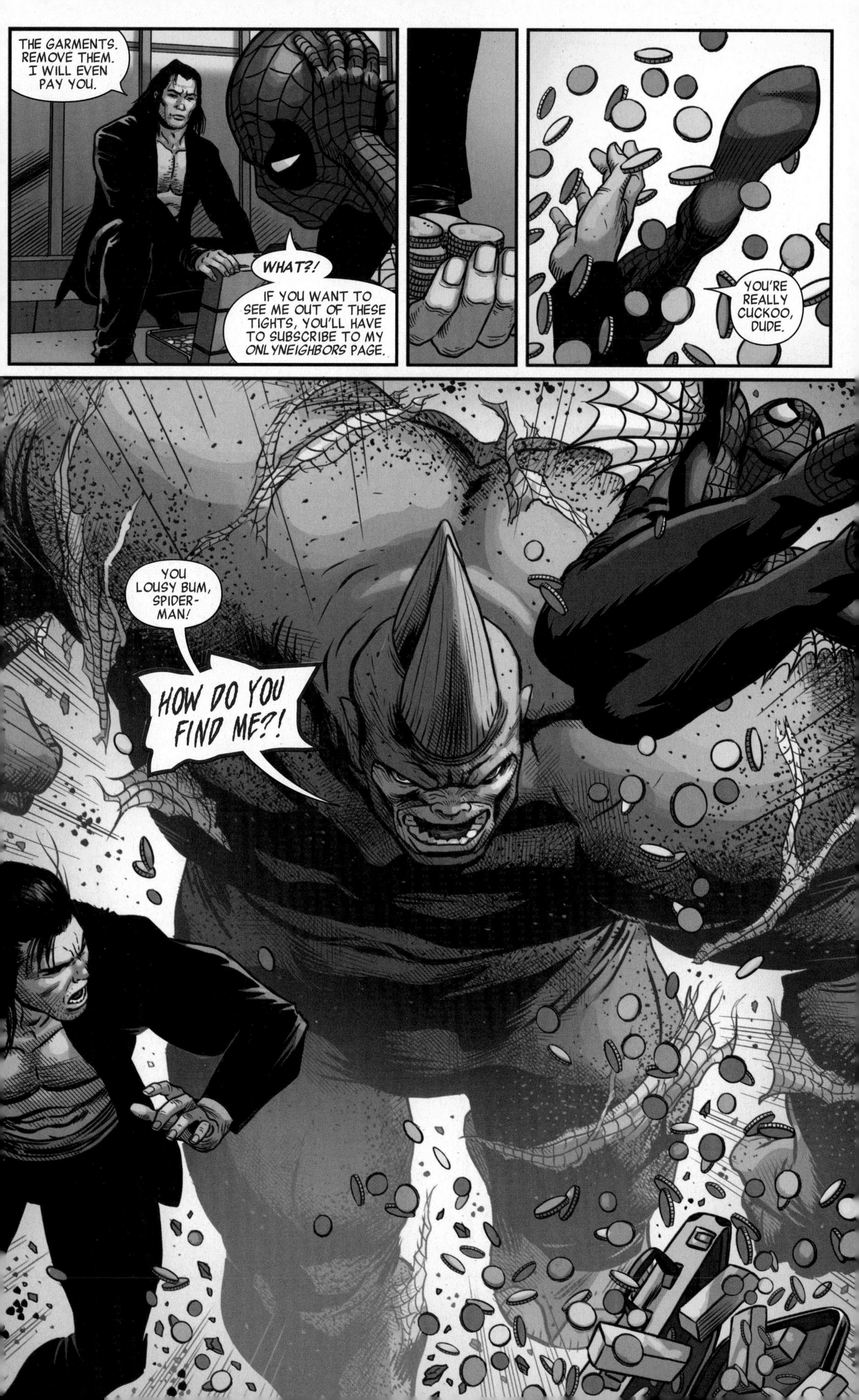
THE GARMENTS. REMOVE THEM. I WILL EVEN PAY YOU.
WHAT?!
IF YOU WANT TO SEE ME OUT OF THESE TIGHTS, YOU'LL HAVE TO SUBSCRIBE TO MY ONLYNEIGHBORS PAGE.
YOU'RE REALLY CUCKOO, DUDE.
YOU LOUSY BUM, SPIDER-MAN!
HOW DO YOU FIND ME?!

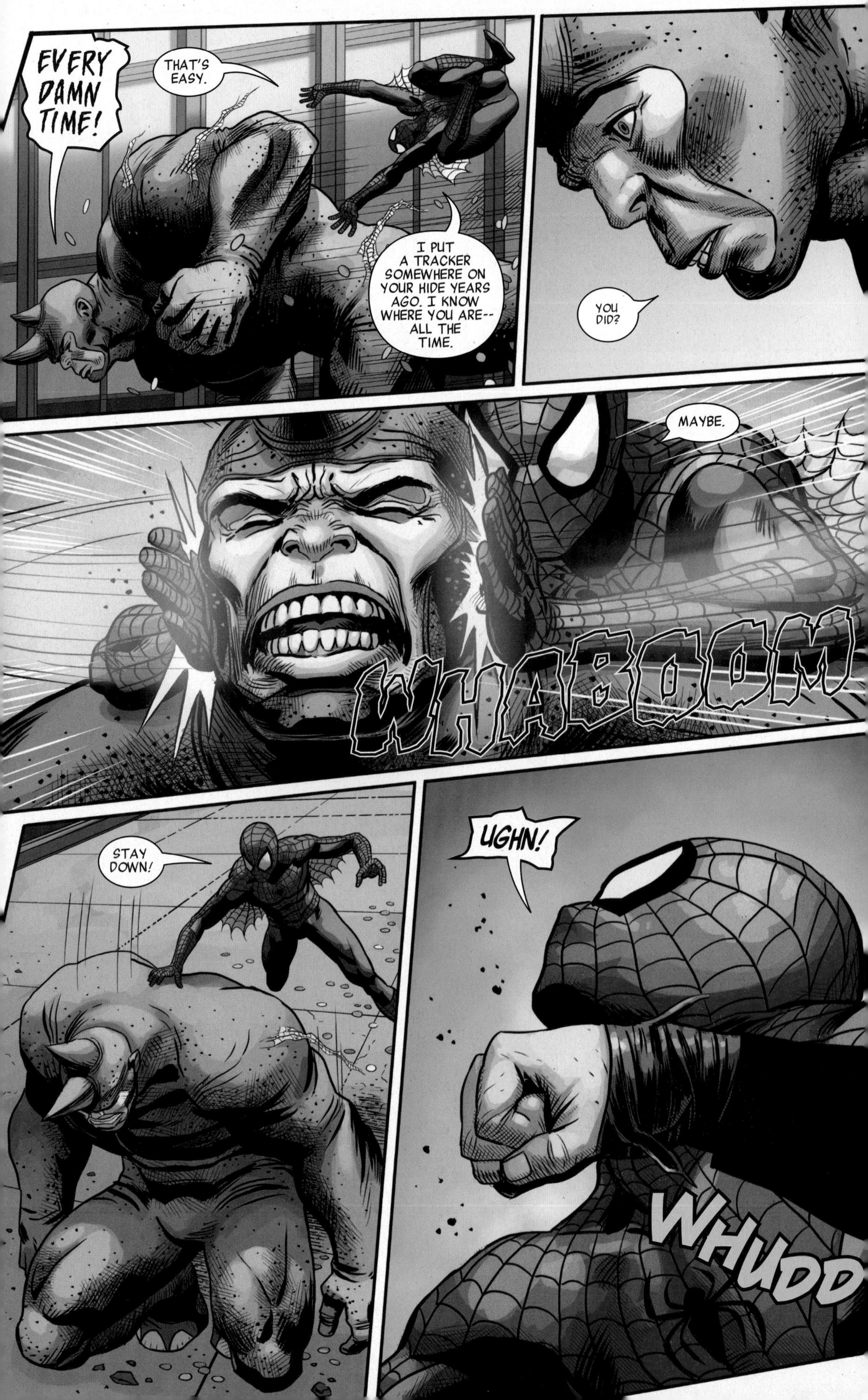
EVERY DAMN TIME!
THAT'S EASY.
I PUT A TRACKER SOMEWHERE ON YOUR HIDE YEARS AGO. I KNOW WHERE YOU ARE-- ALL THE TIME.
YOU DID?
MAYBE.
WHABOOM
STAY DOWN!
UGHN!
WHUDD

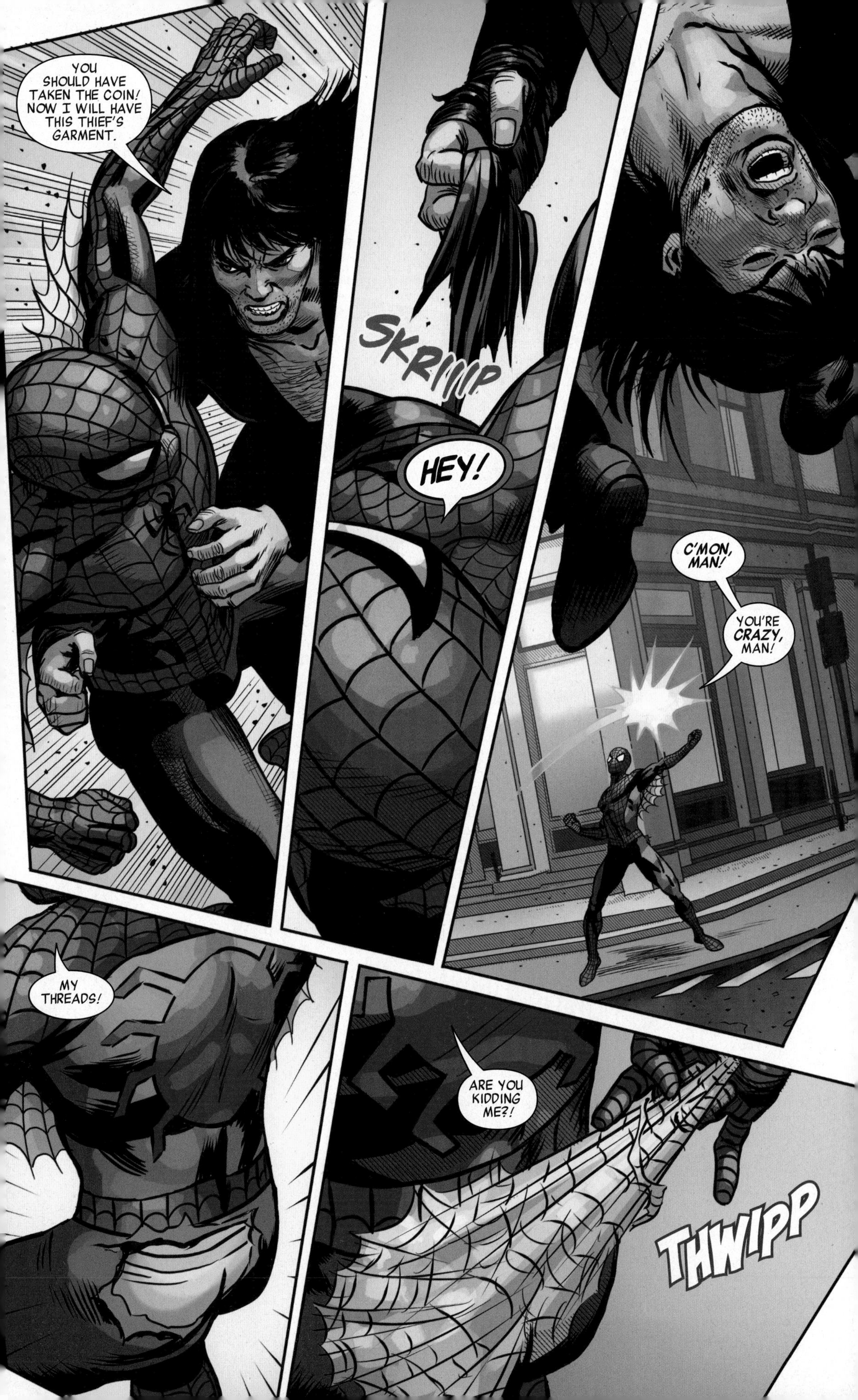
YOU SHOULD HAVE TAKEN THE COIN! NOW I WILL HAVE THIS THIEF'S GARMENT.
SKRIIIIP
HEY!
C'MON, MAN!
YOU'RE CRAZY, MAN!
MY THREADS!
ARE YOU KIDDING ME?!
THWIPP

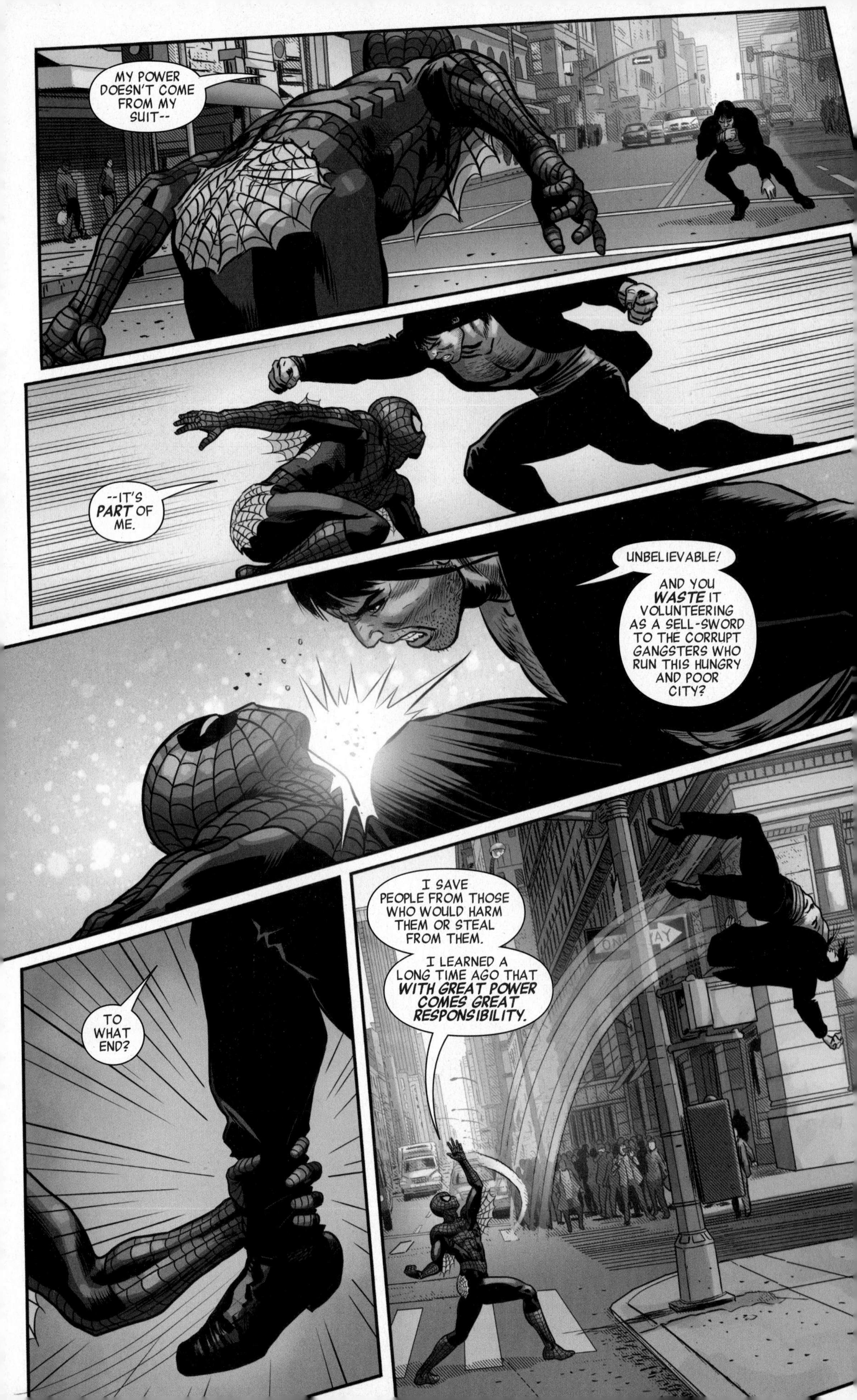
MY POWER DOESN'T COME FROM MY SUIT--
--IT'S *PART* OF ME.
UNBELIEVABLE!
AND YOU ***WASTE*** IT VOLUNTEERING AS A SELL-SWORD TO THE CORRUPT GANGSTERS WHO RUN THIS HUNGRY AND POOR CITY?
TO WHAT END?
I SAVE PEOPLE FROM THOSE WHO WOULD HARM THEM OR STEAL FROM THEM.
I LEARNED A LONG TIME AGO THAT ***WITH GREAT POWER COMES GREAT RESPONSIBILITY.***

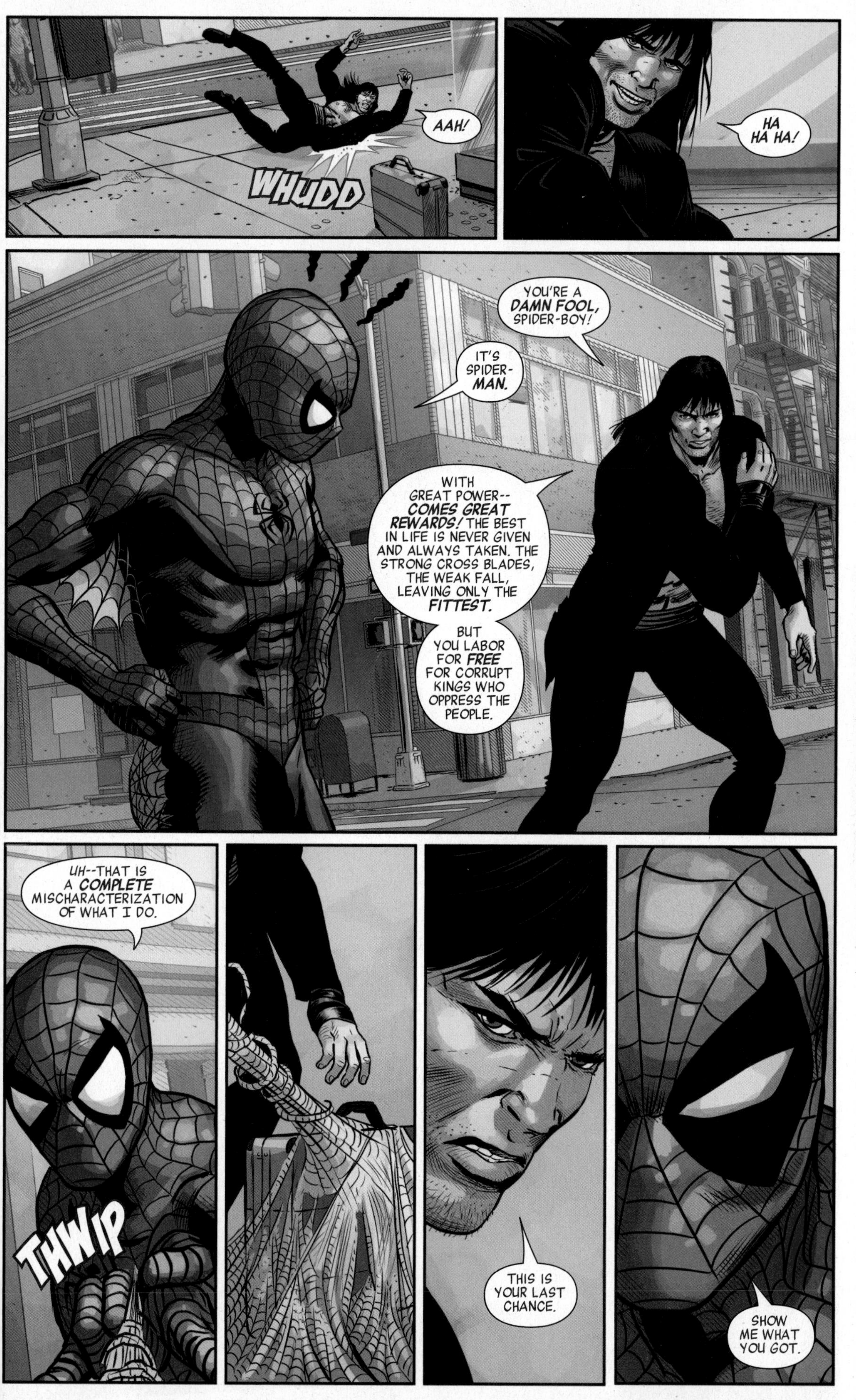
AAH!
WHUDD
HA HA HA!
YOU'RE A DAMN FOOL, SPIDER-BOY!
IT'S SPIDER-MAN.
WITH GREAT POWER-- COMES GREAT REWARDS! THE BEST IN LIFE IS NEVER GIVEN AND ALWAYS TAKEN. THE STRONG CROSS BLADES, THE WEAK FALL, LEAVING ONLY THE FITTEST.
BUT YOU LABOR FOR FREE FOR CORRUPT KINGS WHO OPPRESS THE PEOPLE.
UH--THAT IS A COMPLETE MISCHARACTERIZATION OF WHAT I DO.
THWIP
THIS IS YOUR LAST CHANCE.
SHOW ME WHAT YOU GOT.

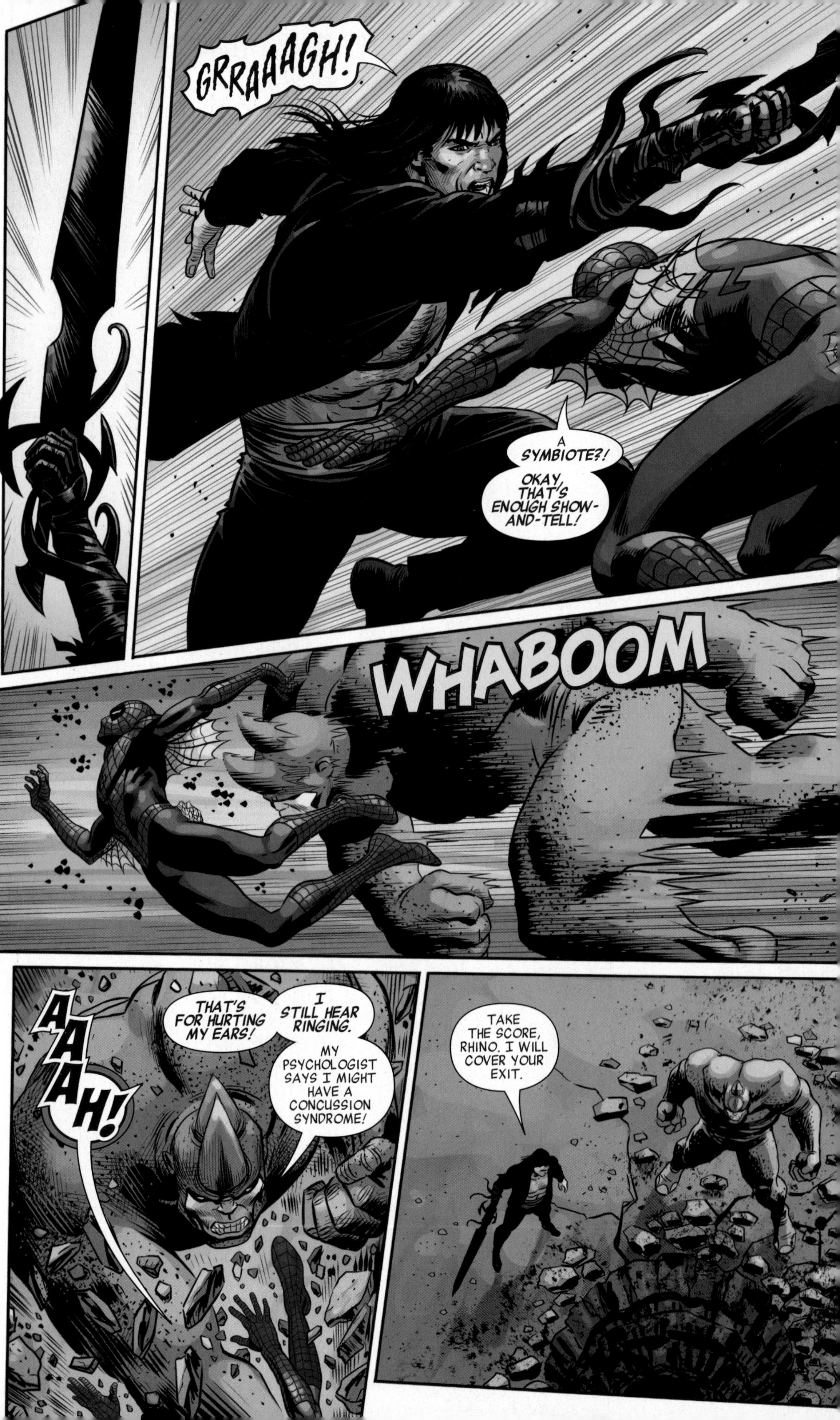
GRRAAAGH!
A SYMBIOTE?!
OKAY, THAT'S ENOUGH SHOW-AND-TELL!
WHABOOM
AAAAH!
THAT'S FOR HURTING MY EARS!
I STILL HEAR RINGING.
MY PSYCHOLOGIST SAYS I MIGHT HAVE A CONCUSSION SYNDROME!
TAKE THE SCORE, RHINO. I WILL COVER YOUR EXIT.

FIRST ROUND'S ON ME!

FREEZE!

FEAR NOT, OFFICER--

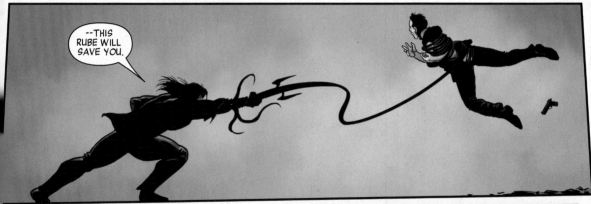

--THIS RUBE WILL SAVE YOU.

AAAHH!

NO!!!

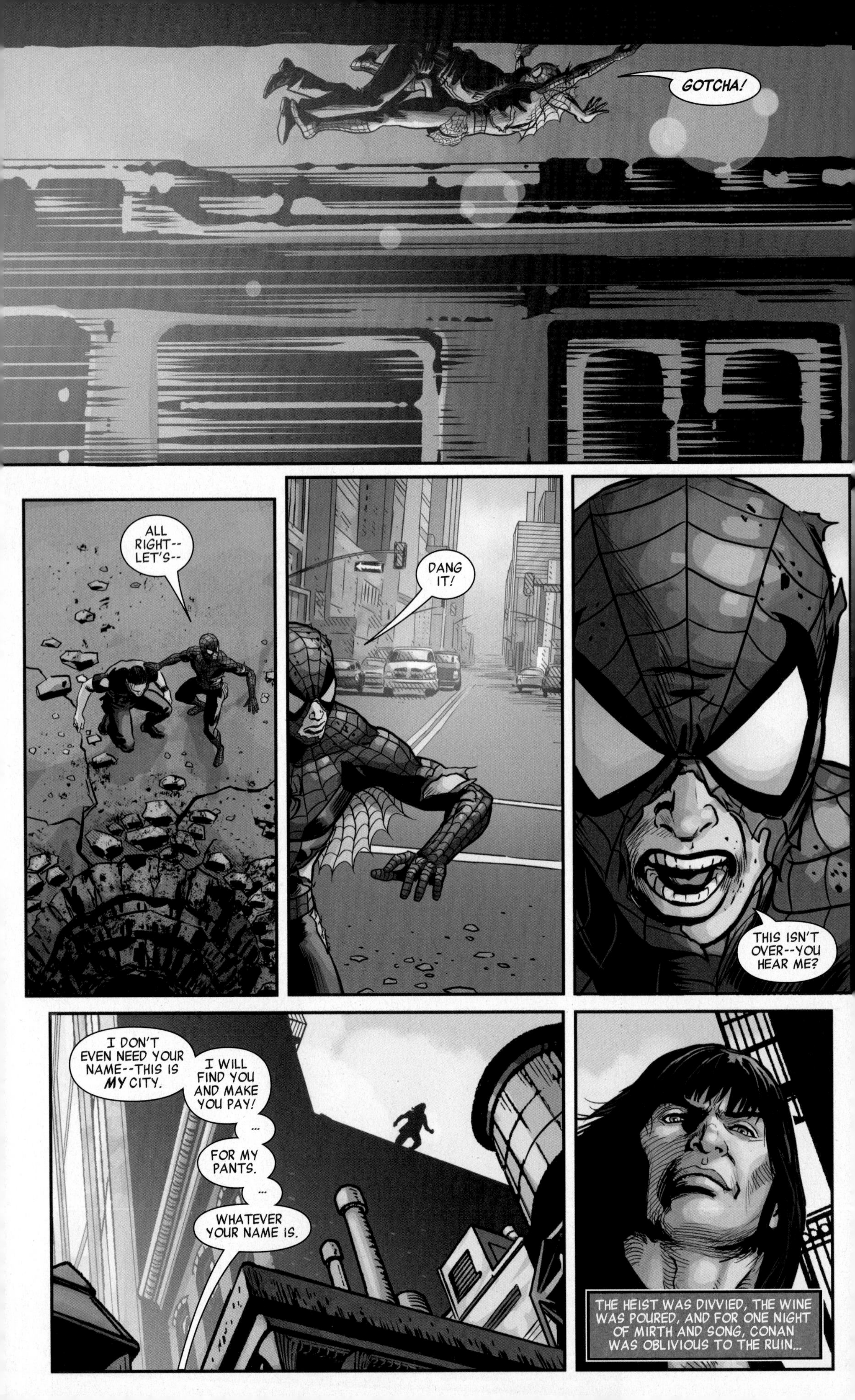
GOTCHA!
ALL RIGHT-- LET'S--
DANG IT!
THIS ISN'T OVER--YOU HEAR ME?
I DON'T EVEN NEED YOUR NAME--THIS IS MY CITY.
I WILL FIND YOU AND MAKE YOU PAY!
...
FOR MY PANTS.
...
WHATEVER YOUR NAME IS.
THE HEIST WAS DIVVIED, THE WINE WAS POURED, AND FOR ONE NIGHT OF MIRTH AND SONG, CONAN WAS OBLIVIOUS TO THE RUIN...

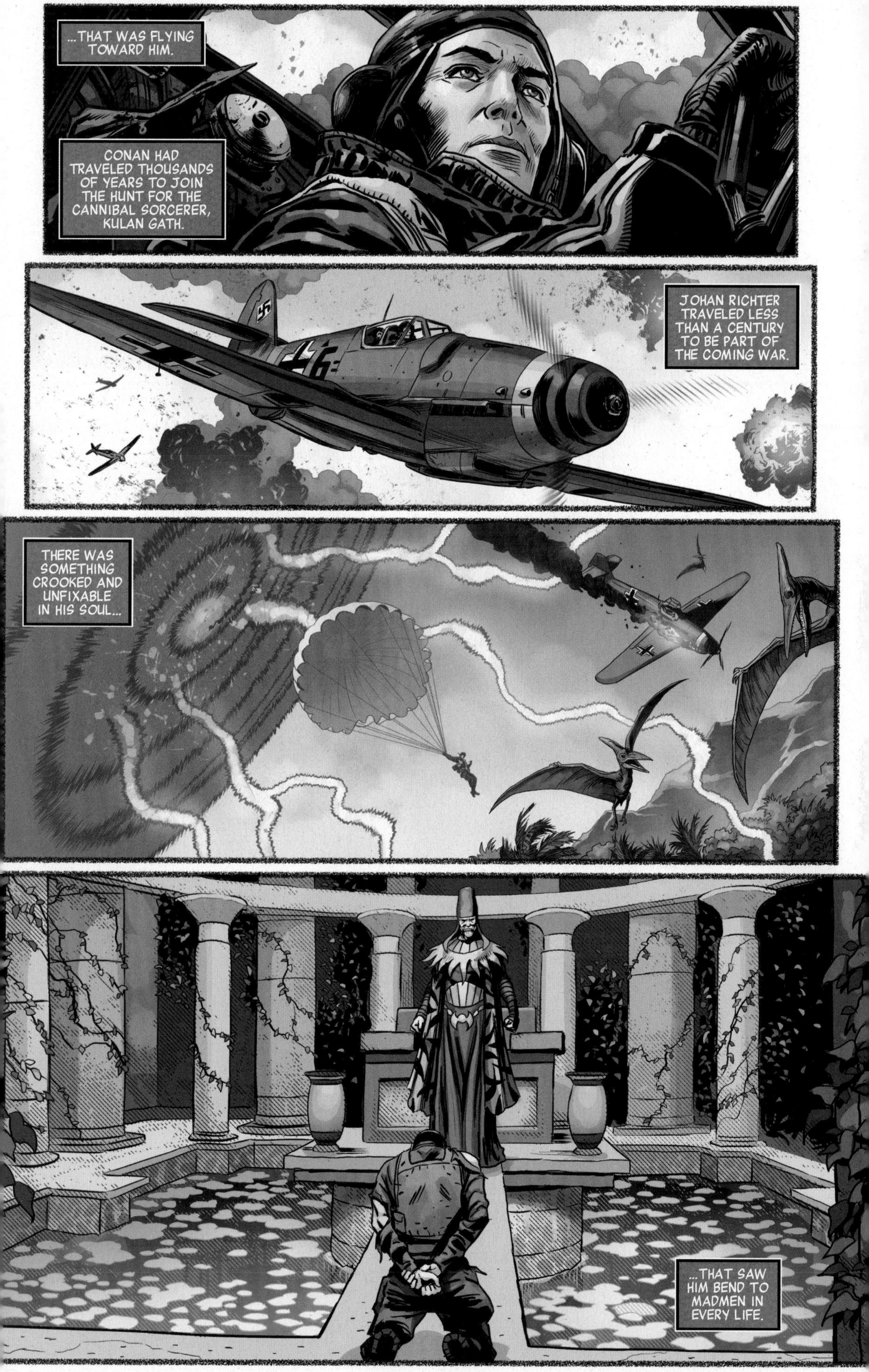
...THAT WAS FLYING TOWARD HIM.
CONAN HAD TRAVELED THOUSANDS OF YEARS TO JOIN THE HUNT FOR THE CANNIBAL SORCERER, KULAN GATH.
JOHAN RICHTER TRAVELED LESS THAN A CENTURY TO BE PART OF THE COMING WAR.
THERE WAS SOMETHING CROOKED AND UNFIXABLE IN HIS SOUL...
...THAT SAW HIM BEND TO MADMEN IN EVERY LIFE.

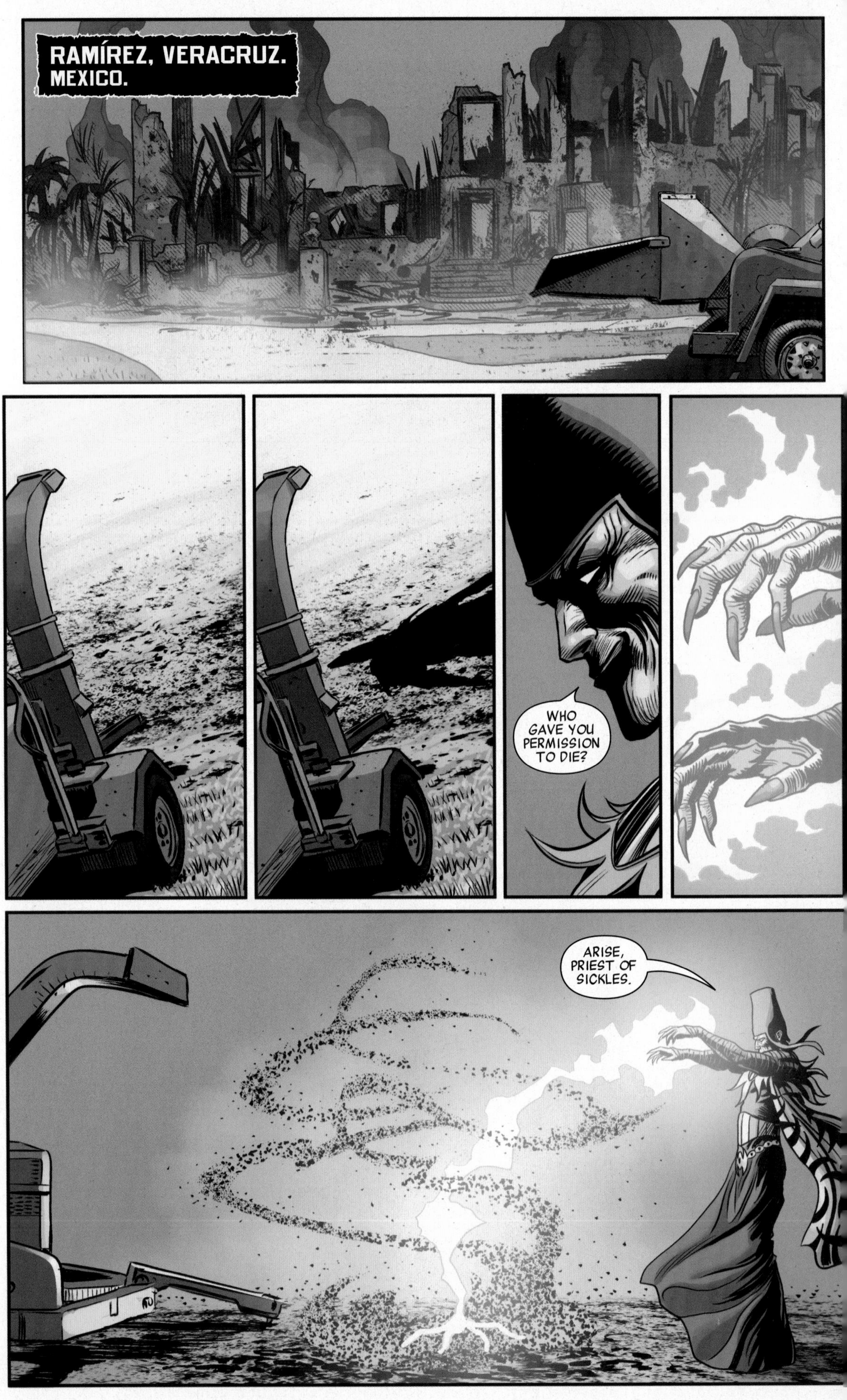
RAMÍREZ, VERACRUZ.
MEXICO.
WHO GAVE YOU PERMISSION TO DIE?
ARISE, PRIEST OF SICKLES.

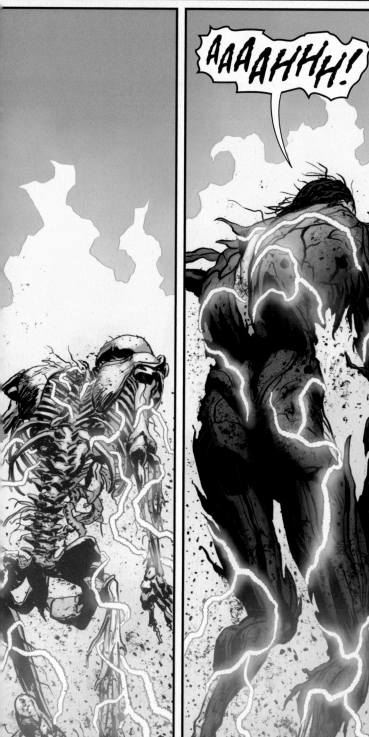

AAAAHHH!

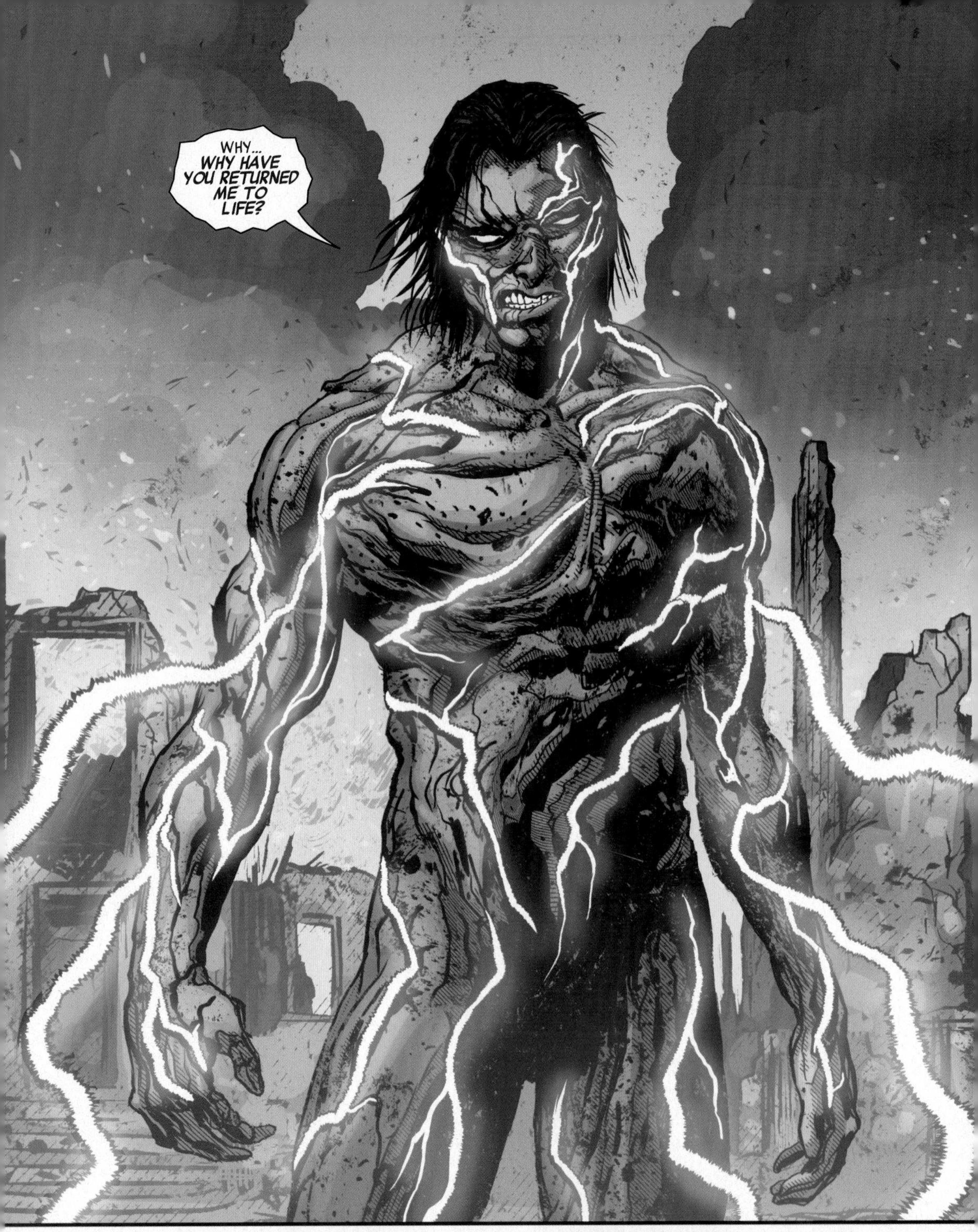
WHY... WHY HAVE YOU RETURNED ME TO LIFE?

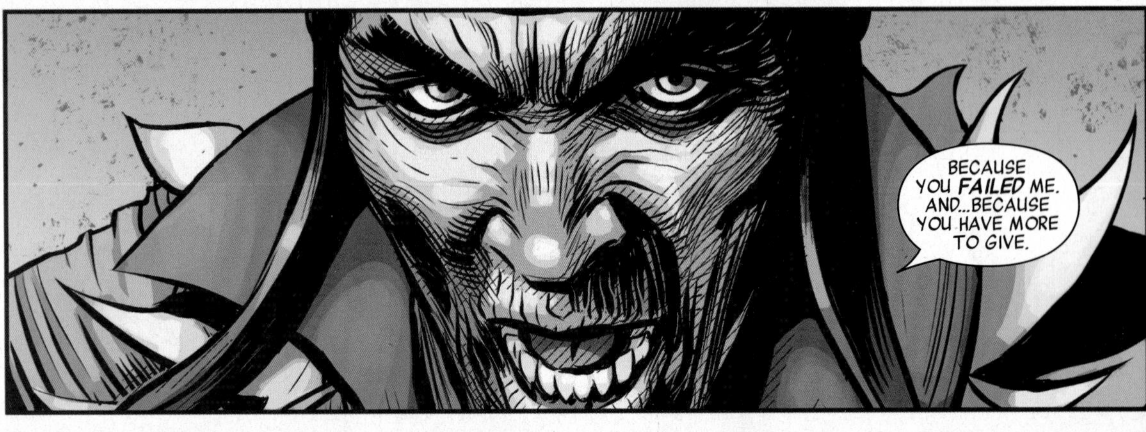
BECAUSE YOU FAILED ME. AND...BECAUSE YOU HAVE MORE TO GIVE.

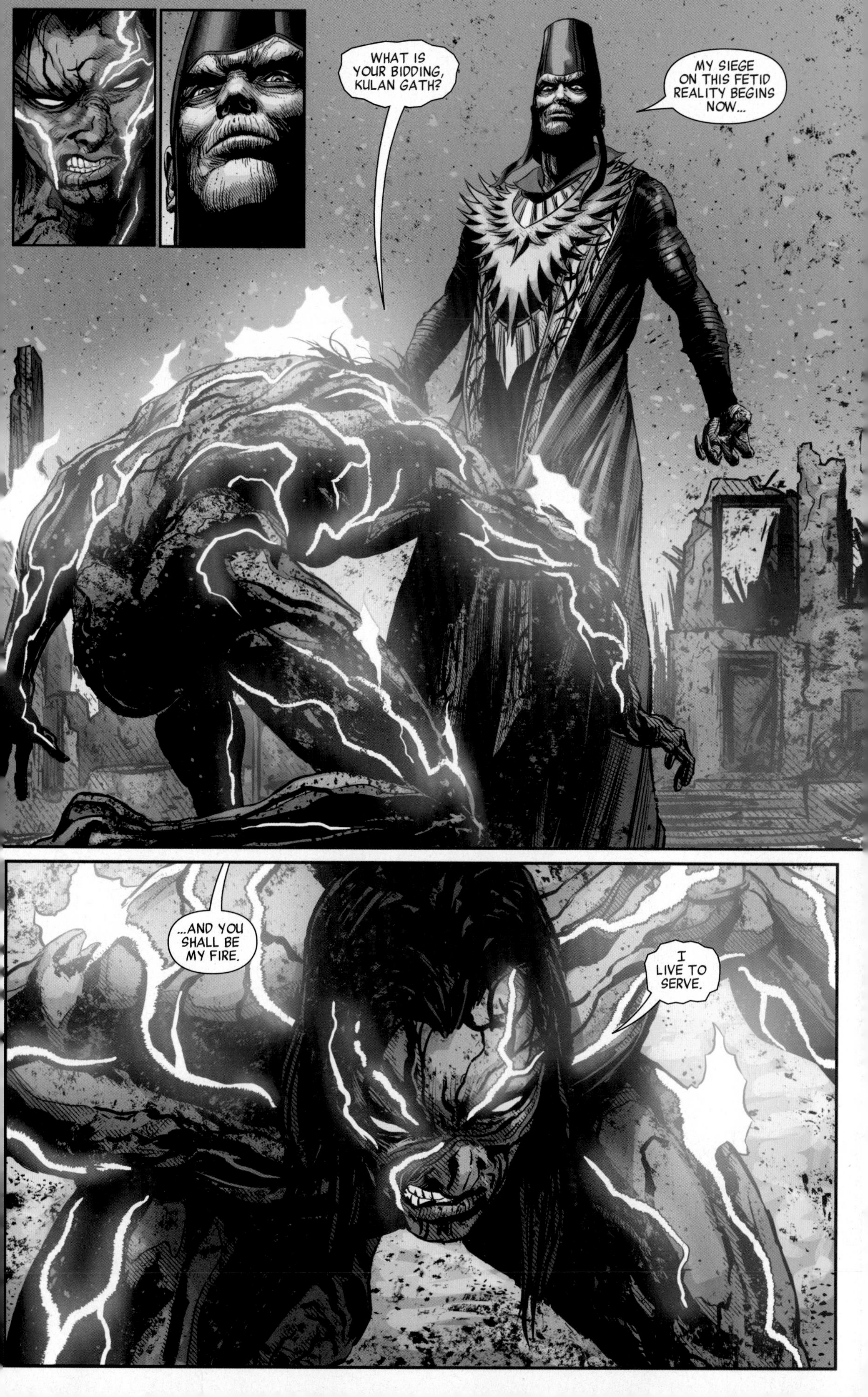
WHAT IS YOUR BIDDING, KULAN GATH?
MY SIEGE ON THIS FETID REALITY BEGINS NOW...
...AND YOU SHALL BE MY FIRE.
I LIVE TO SERVE.

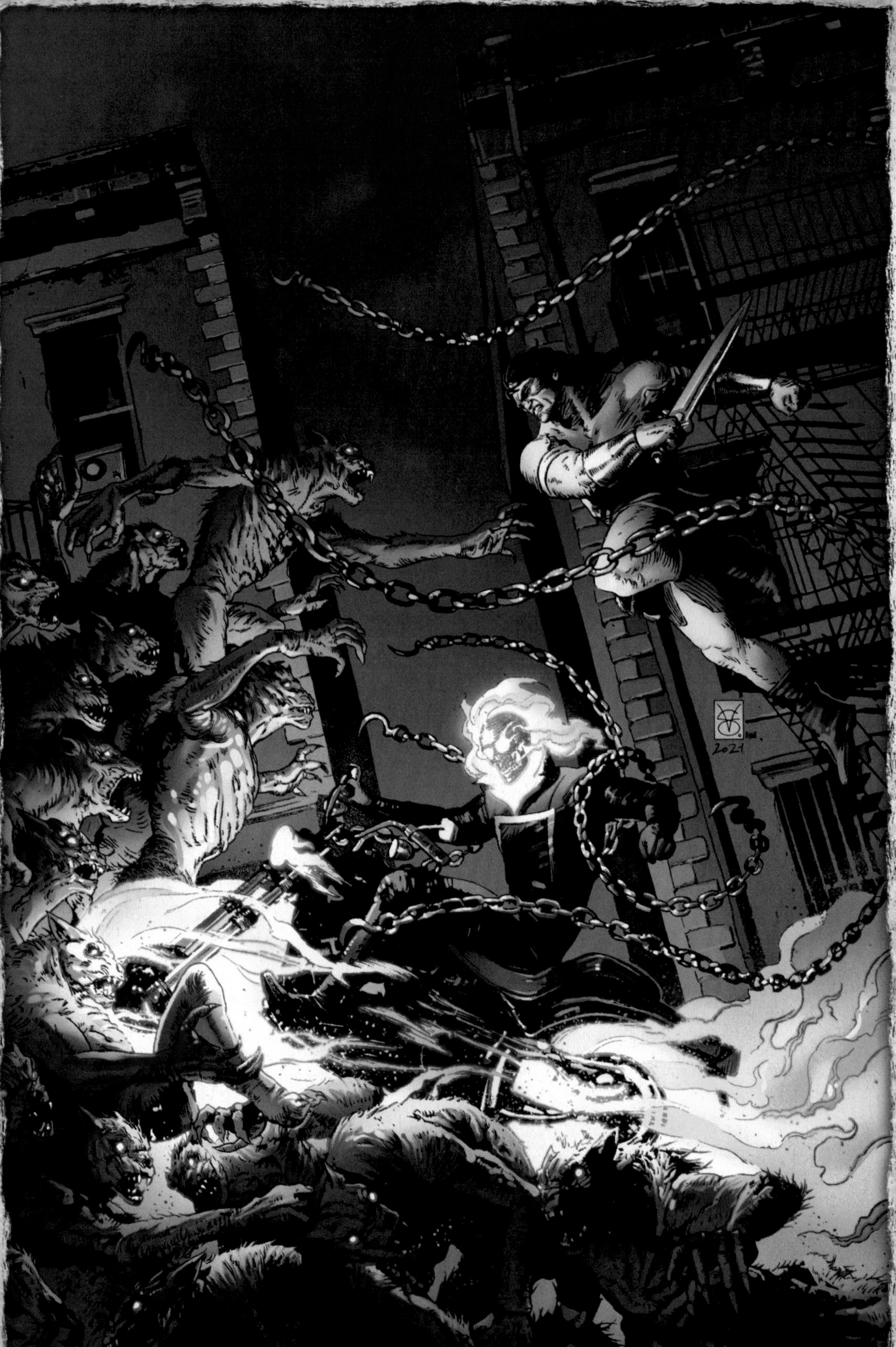

21: DREAM WARRIORS

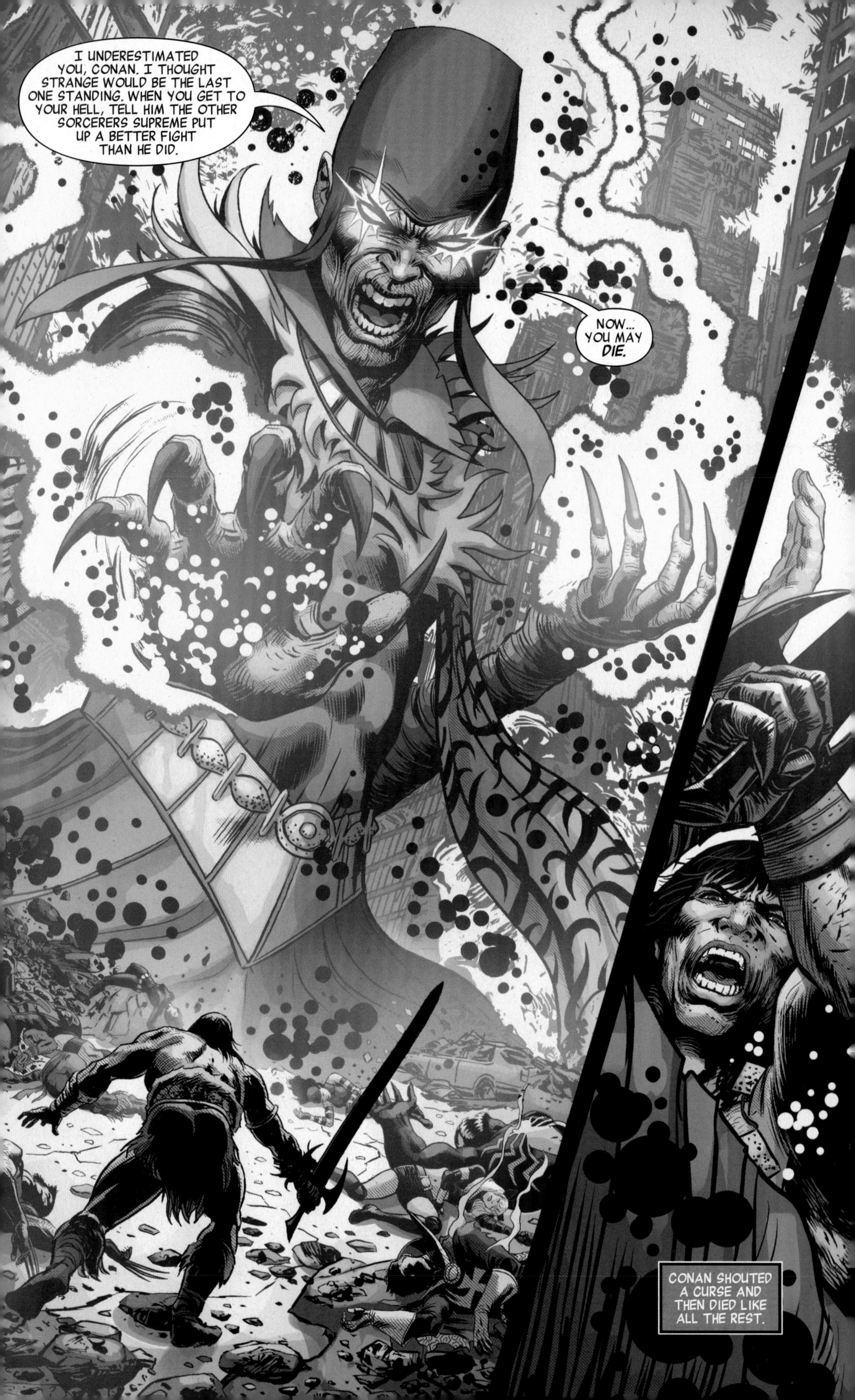
I UNDERESTIMATED YOU, CONAN. I THOUGHT STRANGE WOULD BE THE LAST ONE STANDING. WHEN YOU GET TO YOUR HELL, TELL HIM THE OTHER SORCERERS SUPREME PUT UP A BETTER FIGHT THAN HE DID.
NOW... YOU MAY DIE.
CONAN SHOUTED A CURSE AND THEN DIED LIKE ALL THE REST.

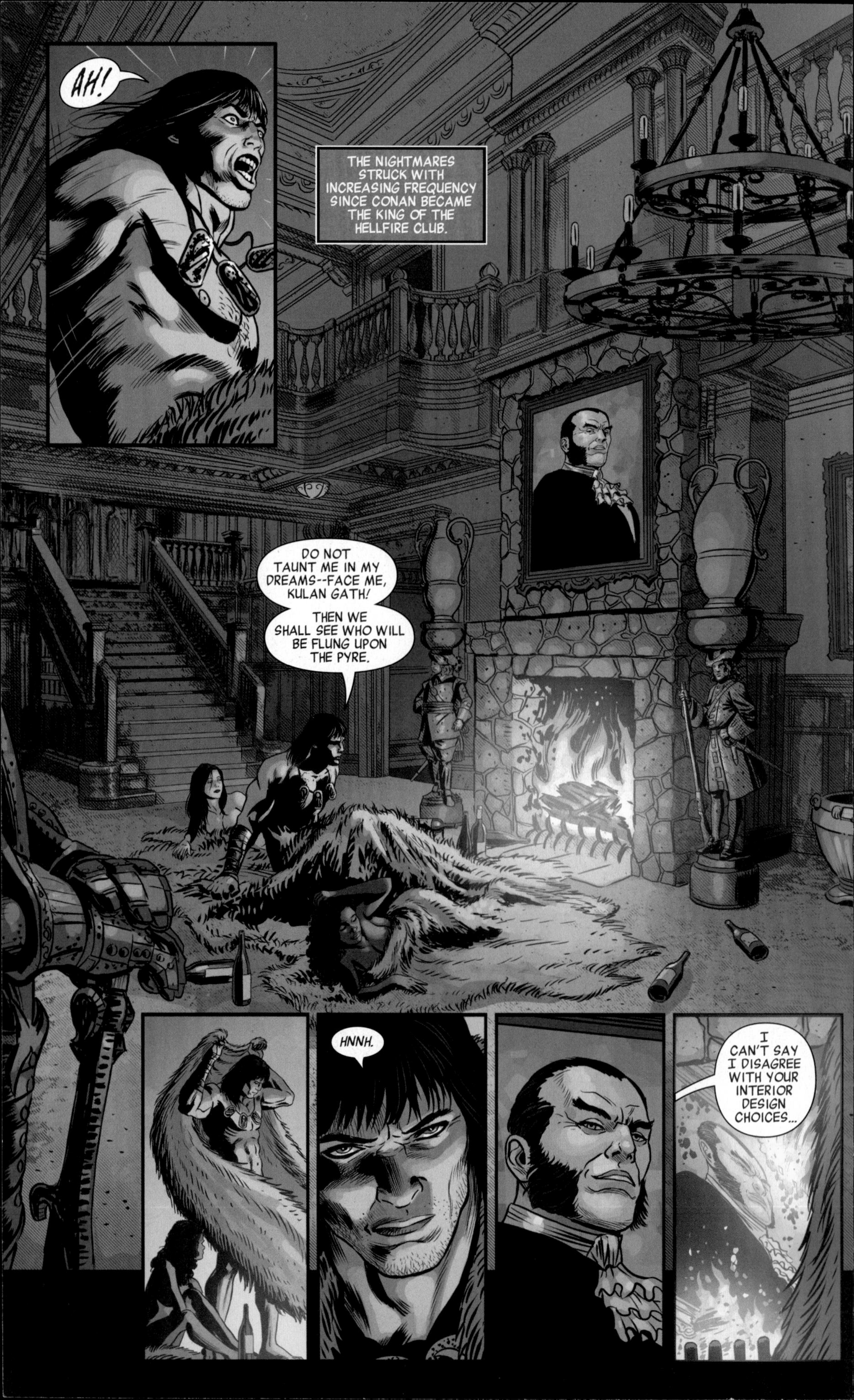
AH!
THE NIGHTMARES STRUCK WITH INCREASING FREQUENCY SINCE CONAN BECAME THE KING OF THE HELLFIRE CLUB.
DO NOT TAUNT ME IN MY DREAMS--FACE ME, KULAN GATH!
THEN WE SHALL SEE WHO WILL BE FLUNG UPON THE PYRE.
HNNH.
I CAN'T SAY I DISAGREE WITH YOUR INTERIOR DESIGN CHOICES...

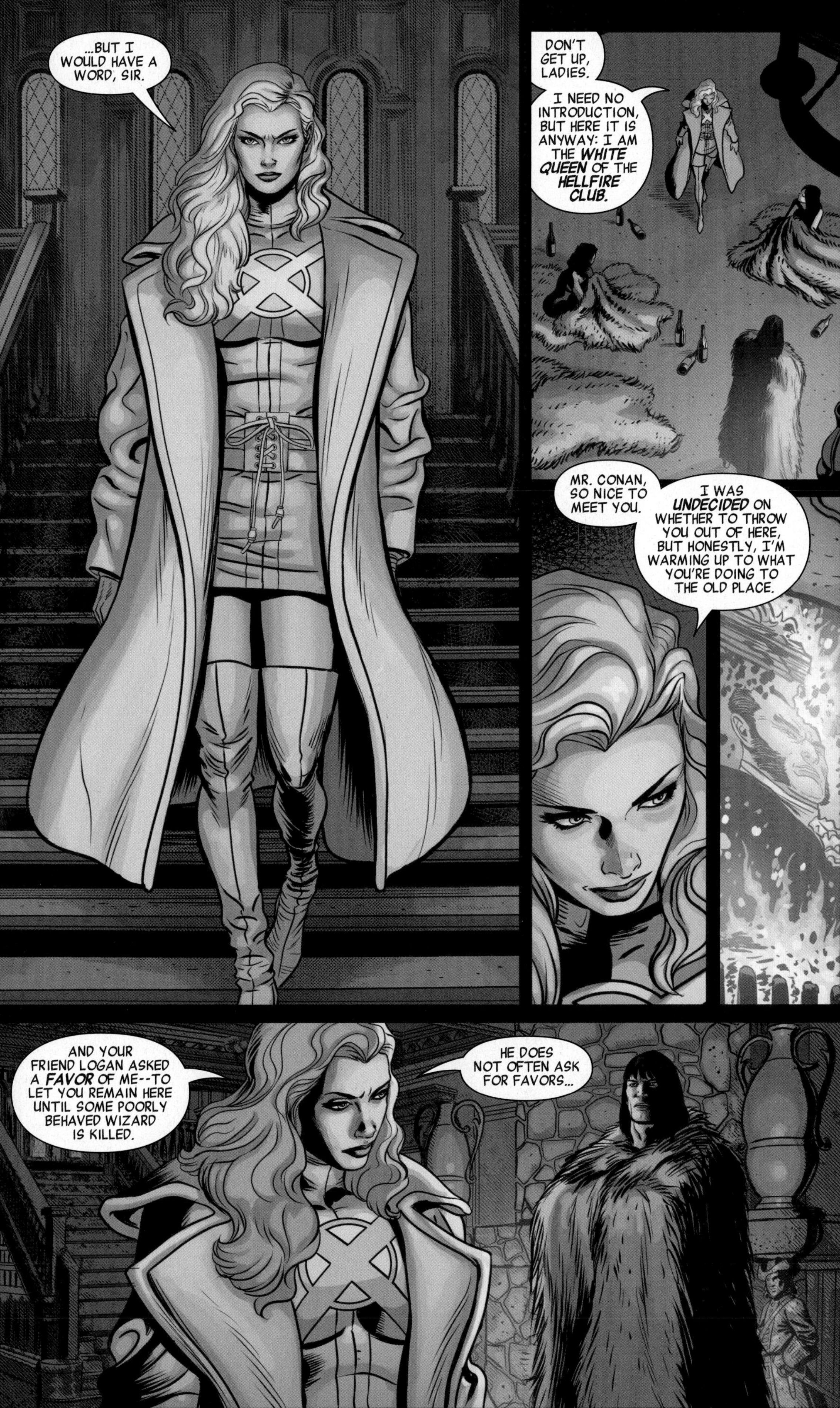
...BUT I WOULD HAVE A WORD, SIR.
DON'T GET UP, LADIES.
I NEED NO INTRODUCTION, BUT HERE IT IS ANYWAY: I AM THE WHITE QUEEN OF THE HELLFIRE CLUB.
MR. CONAN, SO NICE TO MEET YOU.
I WAS UNDECIDED ON WHETHER TO THROW YOU OUT OF HERE, BUT HONESTLY, I'M WARMING UP TO WHAT YOU'RE DOING TO THE OLD PLACE.
AND YOUR FRIEND LOGAN ASKED A FAVOR OF ME--TO LET YOU REMAIN HERE UNTIL SOME POORLY BEHAVED WIZARD IS KILLED.
HE DOES NOT OFTEN ASK FOR FAVORS...

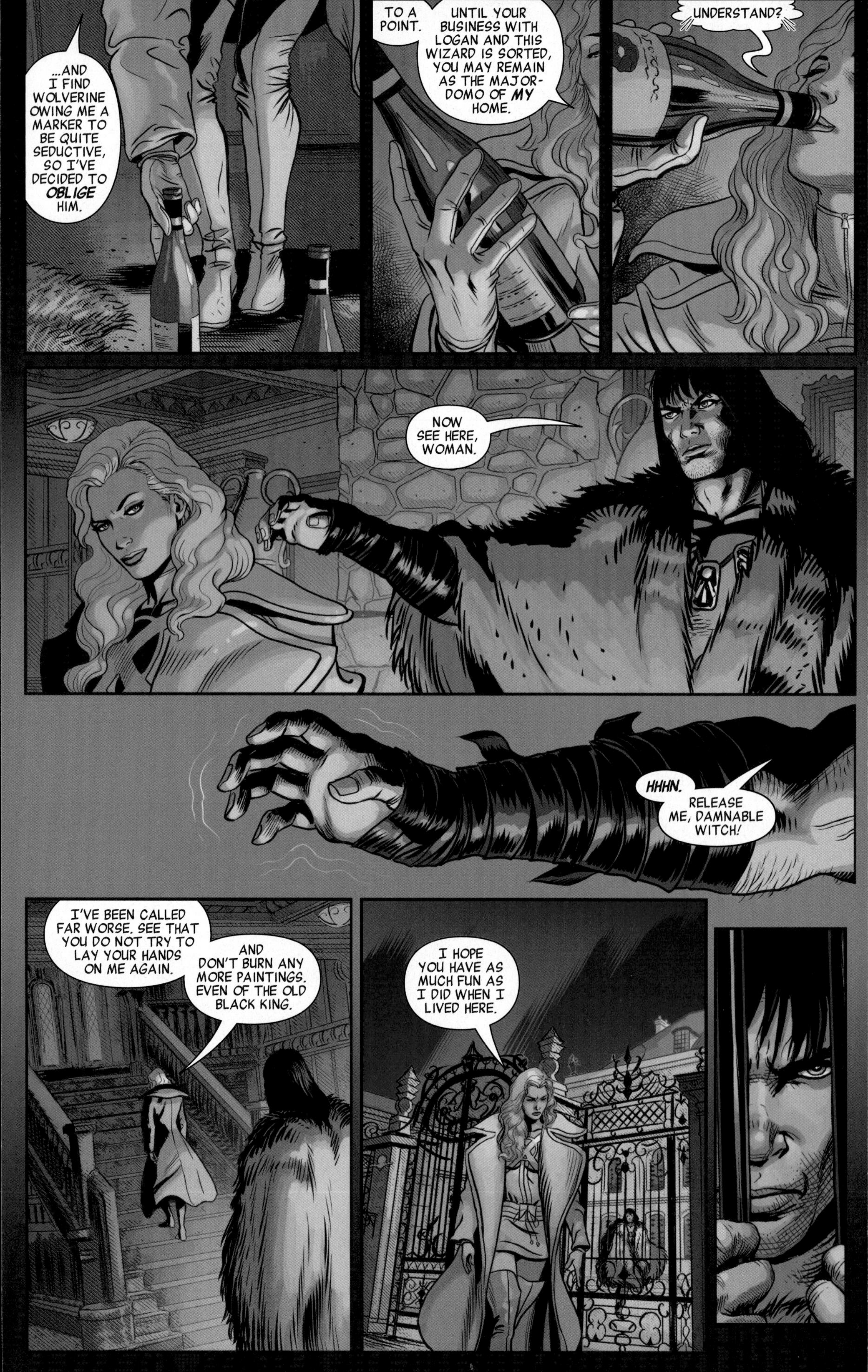
...AND I FIND WOLVERINE OWING ME A MARKER TO BE QUITE SEDUCTIVE, SO I'VE DECIDED TO OBLIGE HIM.
TO A POINT.
UNTIL YOUR BUSINESS WITH LOGAN AND THIS WIZARD IS SORTED, YOU MAY REMAIN AS THE MAJOR-DOMO OF MY HOME.
UNDERSTAND?
NOW SEE HERE, WOMAN.
HHHN. RELEASE ME, DAMNABLE WITCH!
I'VE BEEN CALLED FAR WORSE. SEE THAT YOU DO NOT TRY TO LAY YOUR HANDS ON ME AGAIN.
AND DON'T BURN ANY MORE PAINTINGS. EVEN OF THE OLD BLACK KING.
I HOPE YOU HAVE AS MUCH FUN AS I DID WHEN I LIVED HERE.

THE NIGHT OF MIRTH HAD ENDED EARLY, AND, IN A FOUL MOOD, CONAN STALKED THE STREETS OF THE BIG CITY LOOKING FOR ADVENTURE.

THEY SAY THIS CITY NEVER SLEEPS, BUT THIS NIGHT PROVED THAT TO BE A LIE.

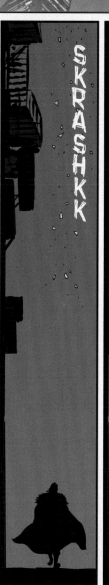

SKRASHKK

HE COMES!

TAKE UP ARMS! HE'S HERE!

SPLAKK

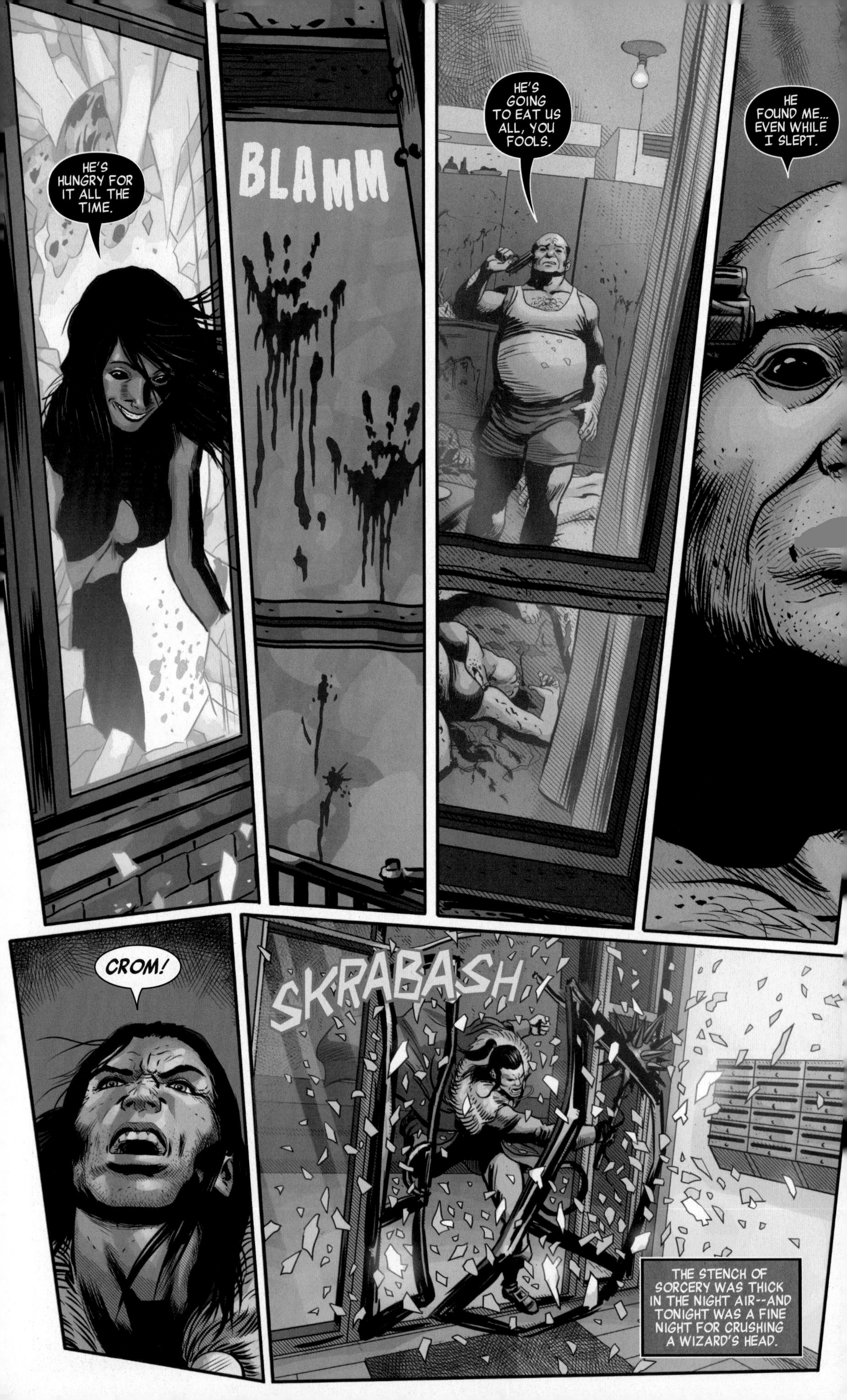
HE'S HUNGRY FOR IT ALL THE TIME.
BLAMM
HE'S GOING TO EAT US ALL, YOU FOOLS.
HE FOUND ME... EVEN WHILE I SLEPT.
CROM!
SKRABASH
THE STENCH OF SORCERY WAS THICK IN THE NIGHT AIR--AND TONIGHT WAS A FINE NIGHT FOR CRUSHING A WIZARD'S HEAD.

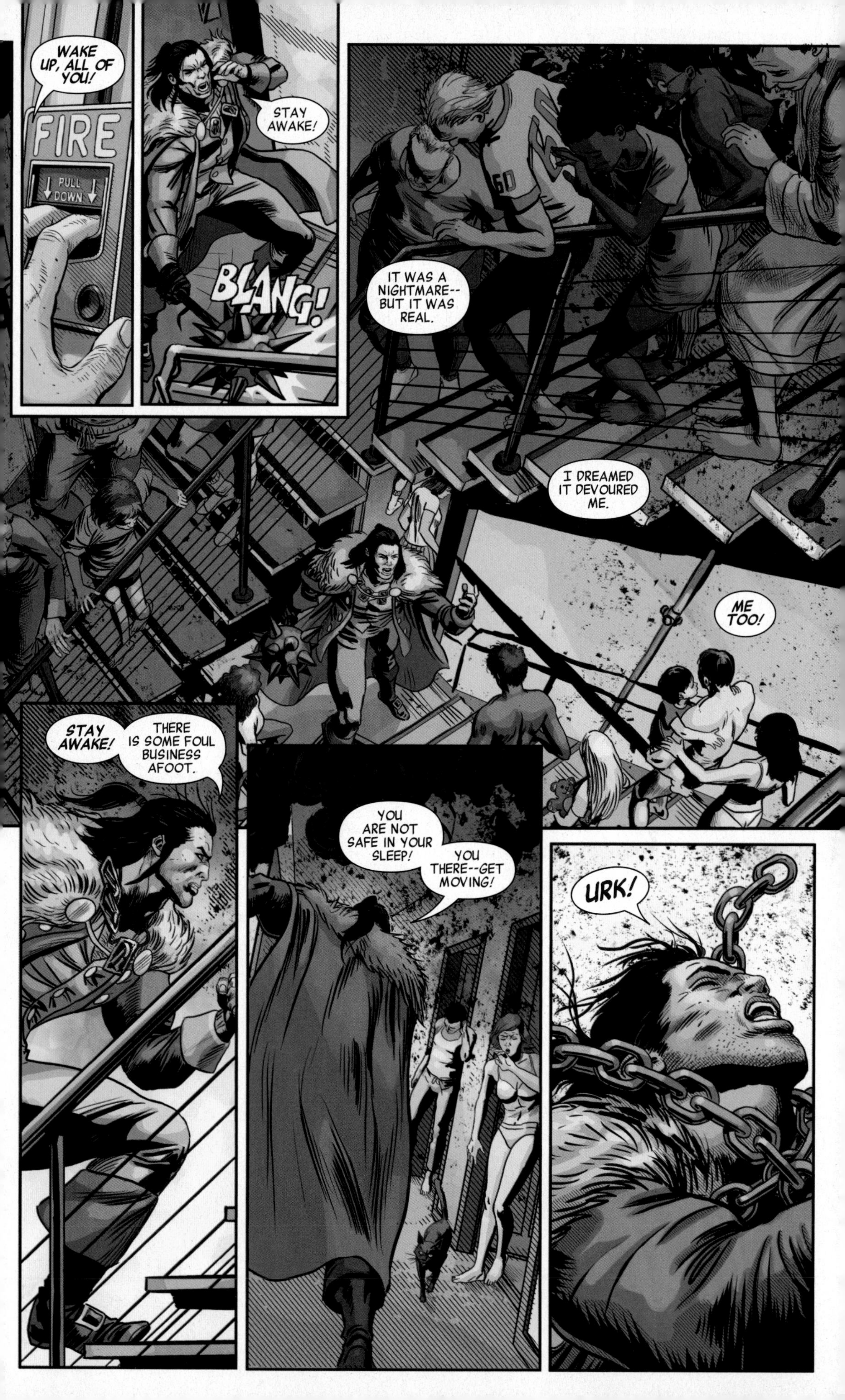
WAKE UP, ALL OF YOU!
FIRE
PULL DOWN
STAY AWAKE!
BLANG!
IT WAS A NIGHTMARE-- BUT IT WAS REAL.
I DREAMED IT DEVOURED ME.
ME TOO!
STAY AWAKE!
THERE IS SOME FOUL BUSINESS AFOOT.
YOU ARE NOT SAFE IN YOUR SLEEP!
YOU THERE--GET MOVING!
URK!

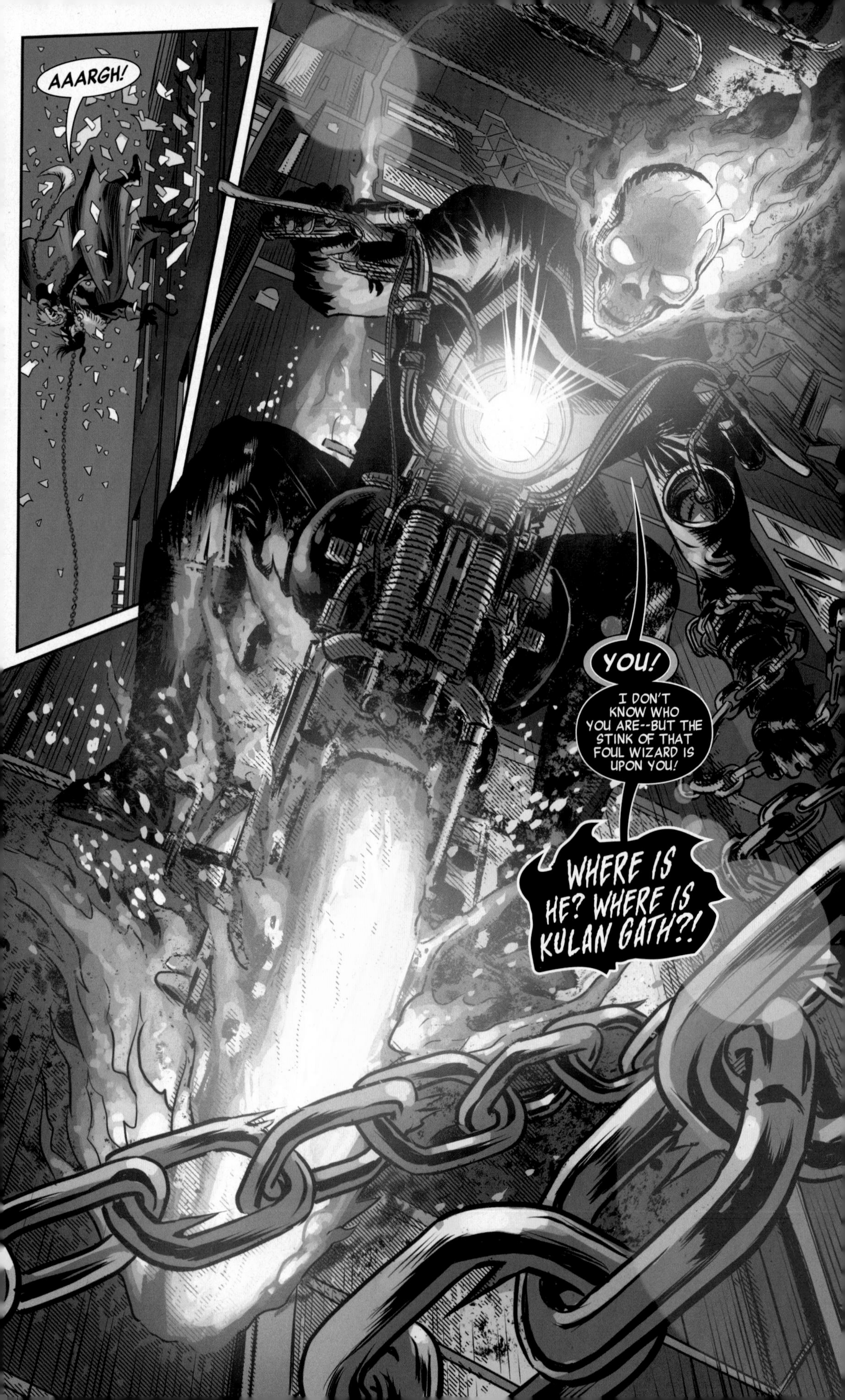
AAARGH!
YOU!
I DON'T KNOW WHO YOU ARE--BUT THE STINK OF THAT FOUL WIZARD IS UPON YOU!
WHERE IS HE? WHERE IS KULAN GATH?!

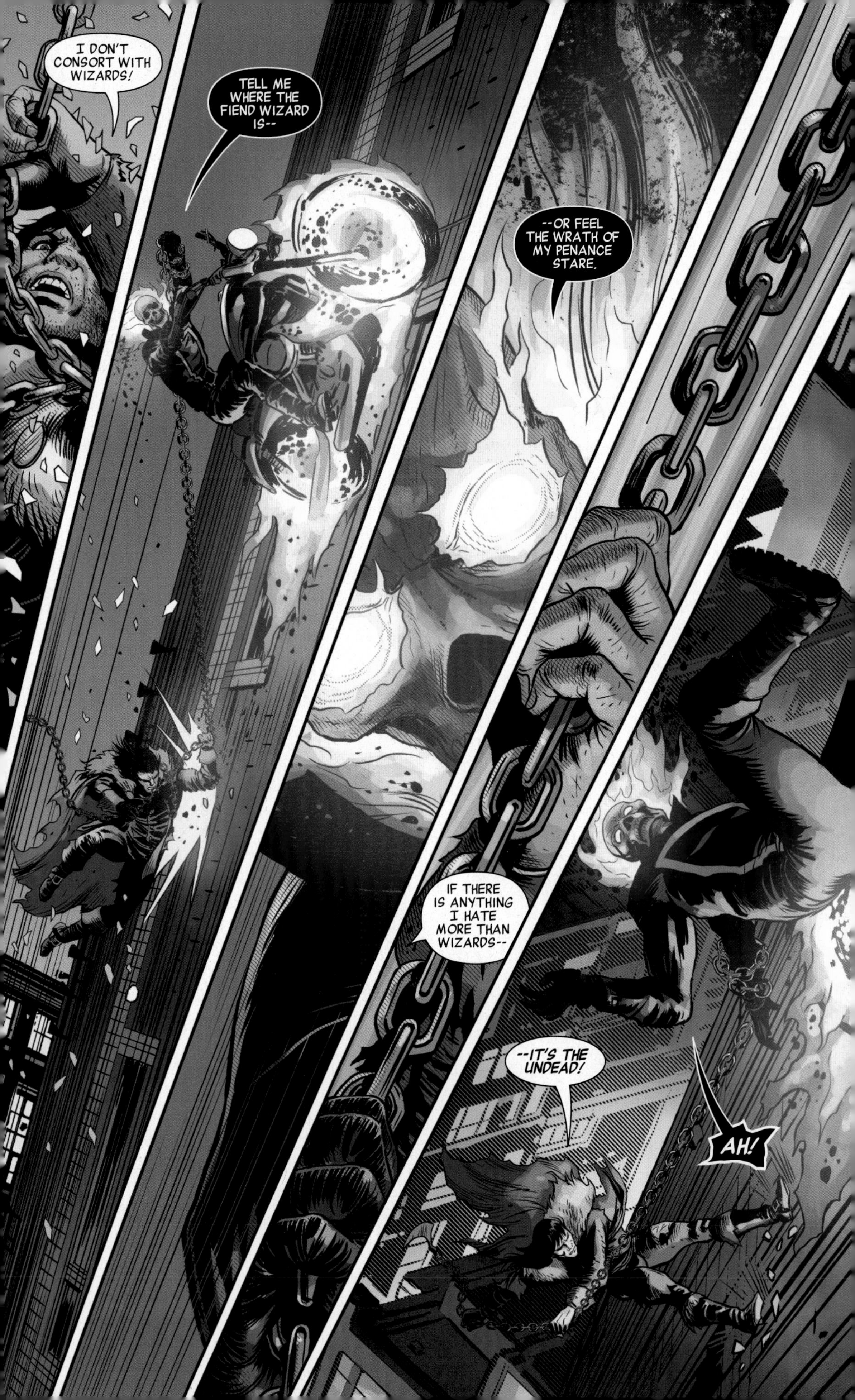
I DON'T CONSORT WITH WIZARDS!
TELL ME WHERE THE FIEND WIZARD IS--
--OR FEEL THE WRATH OF MY PENANCE STARE.
IF THERE IS ANYTHING I HATE MORE THAN WIZARDS--
--IT'S THE UNDEAD!
AH!

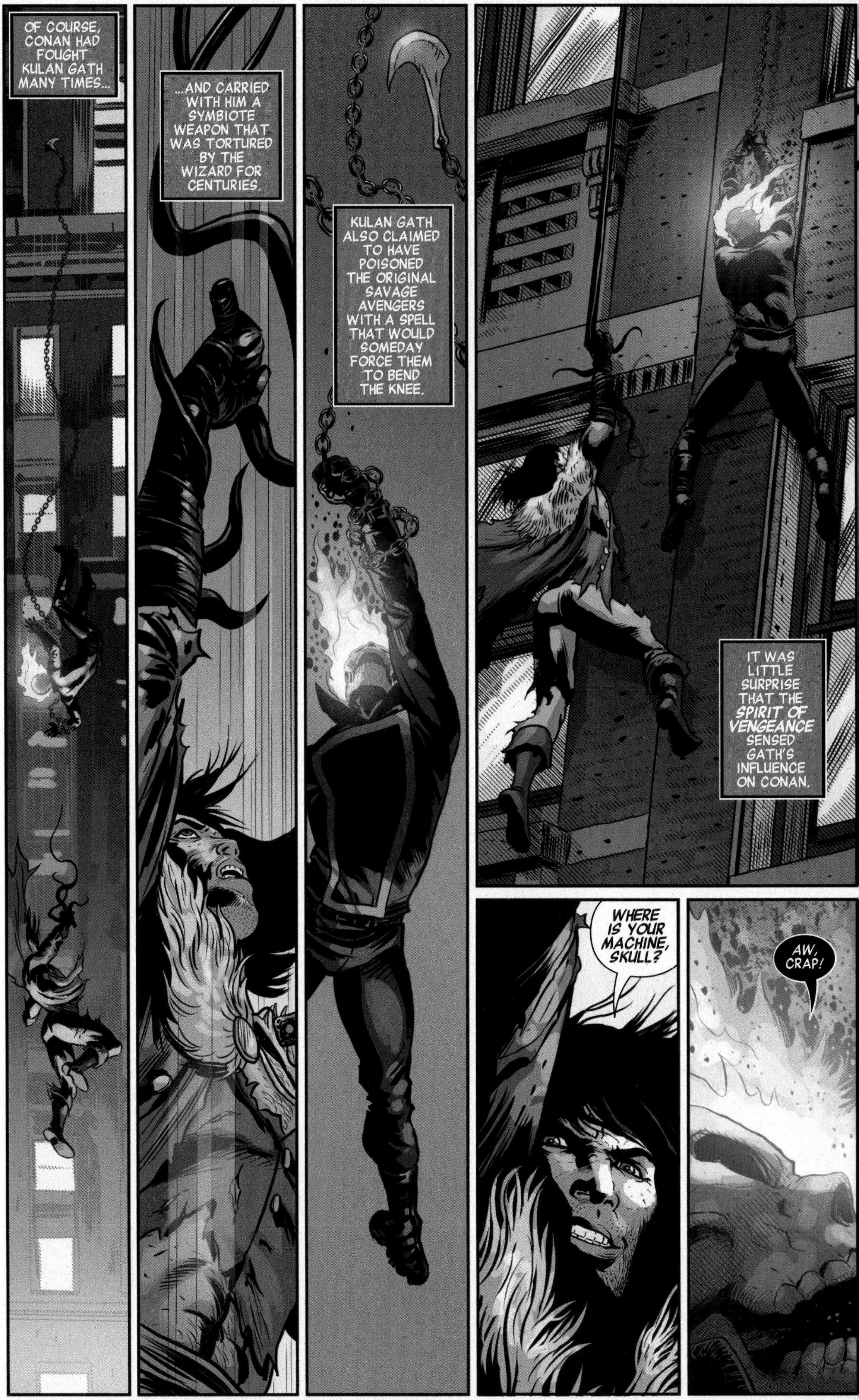
OF COURSE, CONAN HAD FOUGHT KULAN GATH MANY TIMES...
...AND CARRIED WITH HIM A SYMBIOTE WEAPON THAT WAS TORTURED BY THE WIZARD FOR CENTURIES.
KULAN GATH ALSO CLAIMED TO HAVE POISONED THE ORIGINAL SAVAGE AVENGERS WITH A SPELL THAT WOULD SOMEDAY FORCE THEM TO BEND THE KNEE.
IT WAS LITTLE SURPRISE THAT THE SPIRIT OF VENGEANCE SENSED GATH'S INFLUENCE ON CONAN.
WHERE IS YOUR MACHINE, SKULL?
AW, CRAP!

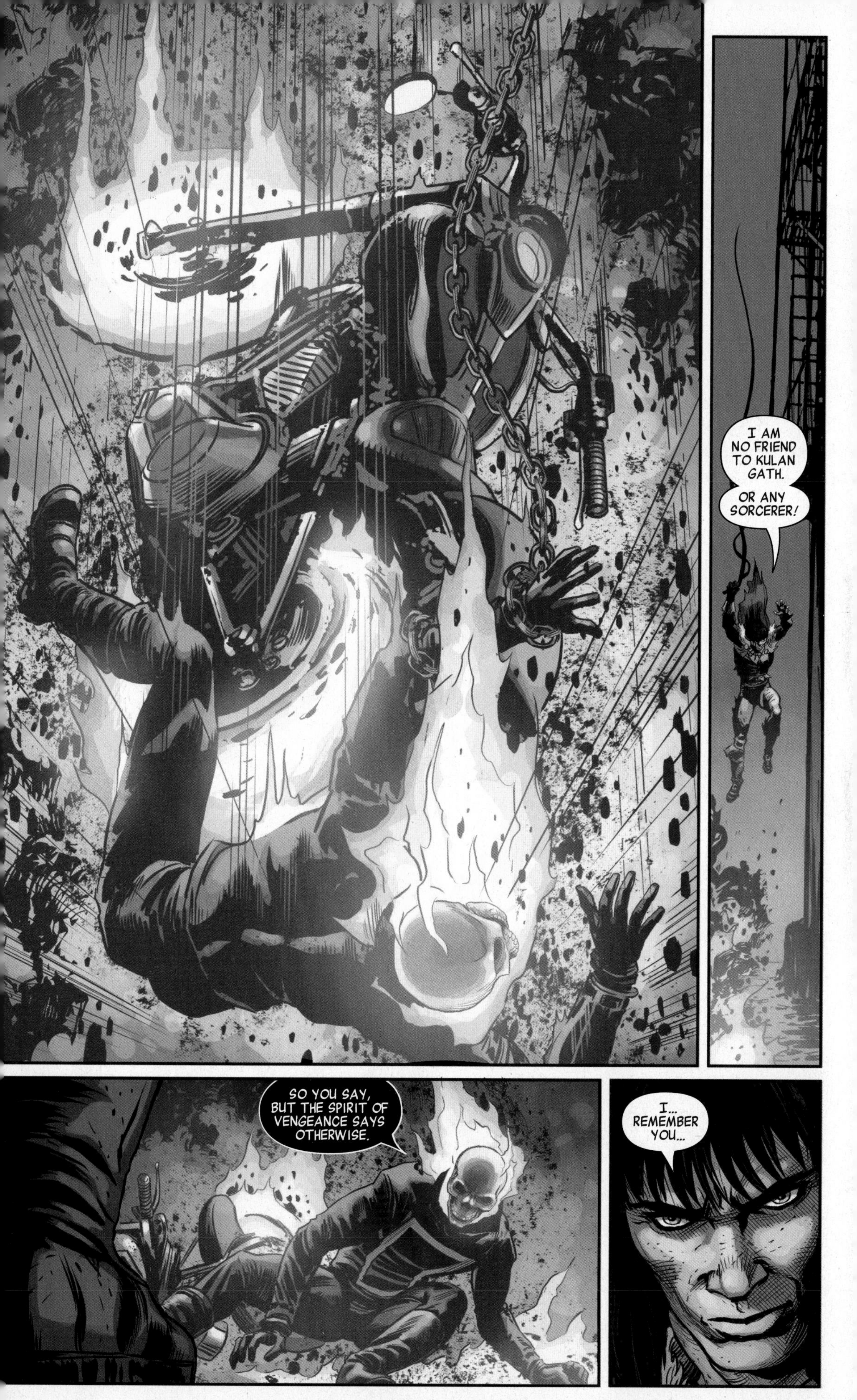

I AM NO FRIEND TO KULAN GATH.
OR ANY SORCERER!
SO YOU SAY, BUT THE SPIRIT OF VENGEANCE SAYS OTHERWISE.
I... REMEMBER YOU...

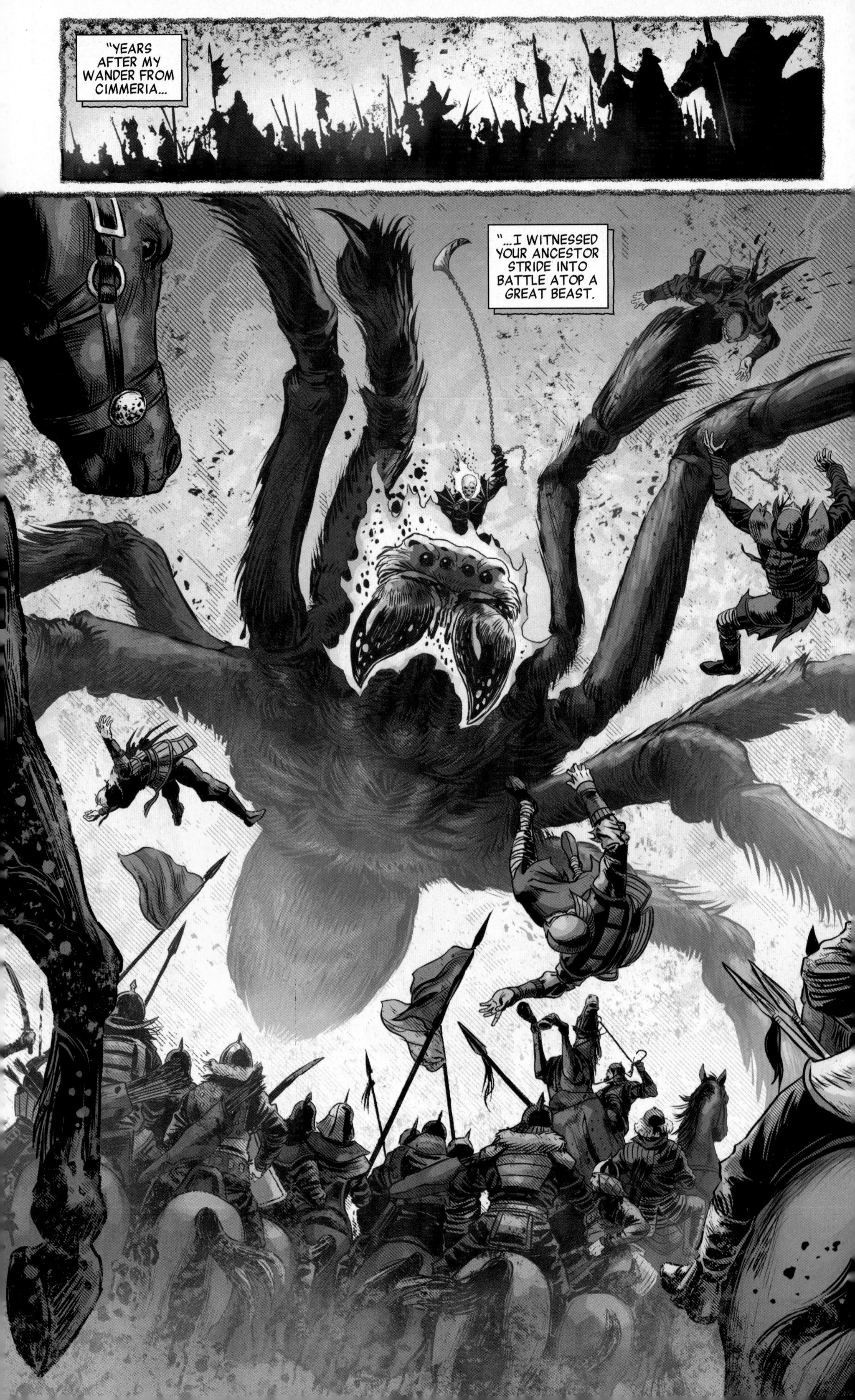
"YEARS AFTER MY WANDER FROM CIMMERIA...
"...I WITNESSED YOUR ANCESTOR STRIDE INTO BATTLE ATOP A GREAT BEAST.

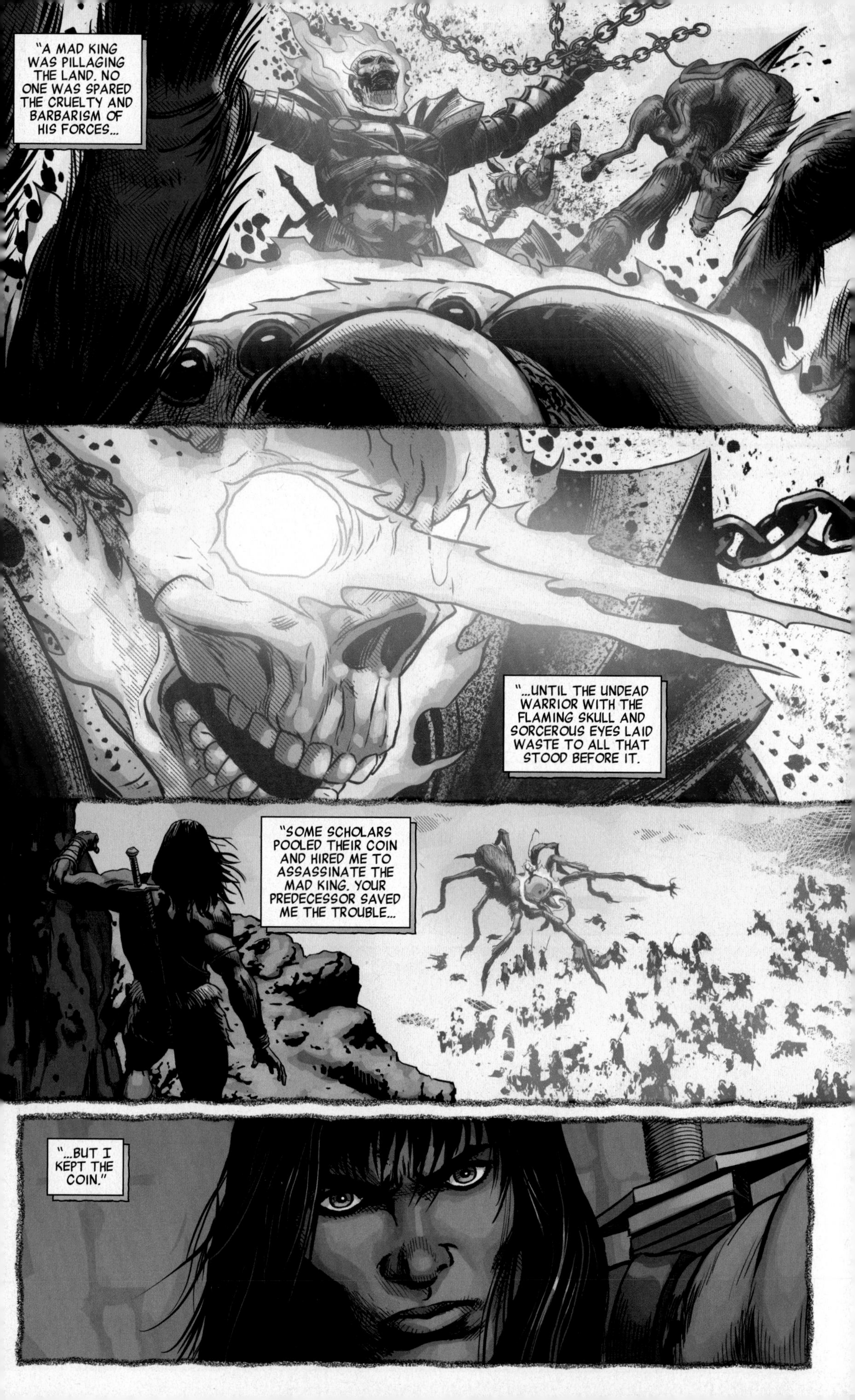
"A MAD KING WAS PILLAGING THE LAND. NO ONE WAS SPARED THE CRUELTY AND BARBARISM OF HIS FORCES...
"...UNTIL THE UNDEAD WARRIOR WITH THE FLAMING SKULL AND SORCEROUS EYES LAID WASTE TO ALL THAT STOOD BEFORE IT.
"SOME SCHOLARS POOLED THEIR COIN AND HIRED ME TO ASSASSINATE THE MAD KING. YOUR PREDECESSOR SAVED ME THE TROUBLE...
"...BUT I KEPT THE COIN."

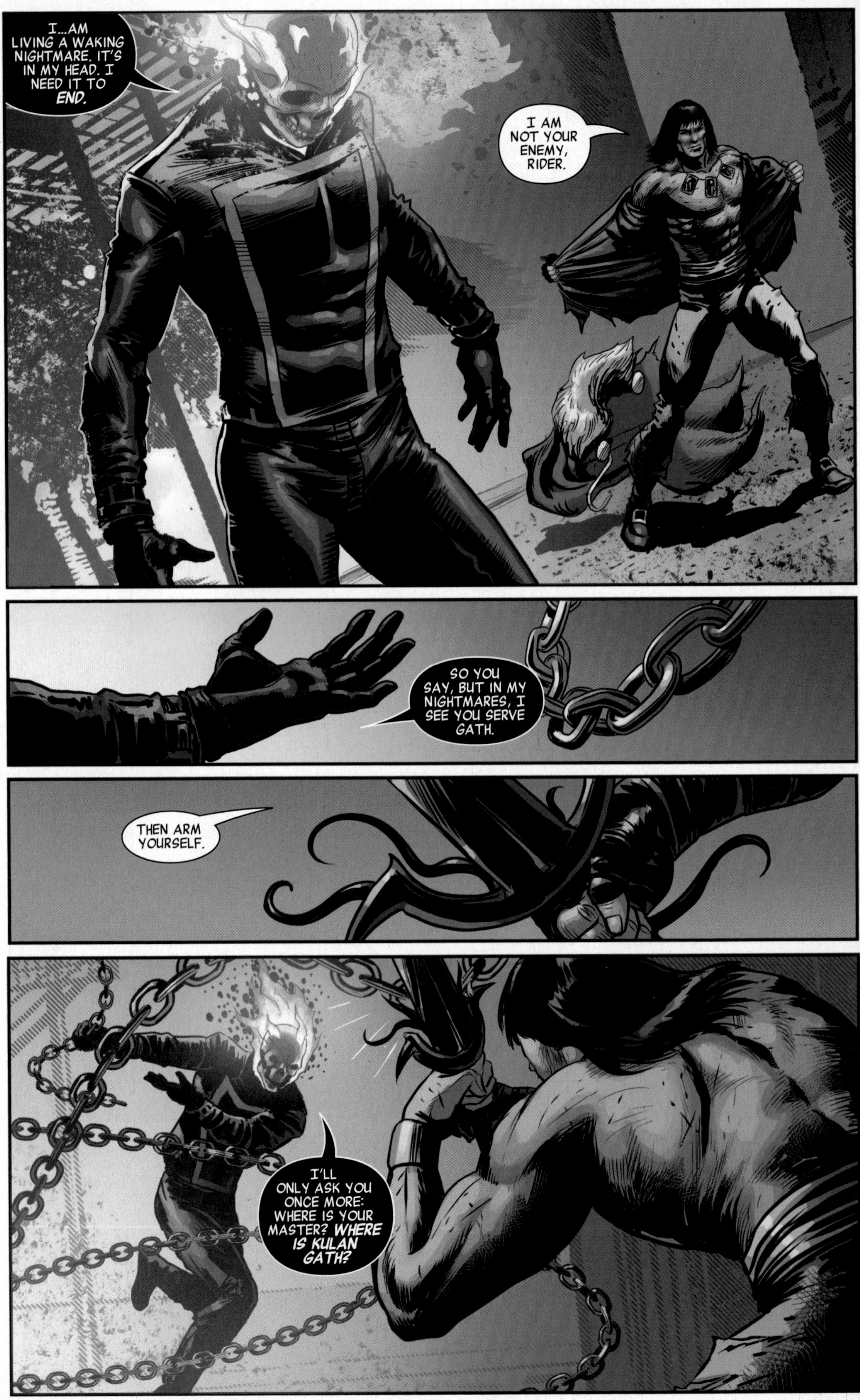
I...AM LIVING A WAKING NIGHTMARE. IT'S IN MY HEAD. I NEED IT TO *END.*
I AM NOT YOUR ENEMY, RIDER.
SO YOU SAY, BUT IN MY NIGHTMARES, I SEE YOU SERVE GATH.
THEN ARM YOURSELF.
I'LL ONLY ASK YOU ONCE MORE: WHERE IS YOUR MASTER? ***WHERE IS KULAN GATH?***

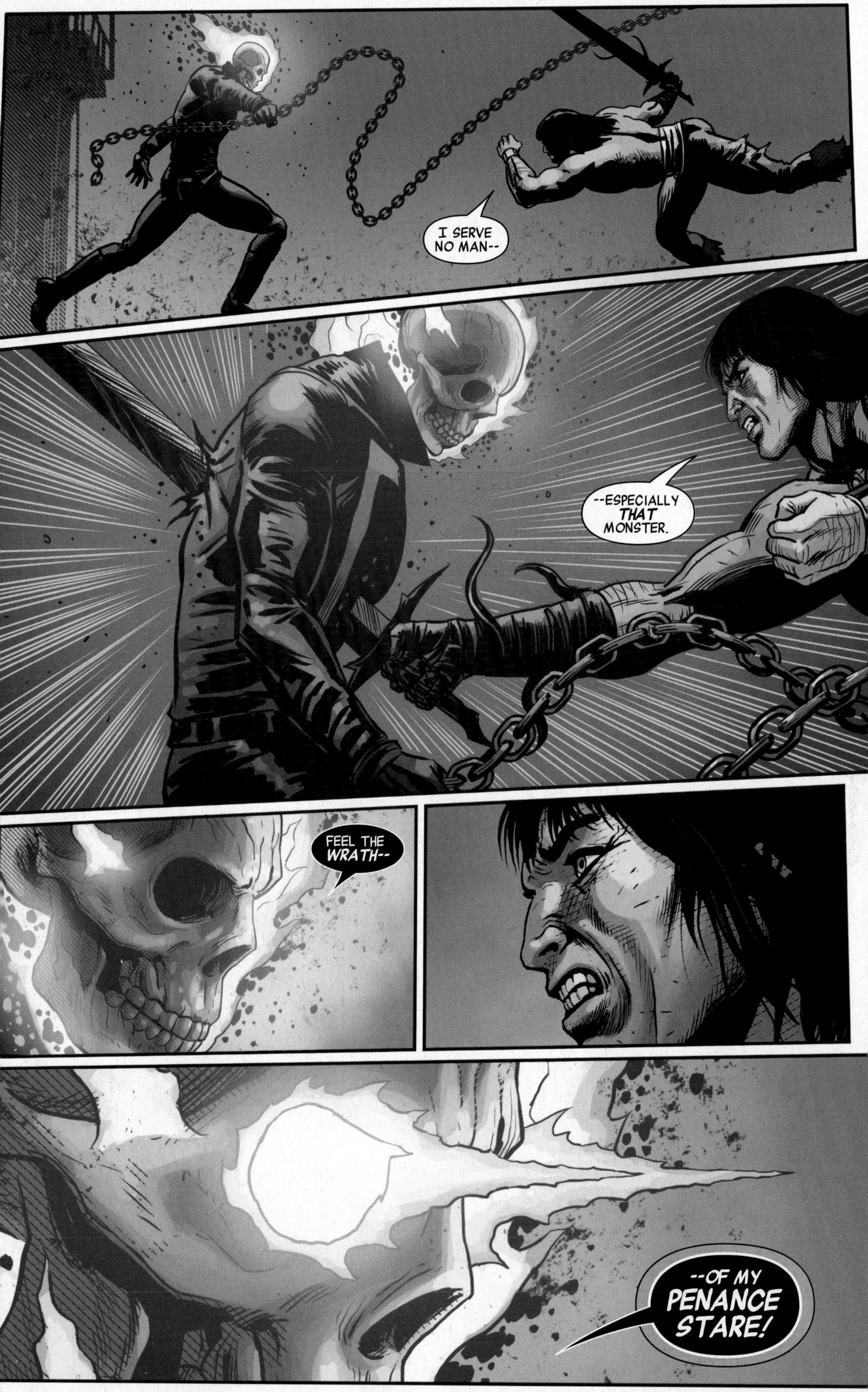
I SERVE NO MAN--
--ESPECIALLY THAT MONSTER.
FEEL THE WRATH--
--OF MY PENANCE STARE!

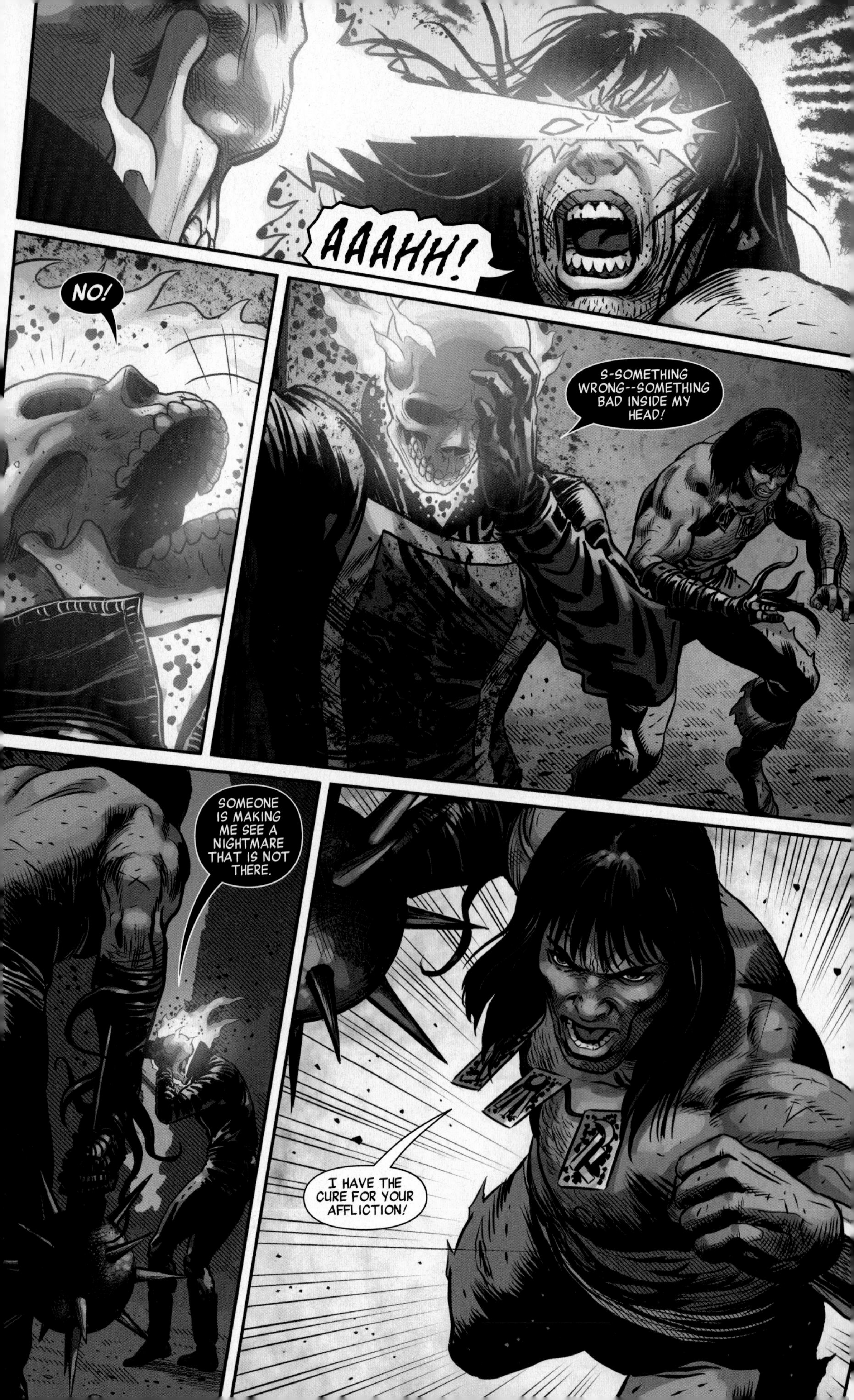
AAAHH!
NO!
S-SOMETHING WRONG--SOMETHING BAD INSIDE MY HEAD!
SOMEONE IS MAKING ME SEE A NIGHTMARE THAT IS NOT THERE.
I HAVE THE CURE FOR YOUR AFFLICTION!

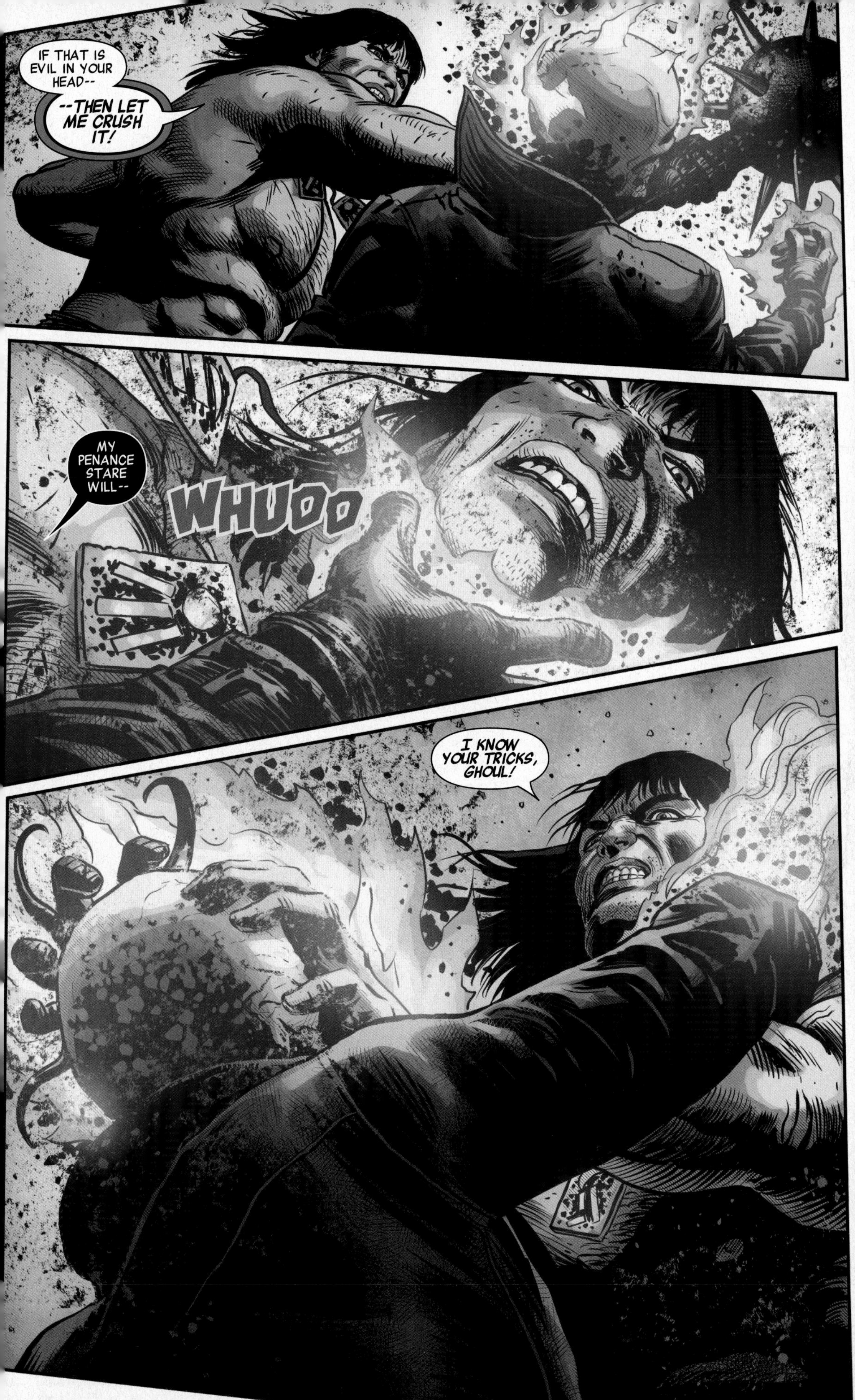
IF THAT IS EVIL IN YOUR HEAD--
--THEN LET ME CRUSH IT!
MY PENANCE STARE WILL--
WHUDD
I KNOW YOUR TRICKS, GHOUL!

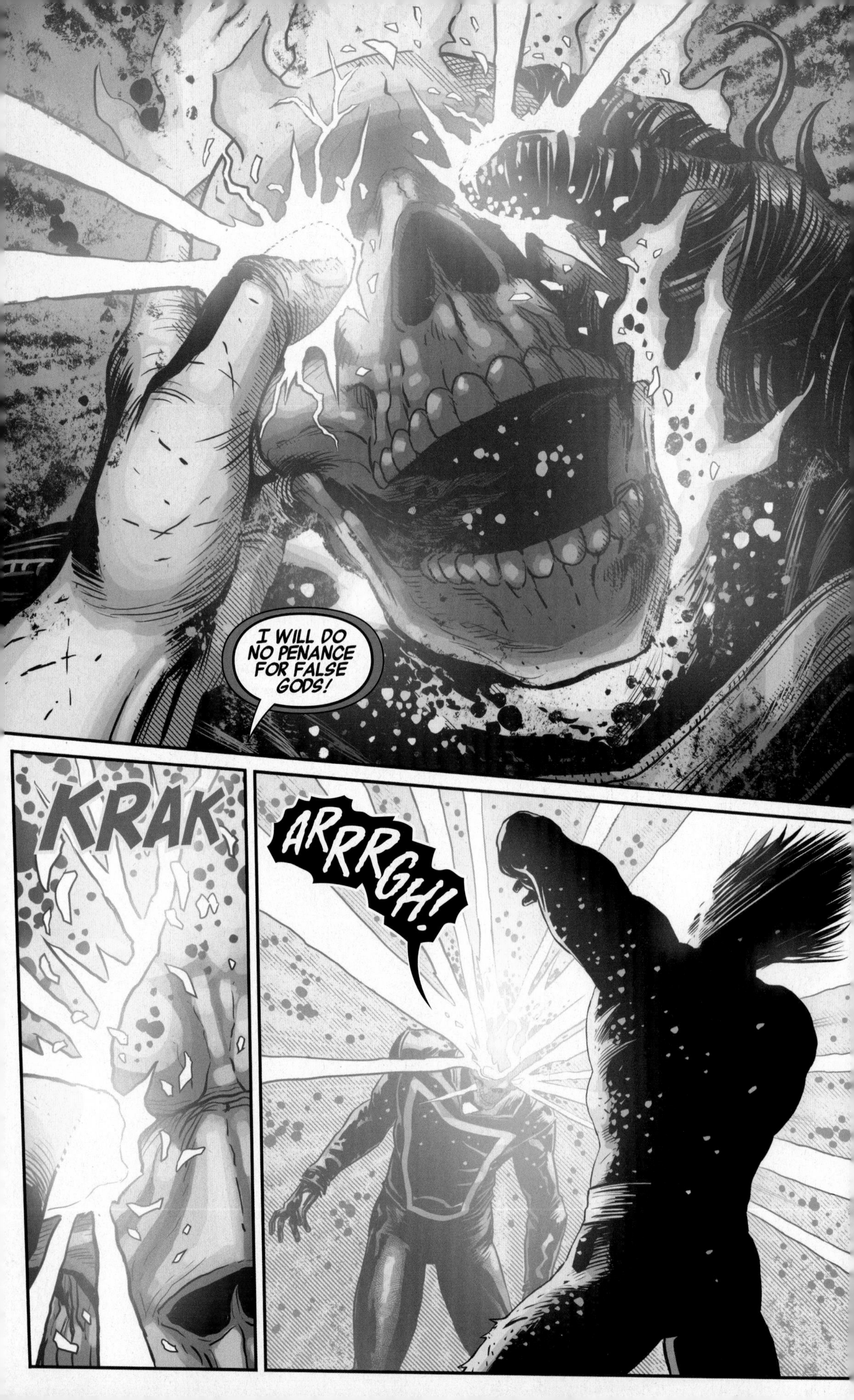
I WILL DO NO PENANCE FOR FALSE GODS!
KRAK
ARRRGH!

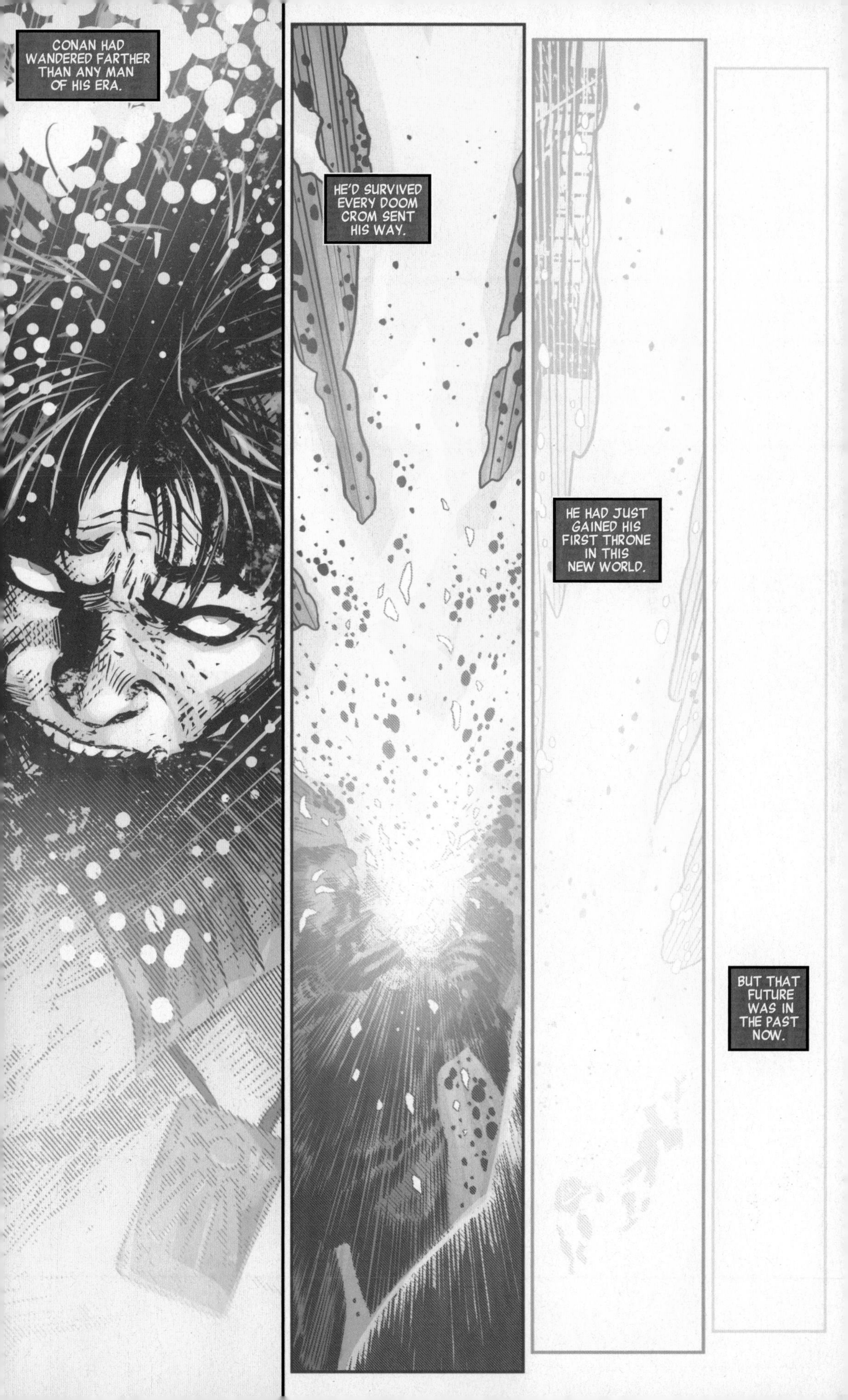
CONAN HAD WANDERED FARTHER THAN ANY MAN OF HIS ERA.
HE'D SURVIVED EVERY DOOM CROM SENT HIS WAY.
HE HAD JUST GAINED HIS FIRST THRONE IN THIS NEW WORLD.
BUT THAT FUTURE WAS IN THE PAST NOW.

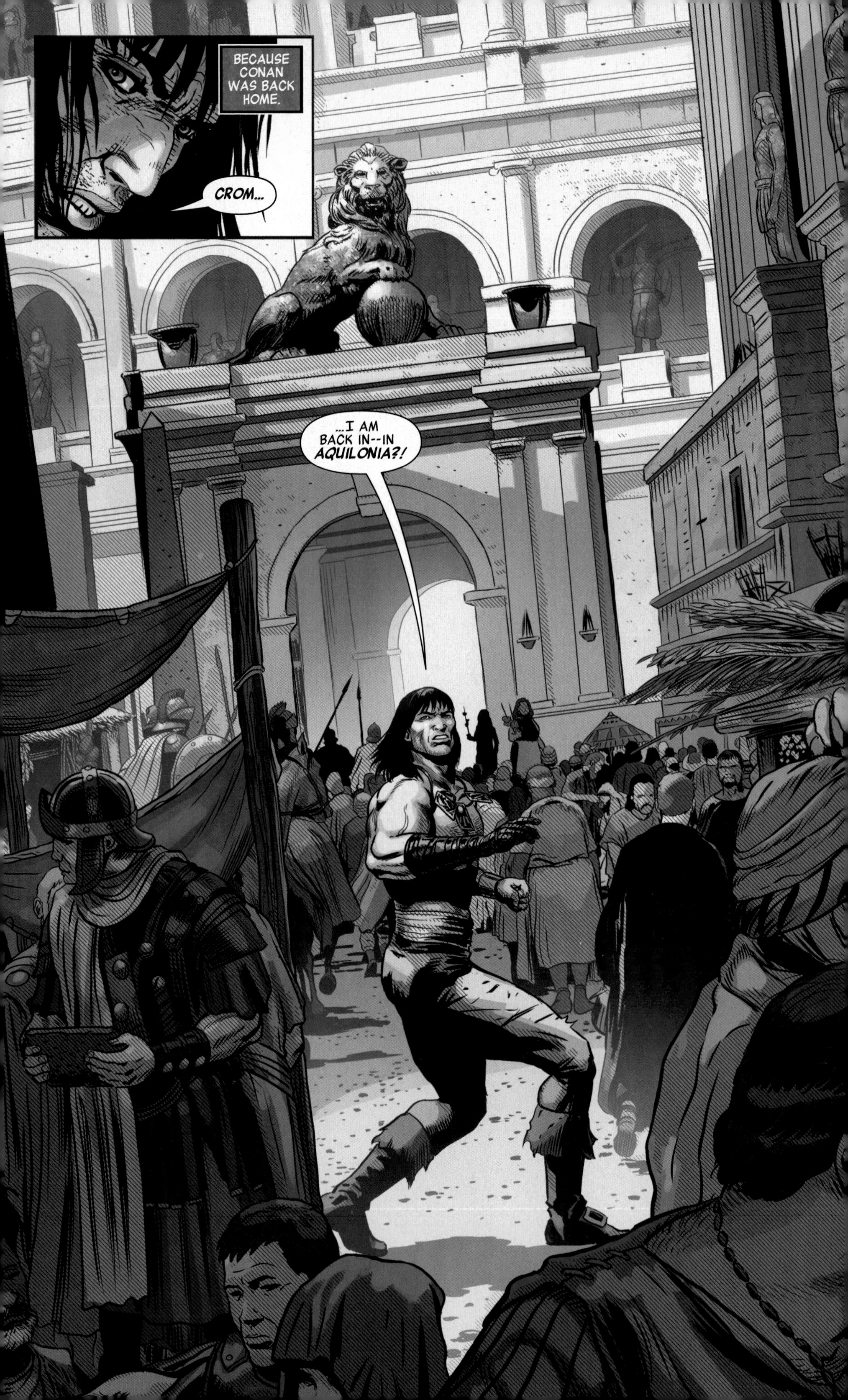
BECAUSE CONAN WAS BACK HOME.
CROM...
...I AM BACK IN--IN AQUILONIA?!

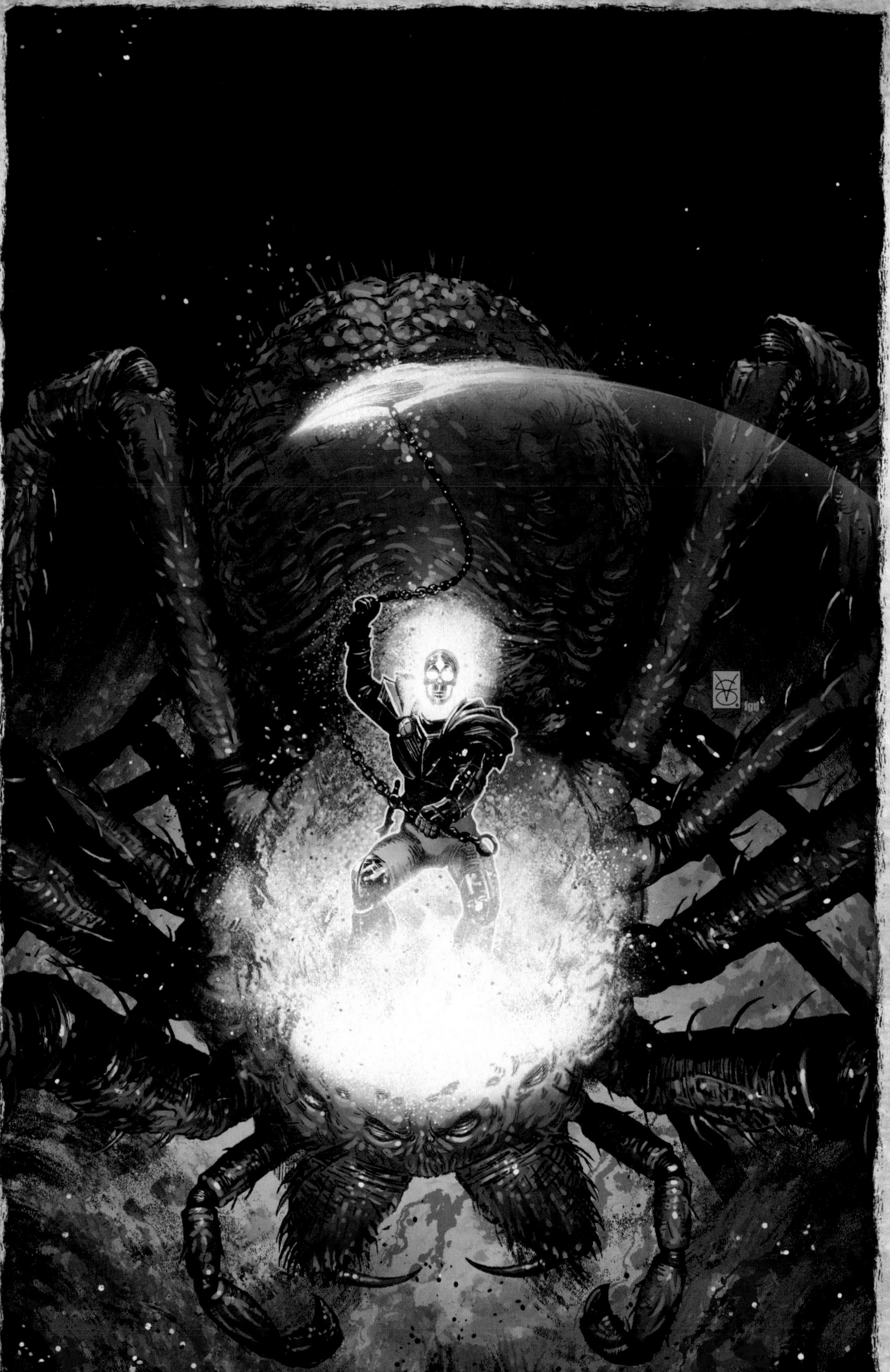

22: A WAKING NIGHTMARE

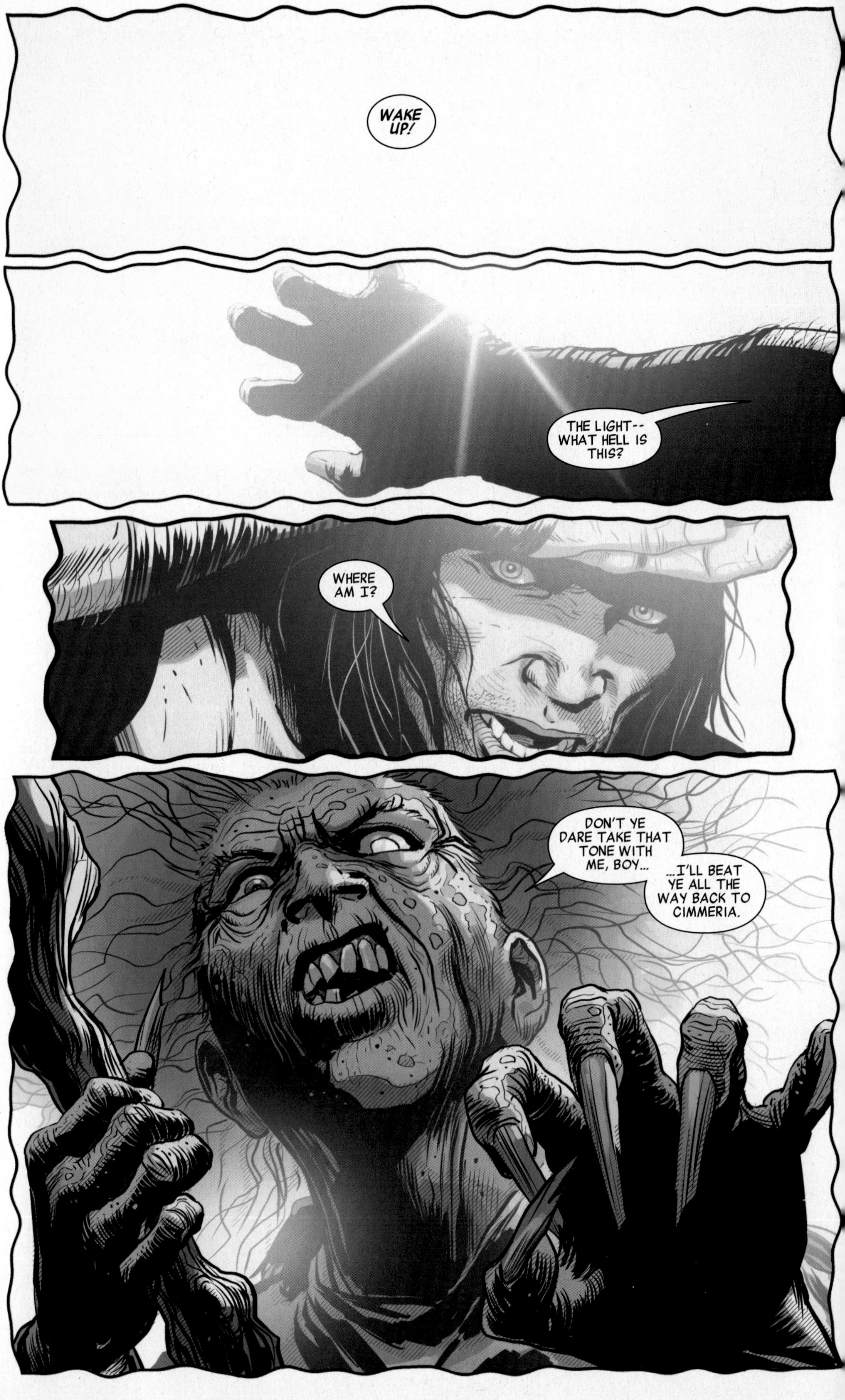
WAKE UP!
THE LIGHT-- WHAT HELL IS THIS?
WHERE AM I?
DON'T YE DARE TAKE THAT TONE WITH ME, BOY...
...I'LL BEAT YE ALL THE WAY BACK TO CIMMERIA.

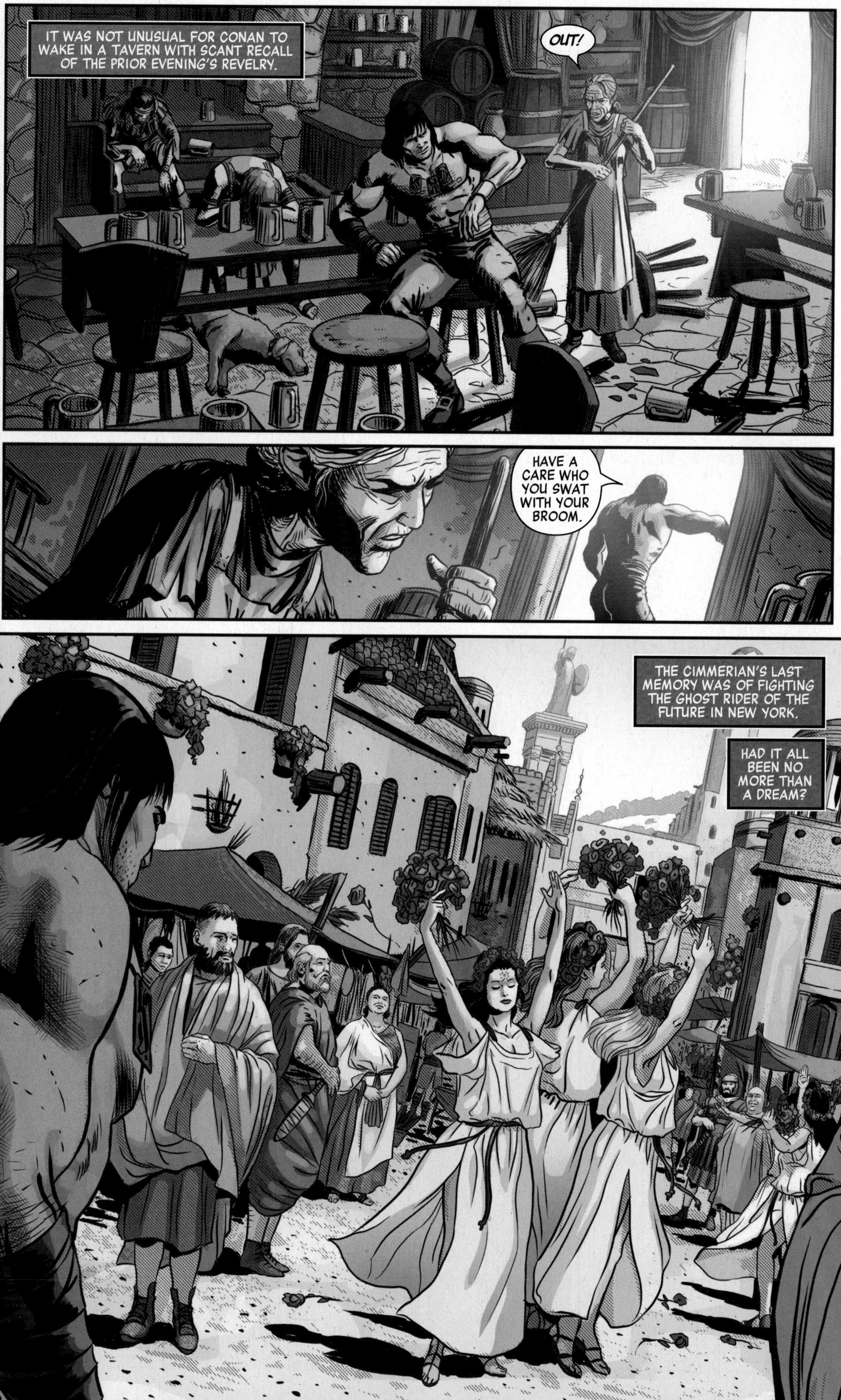
IT WAS NOT UNUSUAL FOR CONAN TO WAKE IN A TAVERN WITH SCANT RECALL OF THE PRIOR EVENING'S REVELRY.
OUT!
HAVE A CARE WHO YOU SWAT WITH YOUR BROOM.
THE CIMMERIAN'S LAST MEMORY WAS OF FIGHTING THE GHOST RIDER OF THE FUTURE IN NEW YORK.
HAD IT ALL BEEN NO MORE THAN A DREAM?

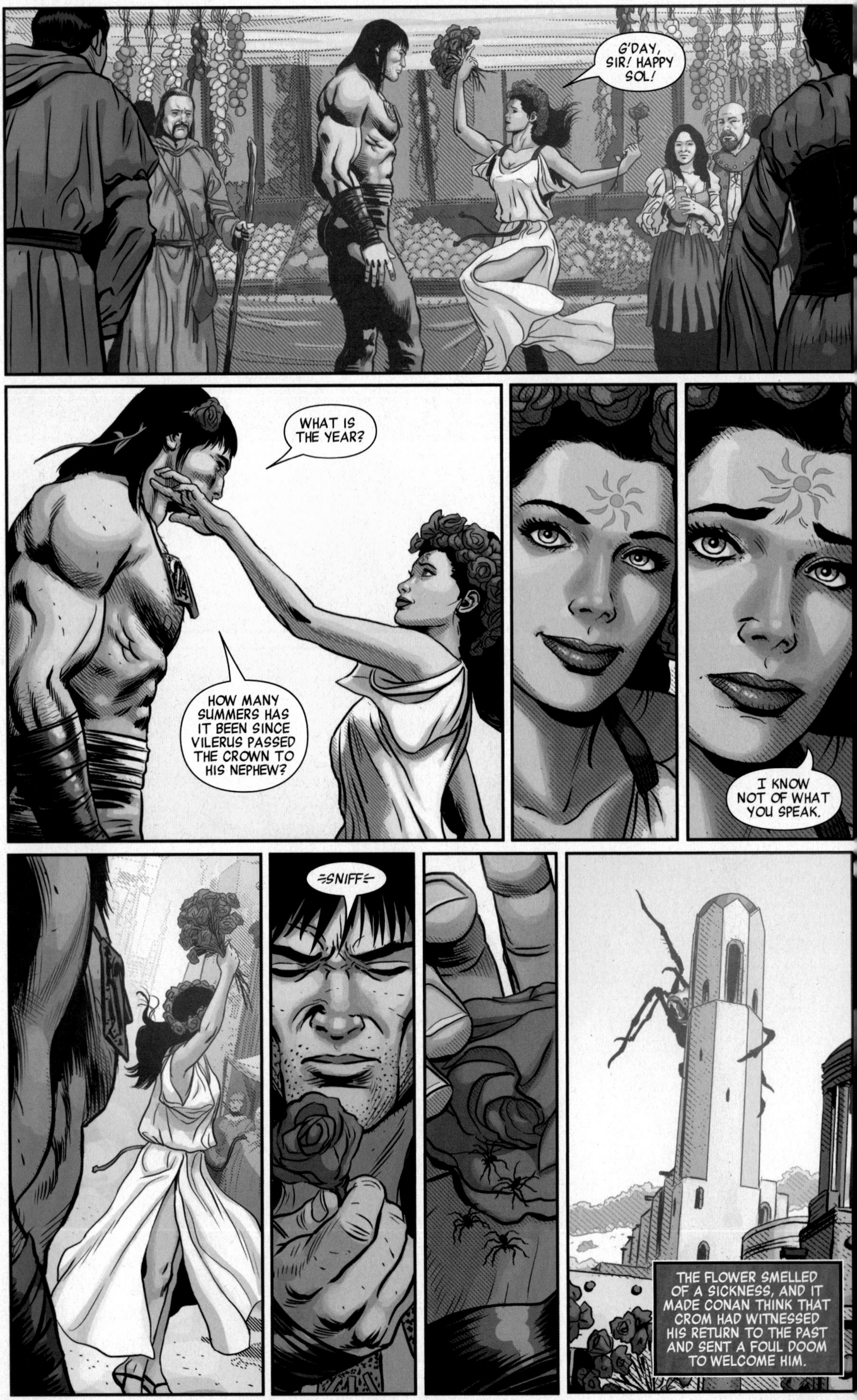
G'DAY, SIR! HAPPY SOL!
WHAT IS THE YEAR?
HOW MANY SUMMERS HAS IT BEEN SINCE VILERUS PASSED THE CROWN TO HIS NEPHEW?
I KNOW NOT OF WHAT YOU SPEAK.
SNIFF
THE FLOWER SMELLED OF A SICKNESS, AND IT MADE CONAN THINK THAT CROM HAD WITNESSED HIS RETURN TO THE PAST AND SENT A FOUL DOOM TO WELCOME HIM.

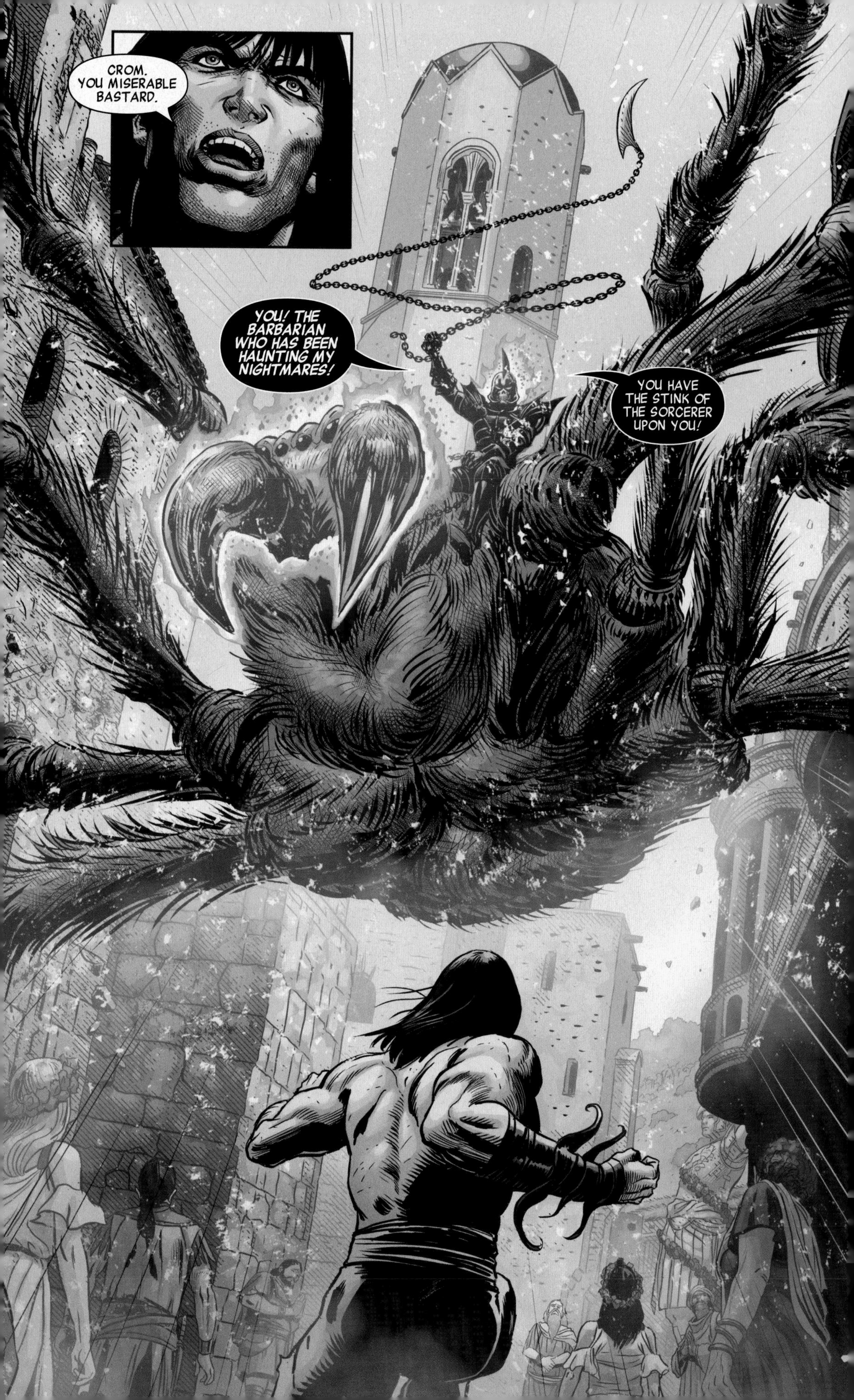
CROM. YOU MISERABLE BASTARD.
YOU! THE BARBARIAN WHO HAS BEEN HAUNTING MY NIGHTMARES!
YOU HAVE THE STINK OF THE SORCERER UPON YOU!

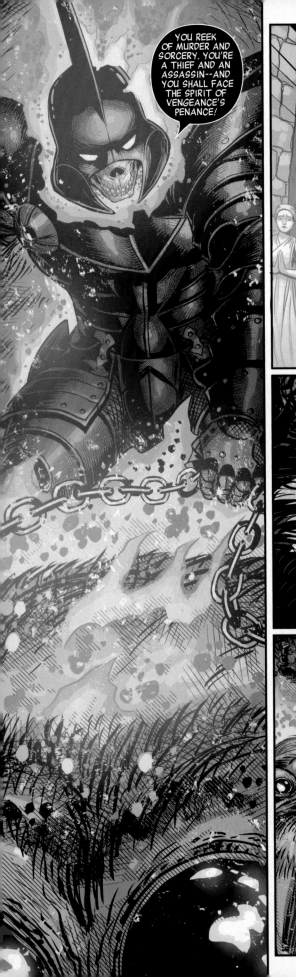

YOU REEK OF MURDER AND SORCERY. YOU'RE A THIEF AND AN ASSASSIN--AND YOU SHALL FACE THE SPIRIT OF VENGEANCE'S PENANCE!

RUN, WOMAN!

GO! WHAT THE DEVIL IS WRONG WITH YOU?

AND YOU, SPIRIT RIDER--

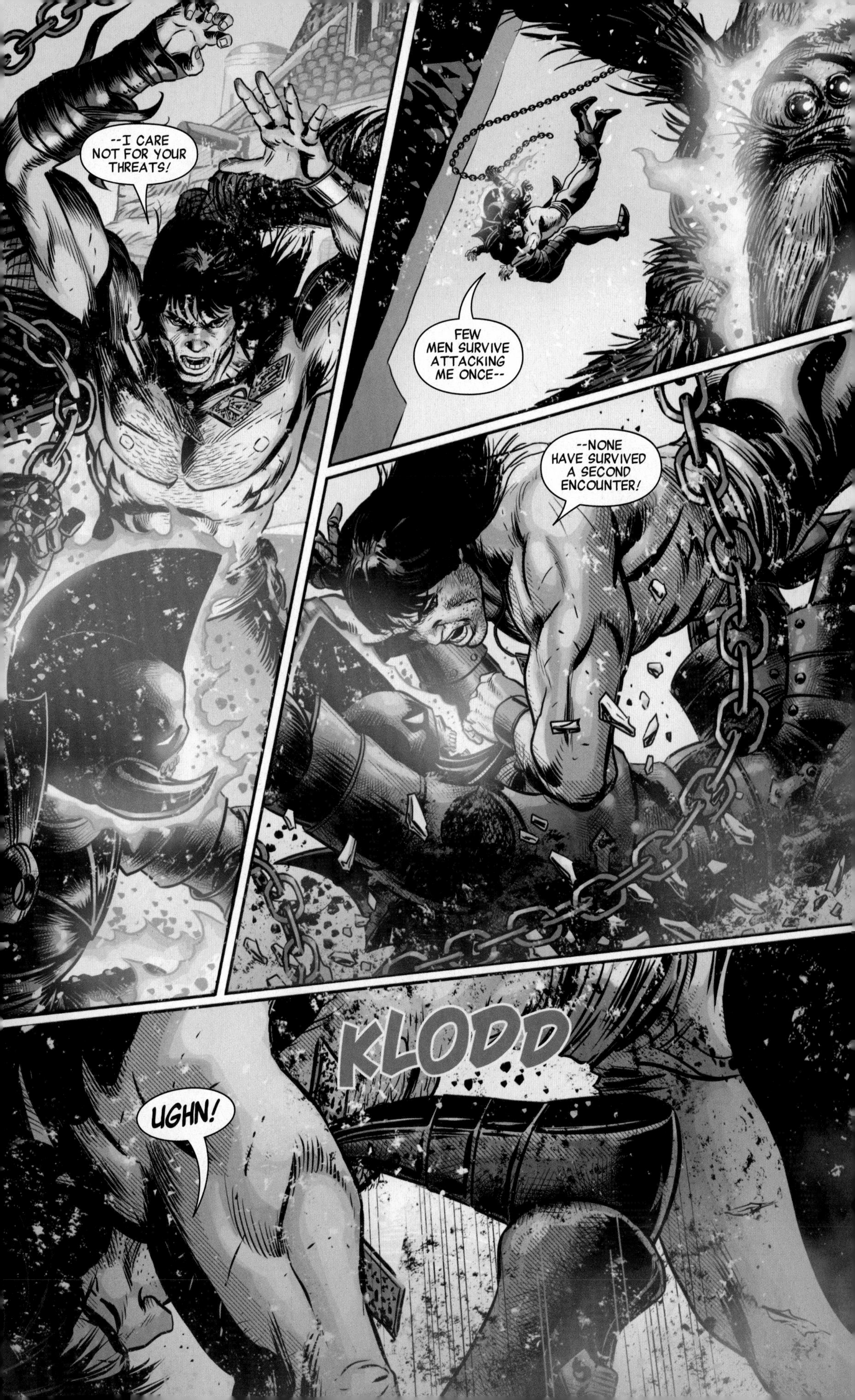
--I CARE NOT FOR YOUR THREATS!
FEW MEN SURVIVE ATTACKING ME ONCE--
--NONE HAVE SURVIVED A SECOND ENCOUNTER!
KLODD
UGHN!

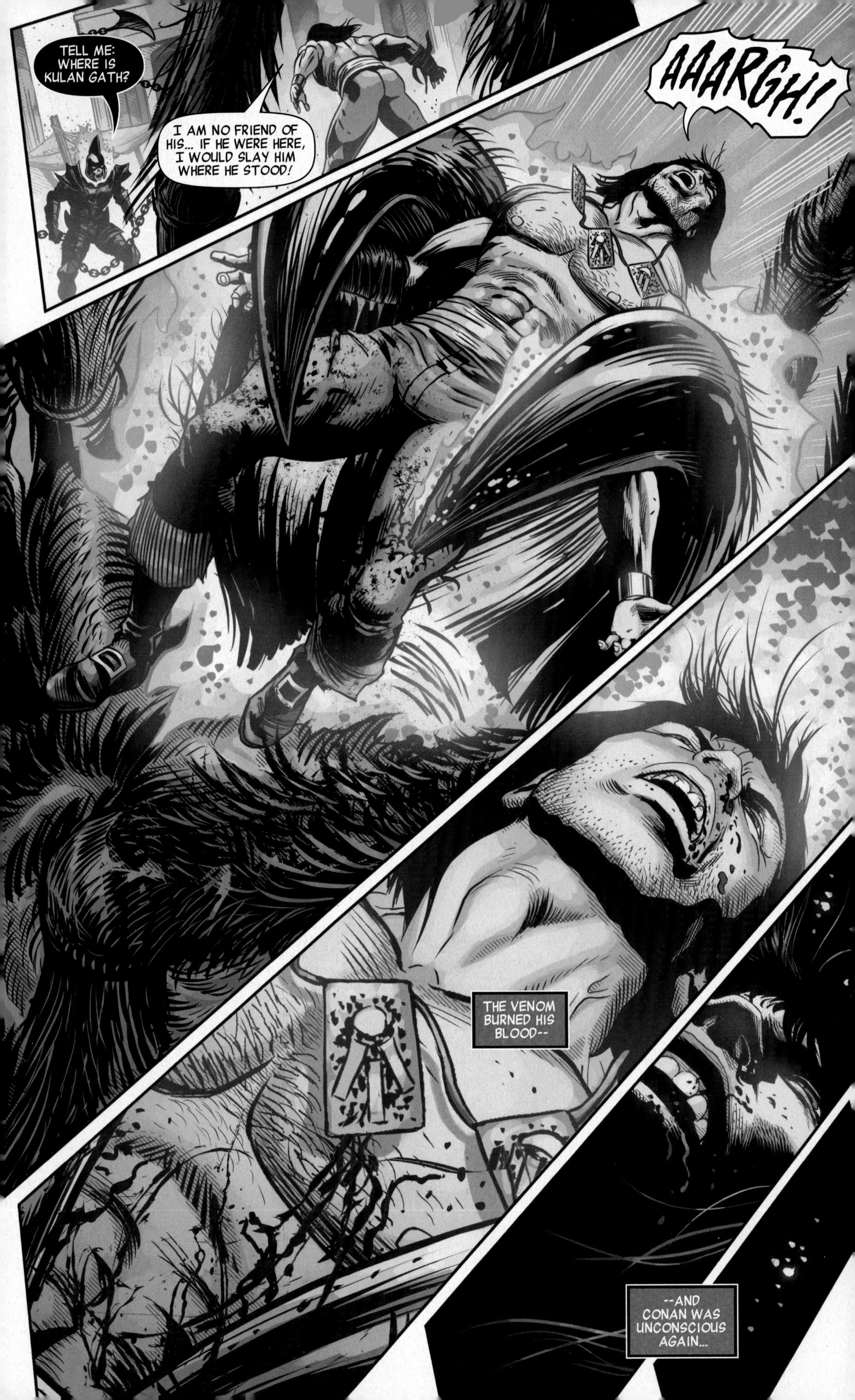
TELL ME: WHERE IS KULAN GATH?
I AM NO FRIEND OF HIS... IF HE WERE HERE, I WOULD SLAY HIM WHERE HE STOOD!
AAARGH!
THE VENOM BURNED HIS BLOOD--
--AND CONAN WAS UNCONSCIOUS AGAIN...

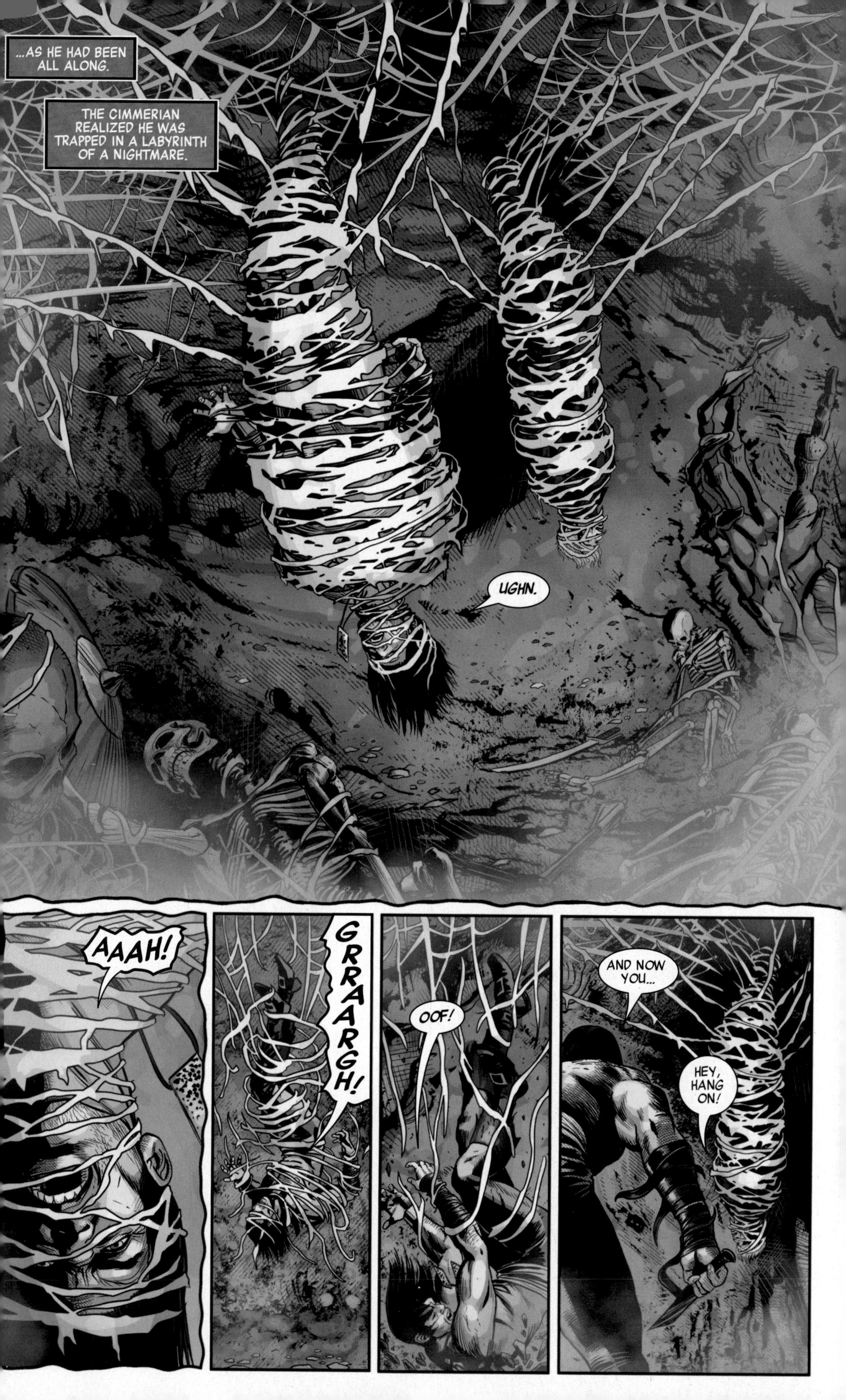
...AS HE HAD BEEN ALL ALONG.
THE CIMMERIAN REALIZED HE WAS TRAPPED IN A LABYRINTH OF A NIGHTMARE.
UGHN.
AAAH!
GRRAARGH!
OOF!
AND NOW YOU...
HEY, HANG ON!

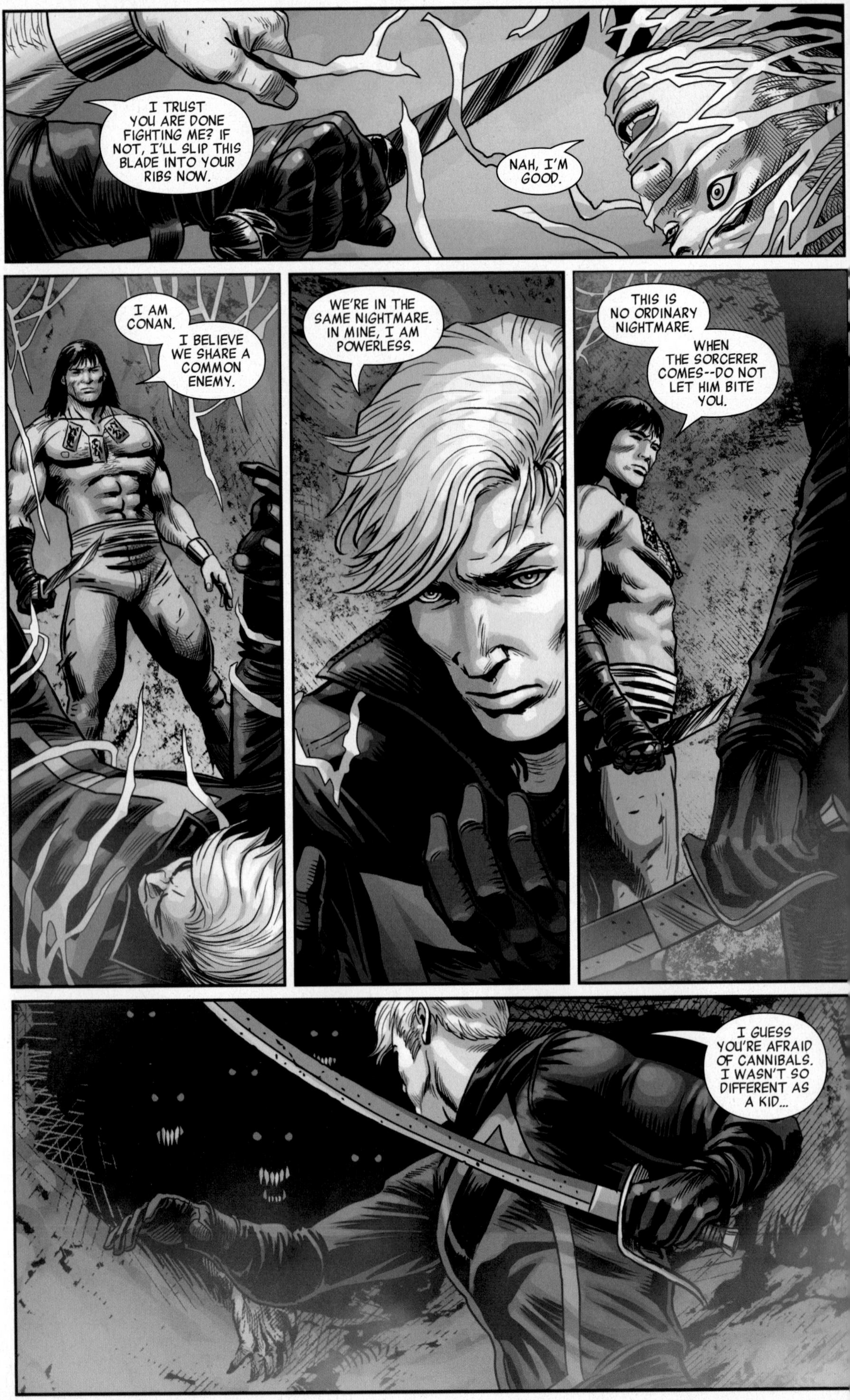
I TRUST YOU ARE DONE FIGHTING ME? IF NOT, I'LL SLIP THIS BLADE INTO YOUR RIBS NOW.
NAH, I'M GOOD.
I AM CONAN.
I BELIEVE WE SHARE A COMMON ENEMY.
WE'RE IN THE SAME NIGHTMARE. IN MINE, I AM POWERLESS.
THIS IS NO ORDINARY NIGHTMARE.
WHEN THE SORCERER COMES--DO NOT LET HIM BITE YOU.
I GUESS YOU'RE AFRAID OF CANNIBALS. I WASN'T SO DIFFERENT AS A KID...

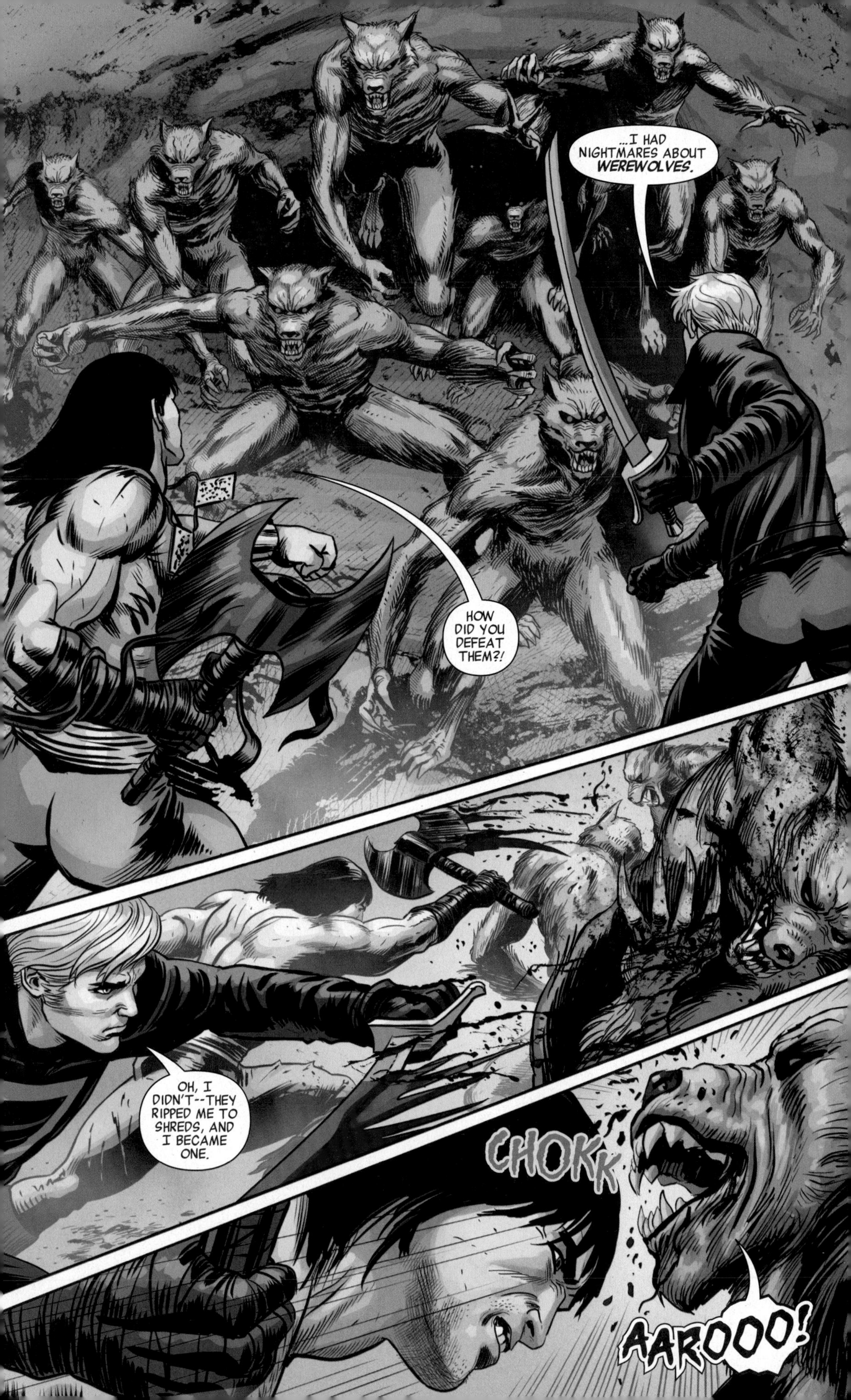
...I HAD NIGHTMARES ABOUT *WEREWOLVES.*
HOW DID YOU DEFEAT THEM?!
OH, I DIDN'T--THEY RIPPED ME TO SHREDS, AND I BECAME ONE.
CHOKK
AAROOO!

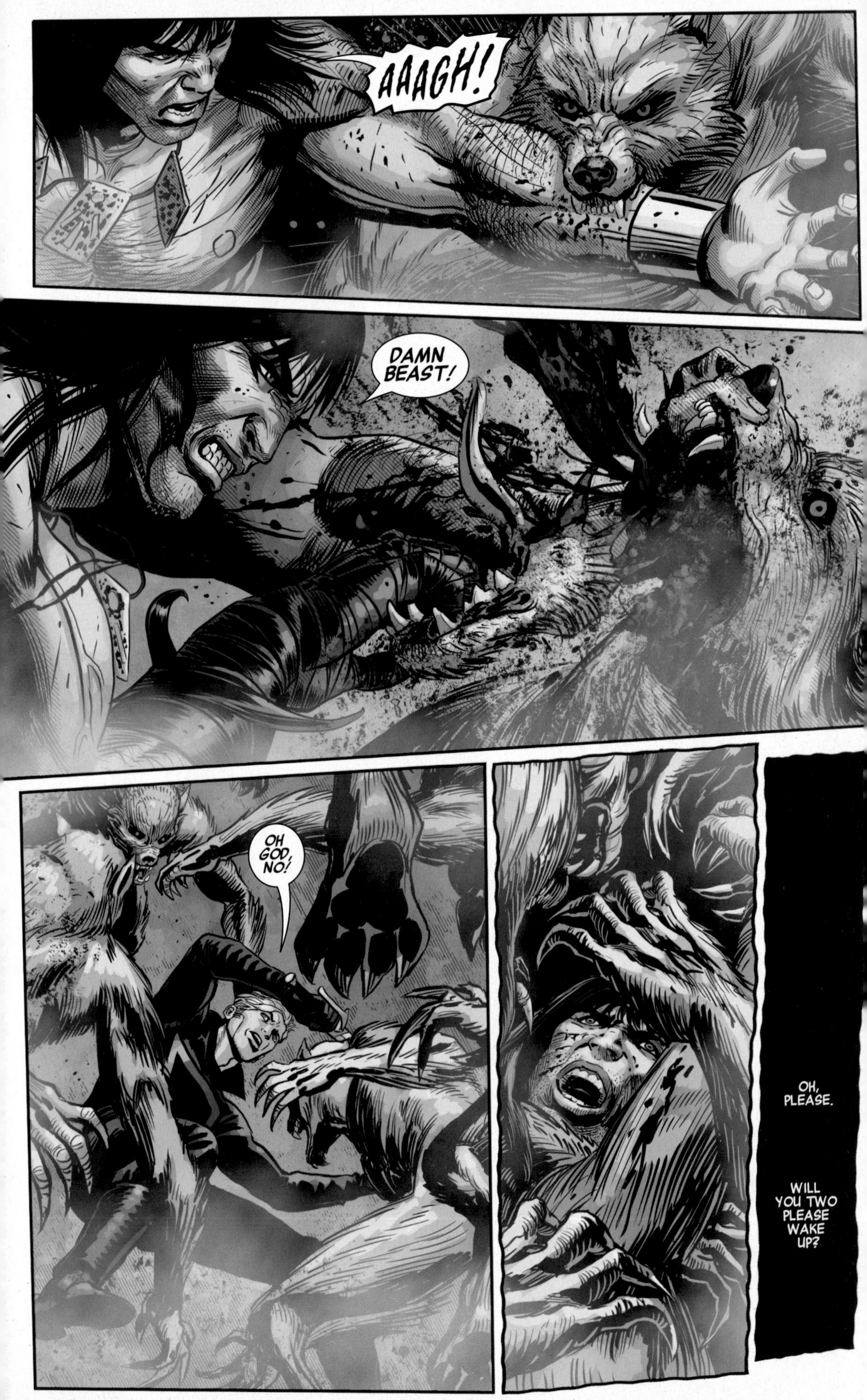
AAAGH!
DAMN BEAST!
OH GOD, NO!
OH, PLEASE.
WILL YOU TWO PLEASE WAKE UP?

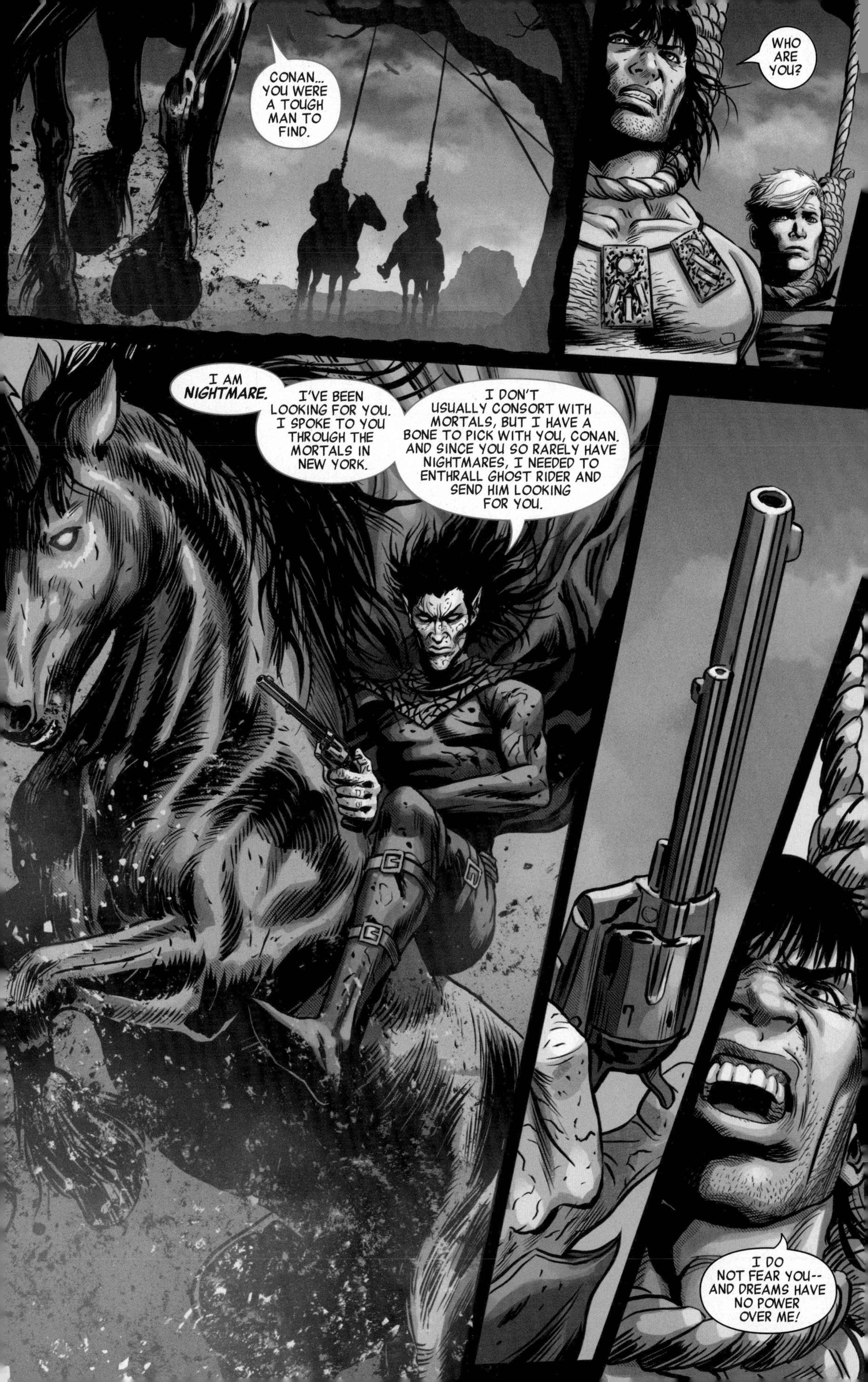
CONAN... YOU WERE A TOUGH MAN TO FIND.
WHO ARE YOU?
I AM NIGHTMARE.
I'VE BEEN LOOKING FOR YOU. I SPOKE TO YOU THROUGH THE MORTALS IN NEW YORK.
I DON'T USUALLY CONSORT WITH MORTALS, BUT I HAVE A BONE TO PICK WITH YOU, CONAN. AND SINCE YOU SO RARELY HAVE NIGHTMARES, I NEEDED TO ENTHRALL GHOST RIDER AND SEND HIM LOOKING FOR YOU.
I DO NOT FEAR YOU-- AND DREAMS HAVE NO POWER OVER ME!

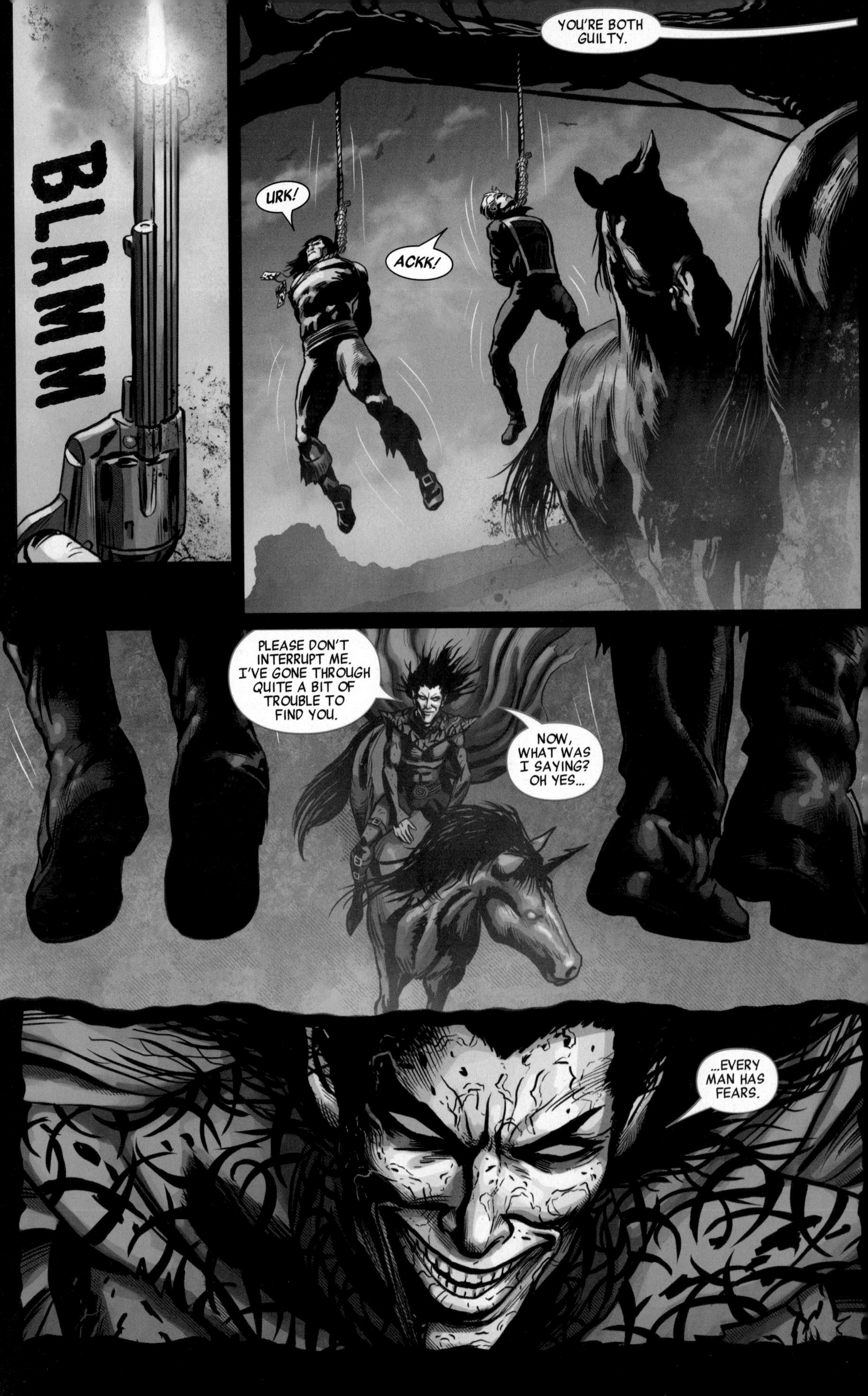
BLAMM
YOU'RE BOTH GUILTY.
URK!
ACKK!
PLEASE DON'T INTERRUPT ME. I'VE GONE THROUGH QUITE A BIT OF TROUBLE TO FIND YOU.
NOW, WHAT WAS I SAYING? OH YES...
...EVERY MAN HAS FEARS.

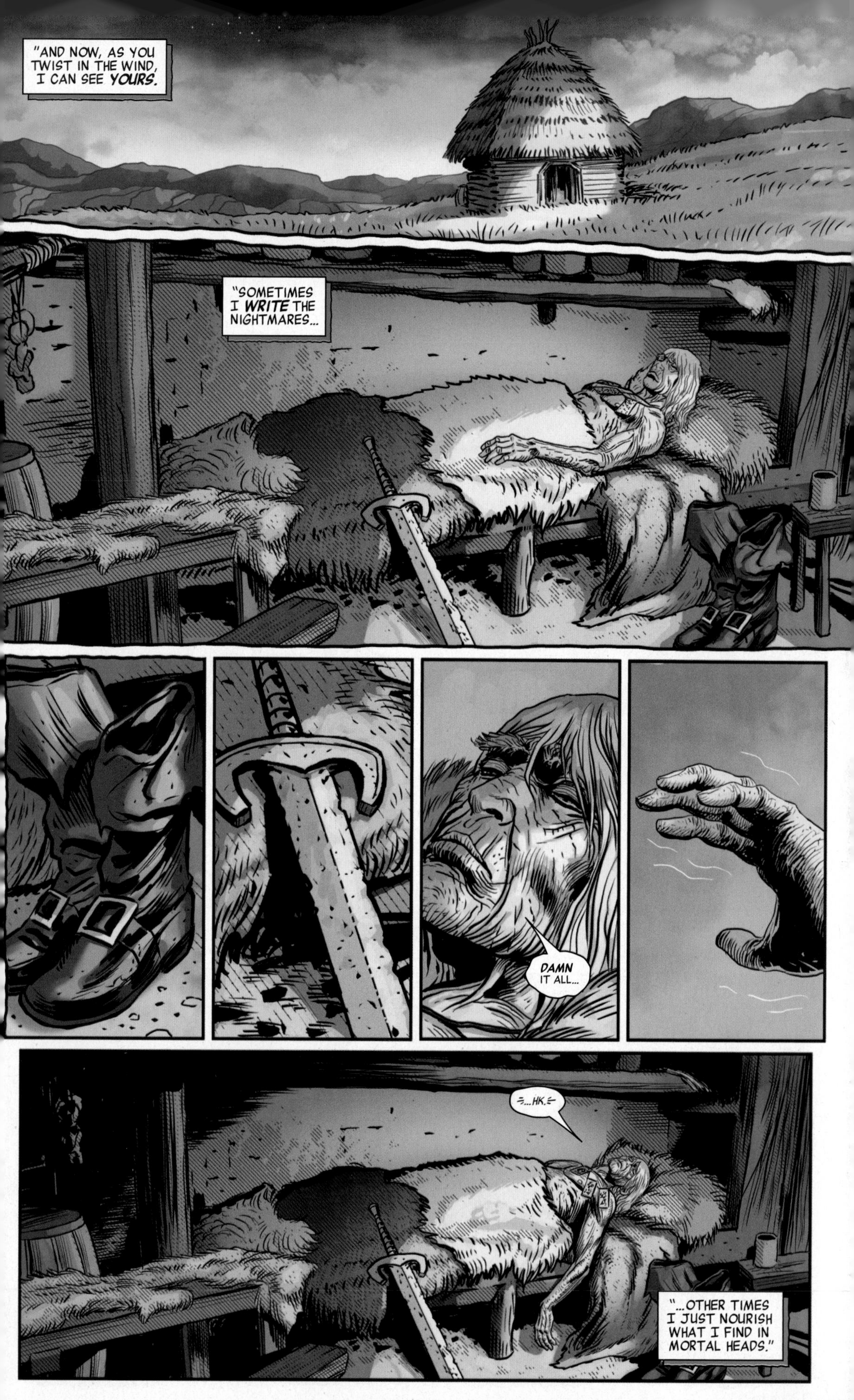
"AND NOW, AS YOU TWIST IN THE WIND, I CAN SEE YOURS.
"SOMETIMES I WRITE THE NIGHTMARES...
DAMN IT ALL...
...HK.
"...OTHER TIMES I JUST NOURISH WHAT I FIND IN MORTAL HEADS."

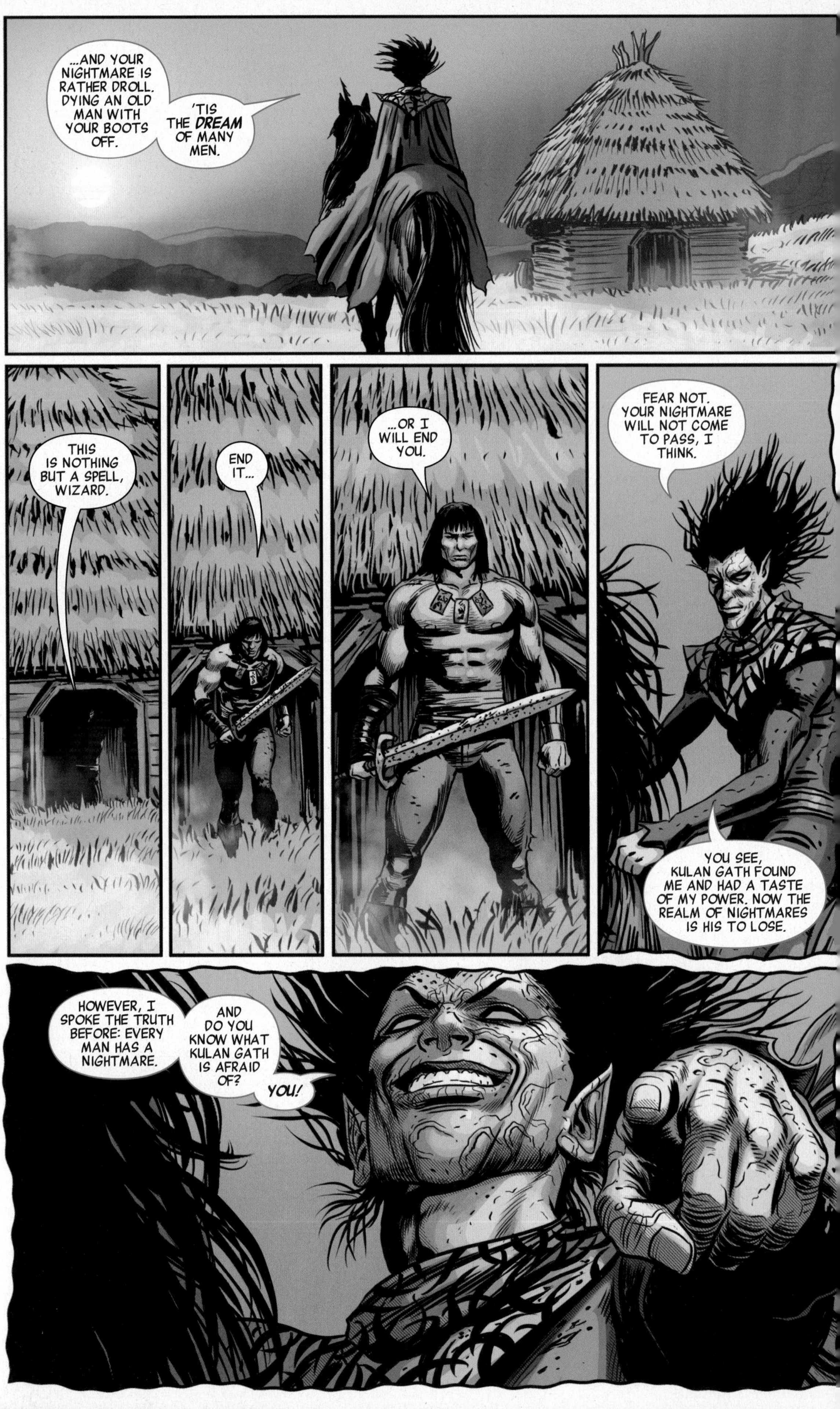
...AND YOUR NIGHTMARE IS RATHER DROLL. DYING AN OLD MAN WITH YOUR BOOTS OFF.
'TIS THE DREAM OF MANY MEN.
THIS IS NOTHING BUT A SPELL, WIZARD.
END IT...
...OR I WILL END YOU.
FEAR NOT. YOUR NIGHTMARE WILL NOT COME TO PASS, I THINK.
YOU SEE, KULAN GATH FOUND ME AND HAD A TASTE OF MY POWER. NOW THE REALM OF NIGHTMARES IS HIS TO LOSE.
HOWEVER, I SPOKE THE TRUTH BEFORE: EVERY MAN HAS A NIGHTMARE.
AND DO YOU KNOW WHAT KULAN GATH IS AFRAID OF?
YOU!

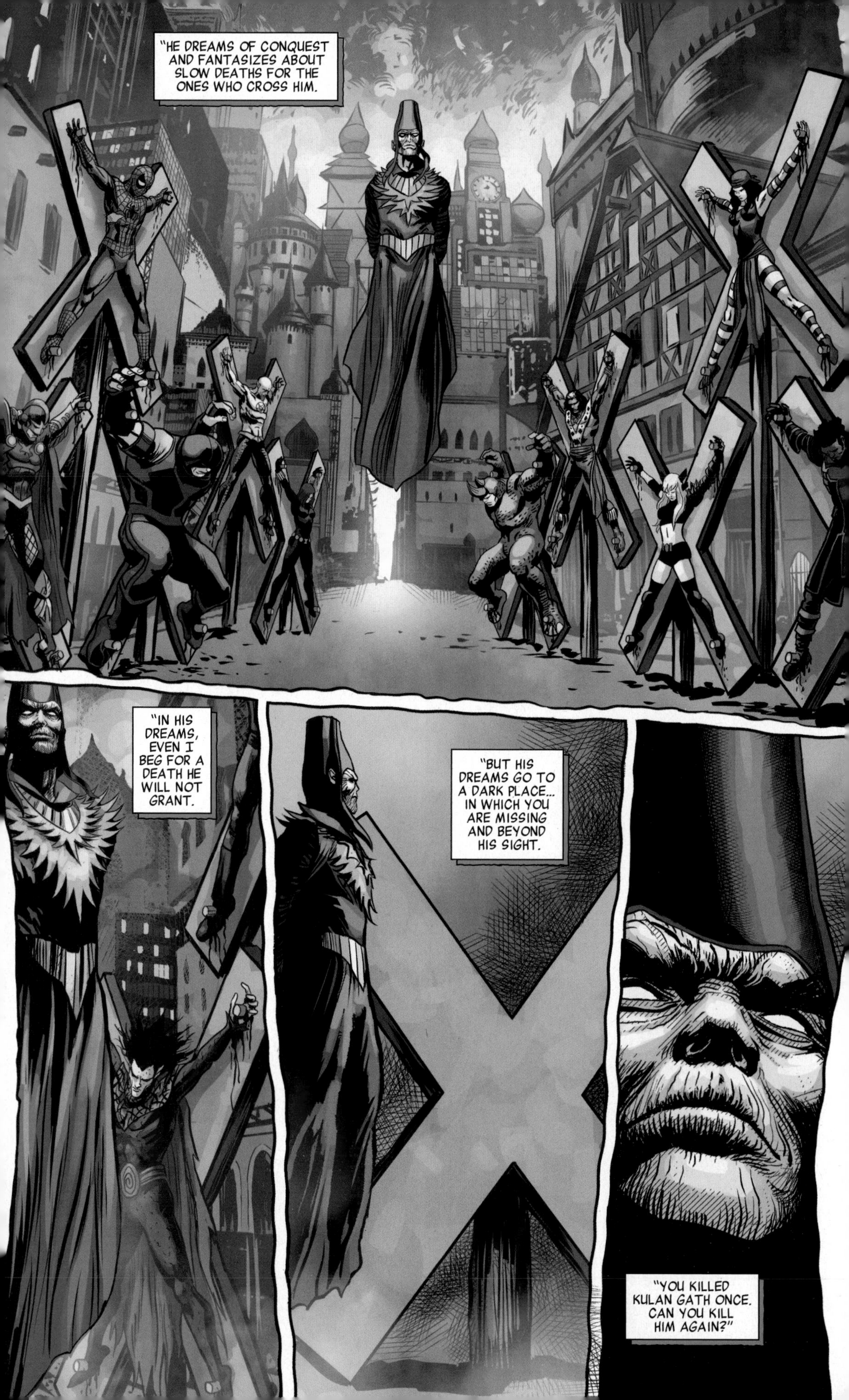
"HE DREAMS OF CONQUEST AND FANTASIZES ABOUT SLOW DEATHS FOR THE ONES WHO CROSS HIM.
"IN HIS DREAMS, EVEN I BEG FOR A DEATH HE WILL NOT GRANT.
"BUT HIS DREAMS GO TO A DARK PLACE... IN WHICH YOU ARE MISSING AND BEYOND HIS SIGHT.
"YOU KILLED KULAN GATH ONCE. CAN YOU KILL HIM AGAIN?"

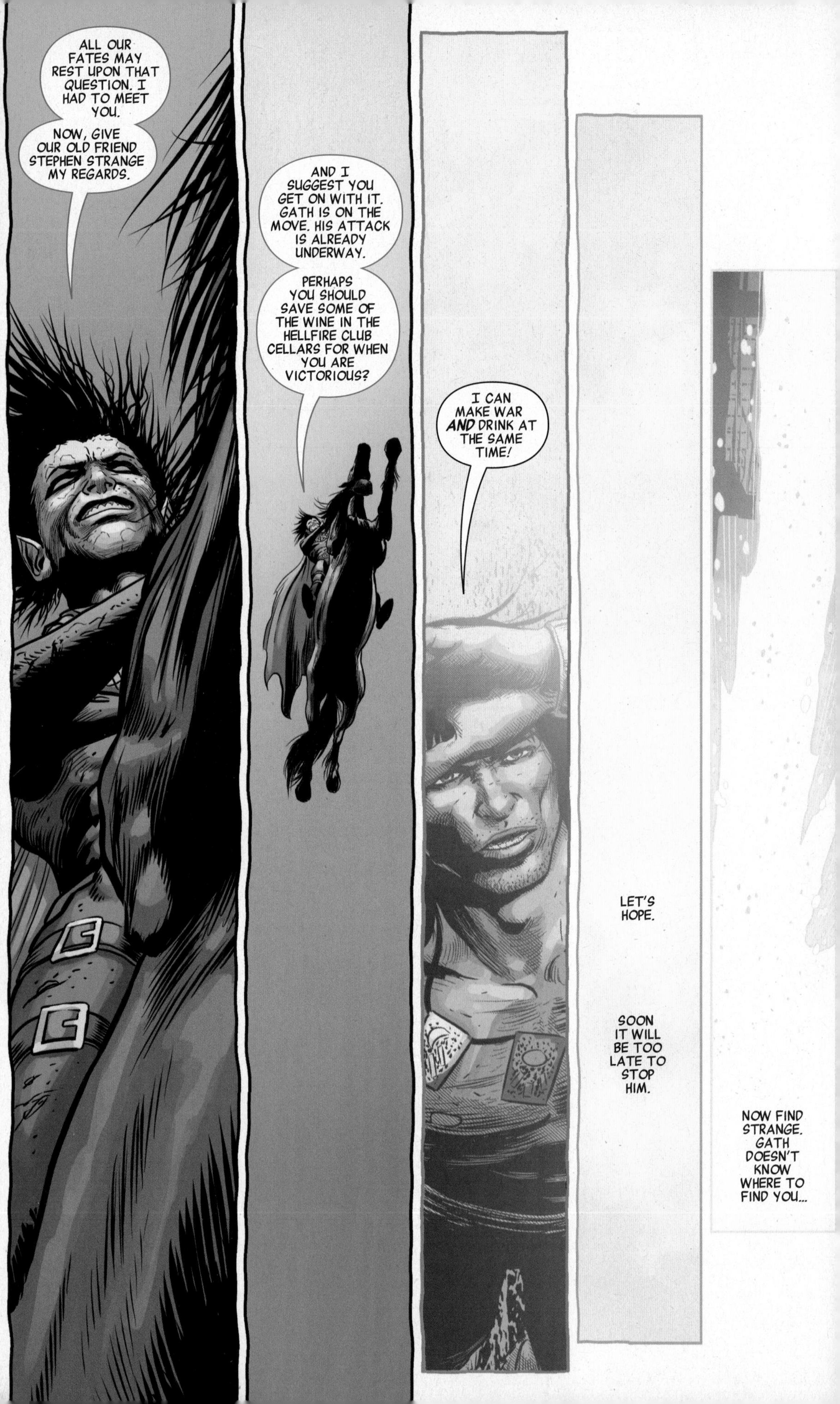

ALL OUR FATES MAY REST UPON THAT QUESTION. I HAD TO MEET YOU.
NOW, GIVE OUR OLD FRIEND STEPHEN STRANGE MY REGARDS.
AND I SUGGEST YOU GET ON WITH IT. GATH IS ON THE MOVE. HIS ATTACK IS ALREADY UNDERWAY.
PERHAPS YOU SHOULD SAVE SOME OF THE WINE IN THE HELLFIRE CLUB CELLARS FOR WHEN YOU ARE VICTORIOUS?
I CAN MAKE WAR AND DRINK AT THE SAME TIME!
LET'S HOPE.
SOON IT WILL BE TOO LATE TO STOP HIM.
NOW FIND STRANGE. GATH DOESN'T KNOW WHERE TO FIND YOU...

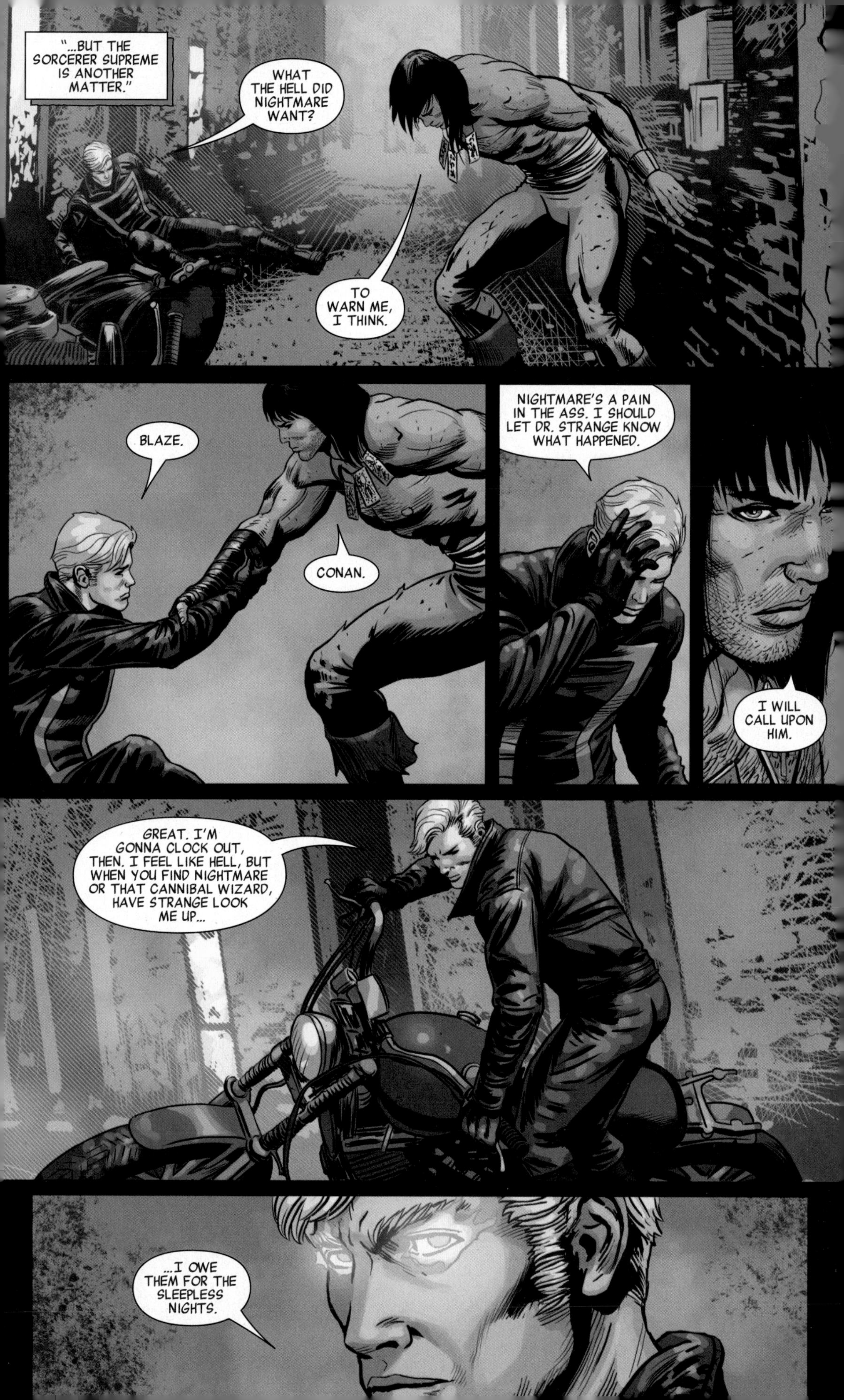
"...BUT THE SORCERER SUPREME IS ANOTHER MATTER."
WHAT THE HELL DID NIGHTMARE WANT?
TO WARN ME, I THINK.
BLAZE.
CONAN.
NIGHTMARE'S A PAIN IN THE ASS. I SHOULD LET DR. STRANGE KNOW WHAT HAPPENED.
I WILL CALL UPON HIM.
GREAT. I'M GONNA CLOCK OUT, THEN. I FEEL LIKE HELL, BUT WHEN YOU FIND NIGHTMARE OR THAT CANNIBAL WIZARD, HAVE STRANGE LOOK ME UP...
...I OWE THEM FOR THE SLEEPLESS NIGHTS.

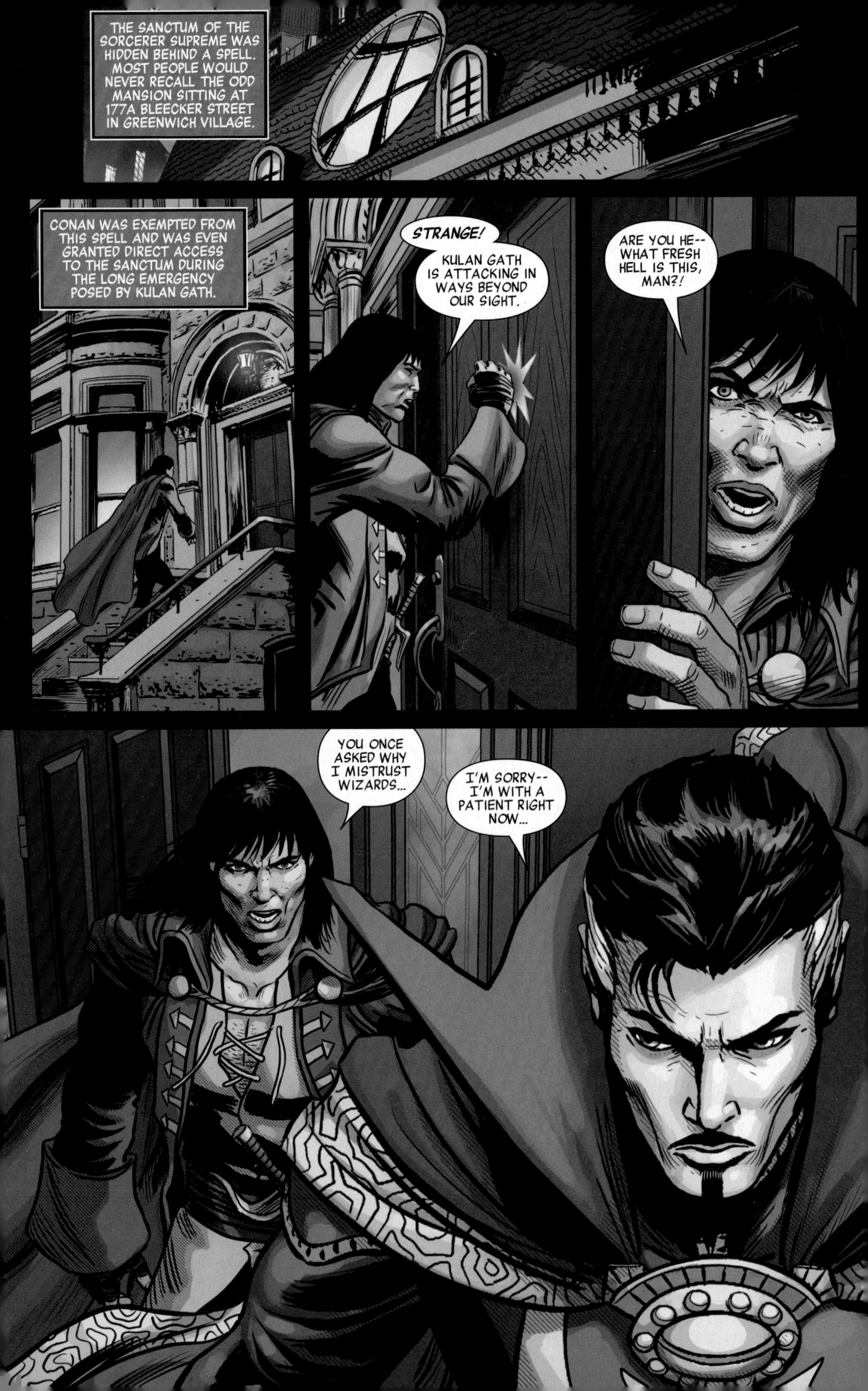
THE SANCTUM OF THE SORCERER SUPREME WAS HIDDEN BEHIND A SPELL. MOST PEOPLE WOULD NEVER RECALL THE ODD MANSION SITTING AT 177A BLEECKER STREET IN GREENWICH VILLAGE.
CONAN WAS EXEMPTED FROM THIS SPELL AND WAS EVEN GRANTED DIRECT ACCESS TO THE SANCTUM DURING THE LONG EMERGENCY POSED BY KULAN GATH.
STRANGE!
KULAN GATH IS ATTACKING IN WAYS BEYOND OUR SIGHT.
ARE YOU HE-- WHAT FRESH HELL IS THIS, MAN?!
YOU ONCE ASKED WHY I MISTRUST WIZARDS...
I'M SORRY-- I'M WITH A PATIENT RIGHT NOW...

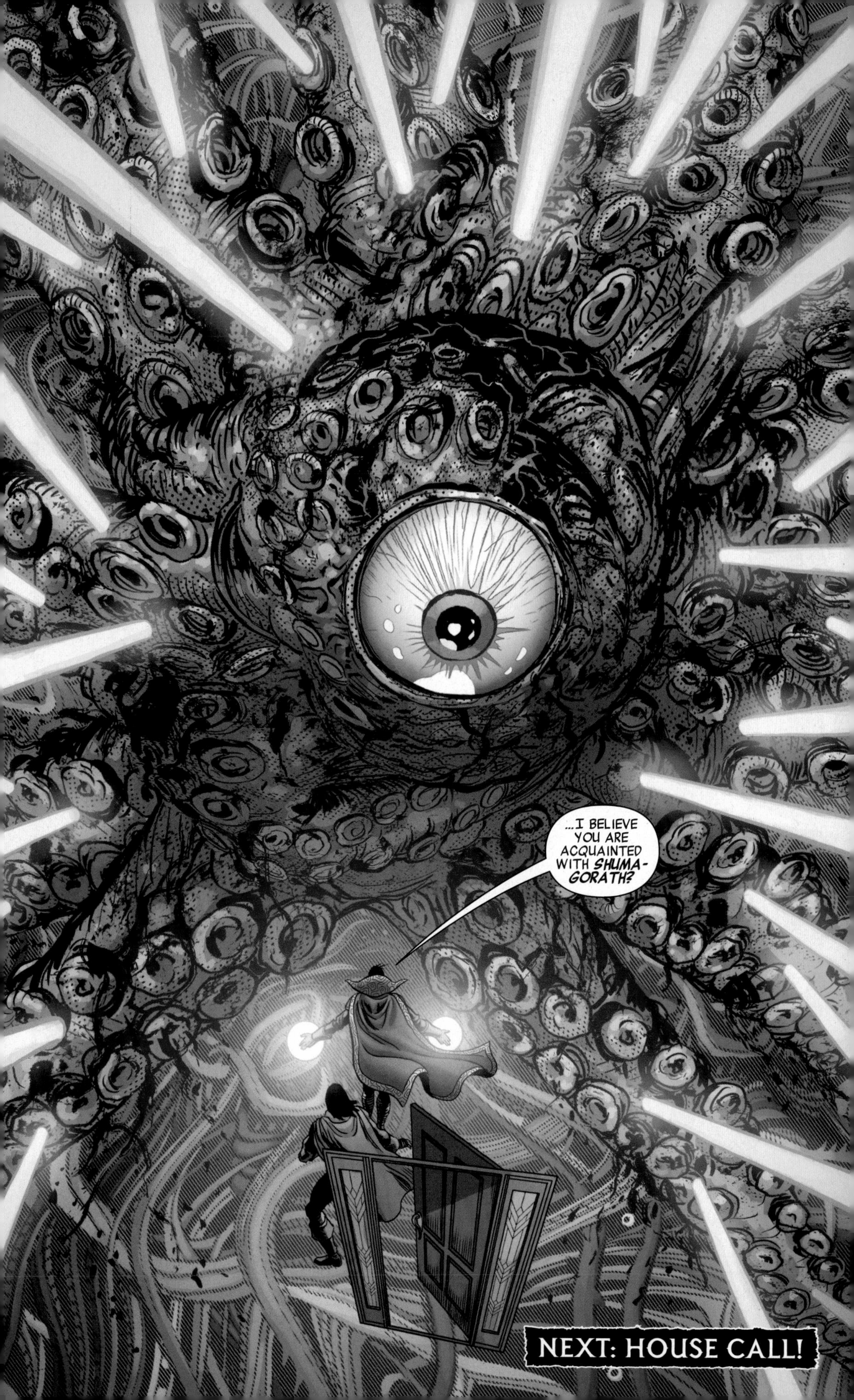
...I BELIEVE YOU ARE ACQUAINTED WITH SHUMA-GORATH?
NEXT: HOUSE CALL!

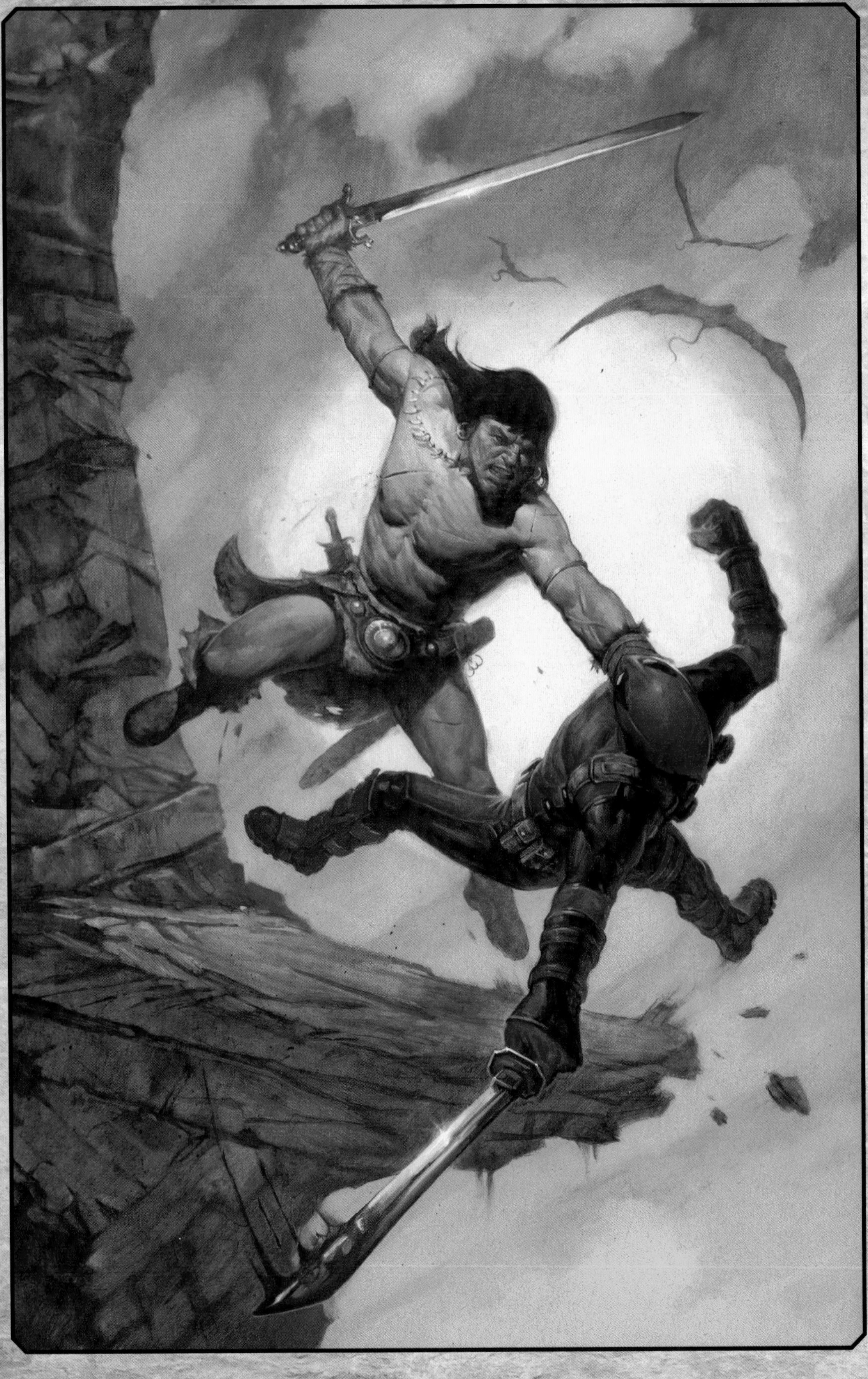

E.M Gist
17 VARIANT

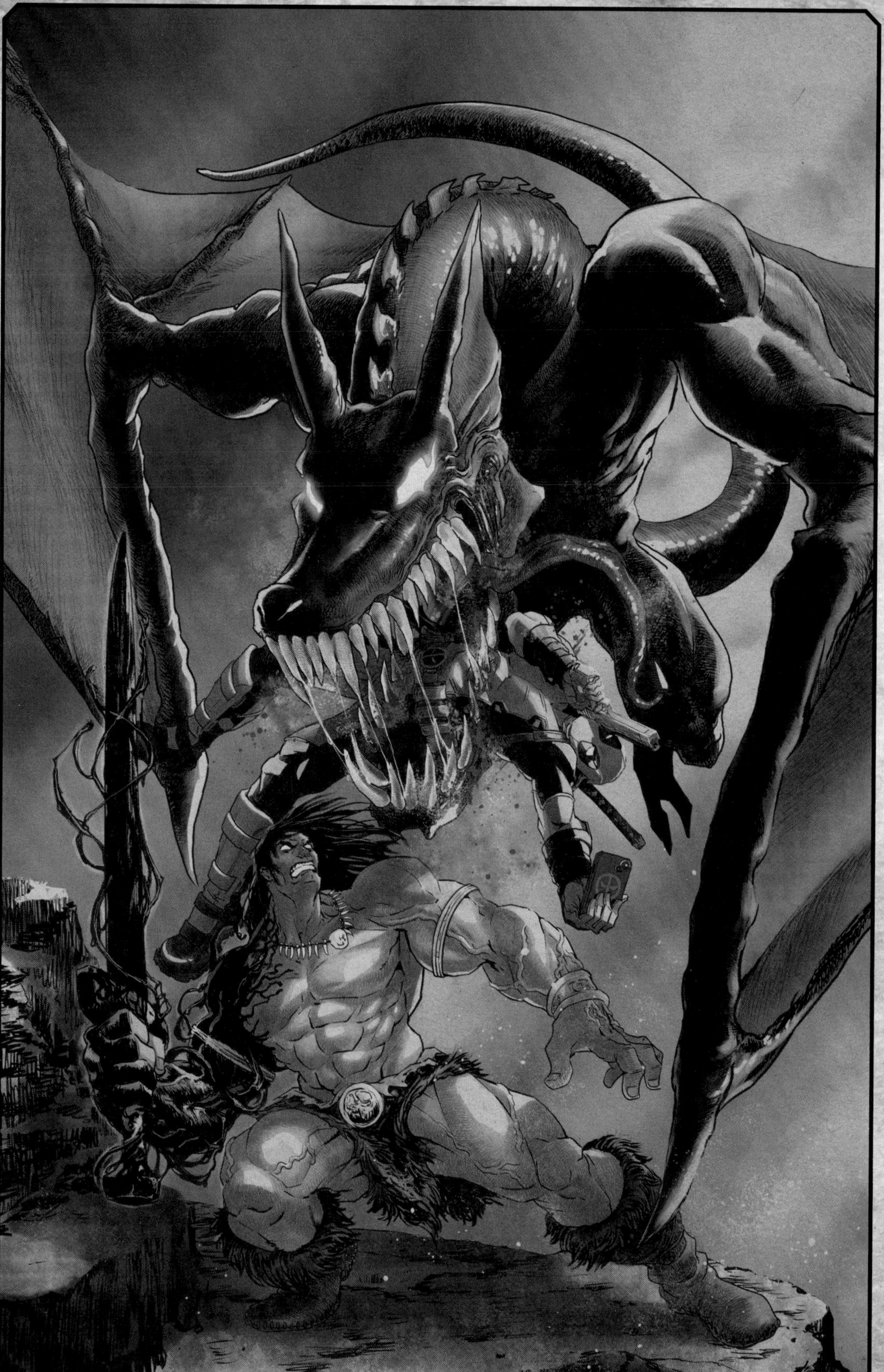

Superlog
18 VARIANT

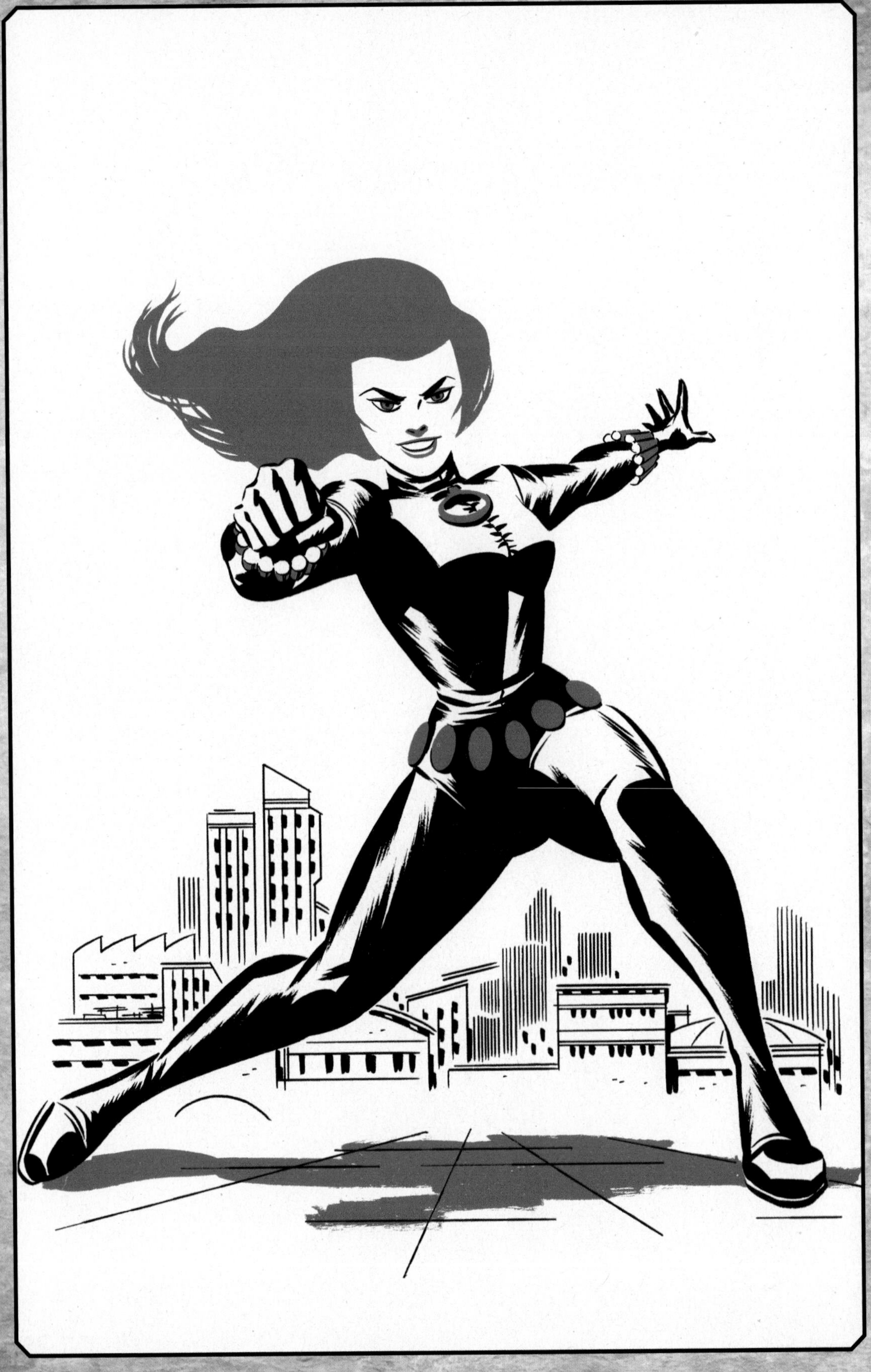

Michael Cho
19 TWO-TONE VARIANT

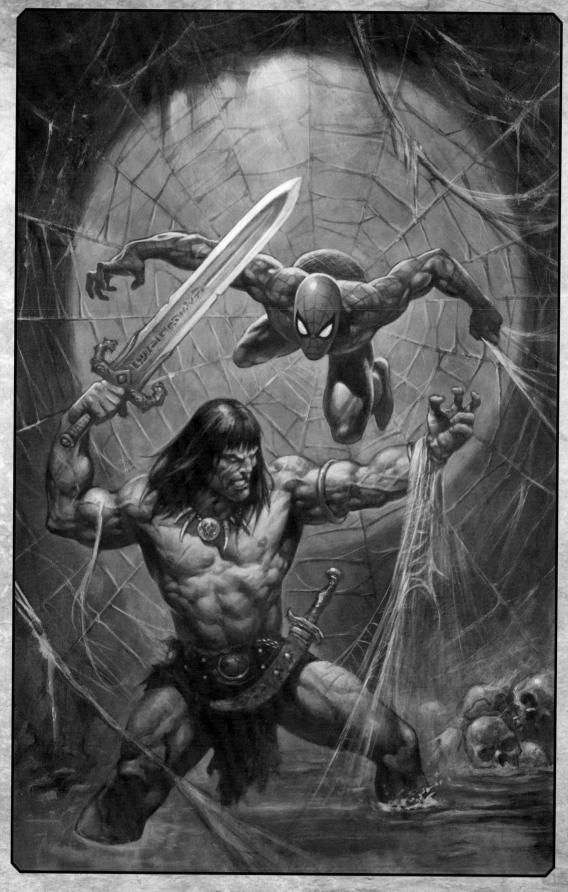

Alex Horley
20 VARIANT

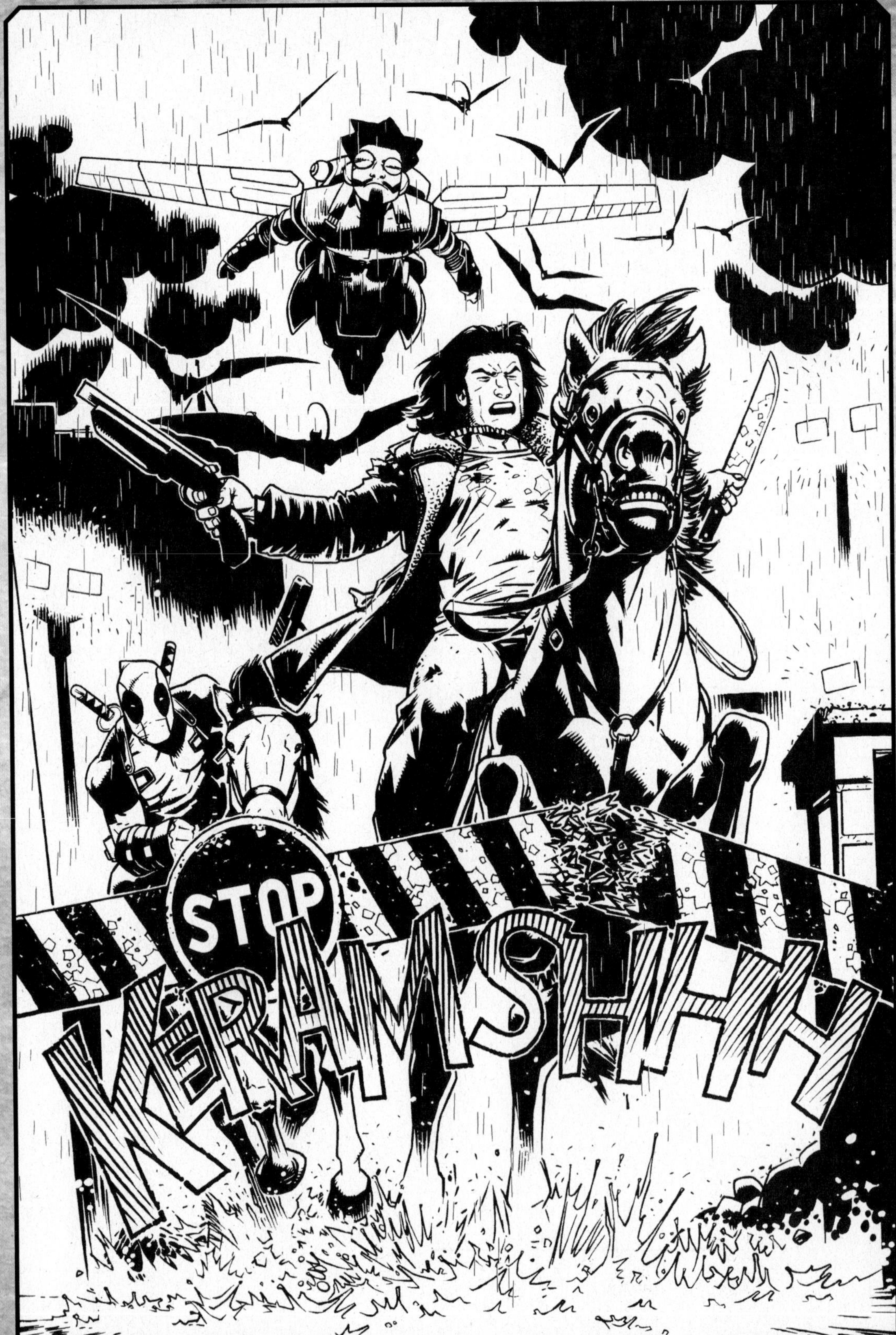

STOP
KERAMSHHH

Kev Walker
17, PAGE 14 INKS

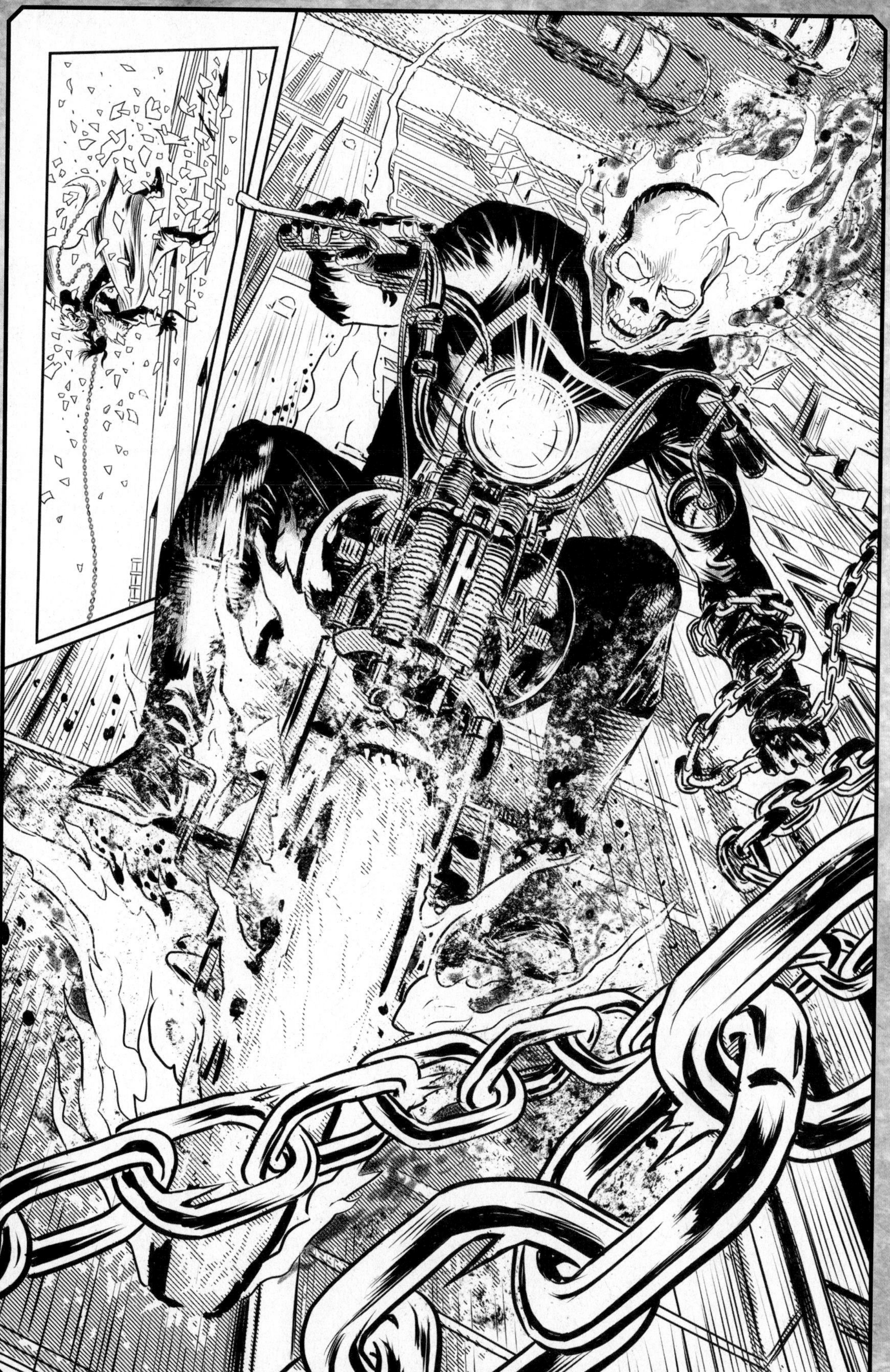

Patch Zircher
21, PAGE 8 INKS

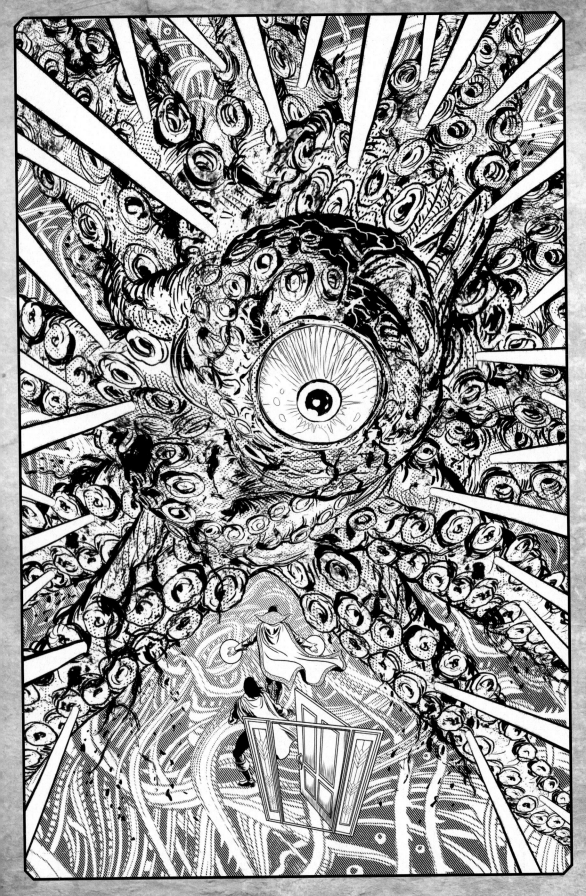

Patch Zircher
22, PAGE 20 INKS